KENYA

WESTVIEW PROFILES • NATIONS OF CONTEMPORARY AFRICA

Larry W. Bowman, Series Editor

Kenya: The Quest for Prosperity, Second Edition,
Norman Miller and Rodger Yeager

*Zaire: Continuity and Political Change
in an Oppressive State,* Winsome J. Leslie

Gabon: Beyond the Colonial Legacy, James F. Barnes

*Guinea-Bissau: Power, Conflict, and Renewal
in a West African Nation,* Joshua B. Forrest

Namibia: The Nation After Independence,
Donald L. Sparks and December Green

Zimbabwe: The Terrain of Contradictory Development,
Christine Sylvester

*Mauritius: Democracy and Development in
the Indian Ocean,* Larry W. Bowman

Niger: Personal Rule and Survival in the Sahel, Robert B. Charlick

*Equatorial Guinea: Colonialism, State Terror, and the Search
for Stability,* Ibrahim K. Sundiata

Mali: A Search for Direction, Pascal James Imperato

Tanzania: An African Experiment,
Second Edition, Rodger Yeager

Cameroon: Dependence and Independence, Mark W. DeLancey

*São Tomé and Príncipe: From Plantation Colony
to Microstate,* Tony Hodges and Malyn Newitt

Zambia: Between Two Worlds, Marcia M. Burdette

Ethiopia: Transition and Development in the Horn of Africa,
Mulatu Wubneh and Yohannis Abate

Mozambique: From Colonialism to Revolution, 1900–1982,
Allen Isaacman and Barbara Isaacman

KENYA

The Quest for Prosperity

SECOND EDITION

Norman Miller
and Rodger Yeager

Westview Press

BOULDER • SAN FRANCISCO • OXFORD

Westview Profiles/Nations of Contemporary Africa

Paperback cover photo: Vendors with vegetables from the wholesale market in Haile Selassie Avenue, Nairobi (photo by David Keith Jones/Images of Africa Photobank).

Published in 1994 in the United States of America by Westview Press, Inc., 5500 Central Avenue, Boulder, Colorado 80301-2877, and in the United Kingdom by Westview Press, 36 Lonsdale Road, Summertown, Oxford OX2 7EW

Library of Congress Cataloging-in-Publication Data
Miller, Norman N., 1933–
  Kenya : the quest for prosperity / Norman Miller and Rodger
Yeager. — 2nd ed.
    p.   cm.
  Includes bibliographical references and index.
  ISBN 0-8133-8201-7. — ISBN 0-8133-8202-5 (pbk.)
    1. Kenya—Politics and government—1963–1978.   2. Kenya—Politics
and government—1978–   3. Kenya—Politics and government—1963–
4. Kenya—Economic conditions—1963–   5. Kenya—Social
conditions—1963–   6. Kenya—Foreign relations.   I. Yeager, Rodger.
II. Title.
DT433.58.M55   1994
967.6204—dc20   93-29882
                                                                                    CIP

Printed and bound in the United States of America

       The paper used in this publication meets the requirements
 (∞)   of the American National Standard for Permanence of Paper
       for Printed Library Materials Z39.48-1984.

10   9   8   7   6   5   4   3   2

To our families

Contents

Tables and Illustrations

Photographs

Preface

This book examines the entrepreneurial, innovative, aggressive approach to life that characterizes modern Kenyan society. Reflecting a mood encountered throughout much of the country, today's Nairobi is a freewheeling, materialistic place where the search for individual advancement shapes the dominant ethic. To the extent that it defines the Kenyan civic culture, this orientation is unique in eastern Africa. It has been both heralded as a harbinger of democratic achievement, social integration, and economic justice and condemned as a deeply embedded cause of political elitism, social conflict, and economic exploitation.

Our view of Kenya is essentially positive, although we believe that a country can be defended and still criticized. The inequities of Kenyan society are not necessarily permanent. The economy faces difficult times but abounds in untapped potential. The political system, increasingly repressive, is nevertheless alive with demands for democratic reform. The overstressed environment still offers the promise of sustainable resource use for the benefit of present and future generations. Events in the international arena are threatening but not overwhelming. Our purpose in the following pages is to describe, explain, and evaluate these divergent tendencies.

In addition to the organizations, friends, and colleagues acknowledged in the first edition, we thank several institutions and individuals for helping make this second edition possible. Under the auspices of the African-Caribbean Institute, our most recent work in Kenya and in other African countries focuses on public-policy problems of natural resource conservation, health, and biodiversity management. We are grateful to the Ford Foundation, the United Nations Environment Programme (UNEP), and the United States Agency for International Development (USAID) for their financial support of this effort. In Nairobi, the assistance of the following persons was especially appreciated: Ford Foundation country representatives Goran Hyden, Diana Rocheleau, and Eric

Rusten; John Gaudet, Larry Hausman, and John Koehring at USAID's regional office for eastern and southern Africa; and Mona Bjorkland of UNEP headquarters. We are also obliged to the researchers and research advisors associated with our Kenyan projects: Mohamud Abdi Jama and J. Keter, University of Nairobi; A. K. Kiriro, National Environment Secretariat; Michael Korir-Koech, Kenyatta University; Francis Lelo, Egerton University; Charles Okidi, Moi University; Fred Owino, International Centre for Research in Agroforestry; Betty Nafuna Wamalwa, UN Development Programme; and David Wasawo, UN Environment Programme.

Both individually and together, we have long enjoyed an excellent working relationship with Westview Press and with its Nations of Contemporary Africa series. Over the years, series editor Larry W. Bowman has continued to encourage and support our work, as have our Westview editors, Barbara Ellington, Miriam Gilbert, Michelle Murphy, and Shena Redmond. To them we are particularly indebted for enabling our thoughts to see the light of day.

In the final analysis, our deepest thanks are reserved for our long-suffering academic associates and students and, above all, for our families, to whom this book is dedicated: Jan Yeager and Judith, Scott, and Amy Miller. Carrying on a tradition established in nearly three decades of friendship and research collaboration in Africa, we have once again agreed to attribute any errors of fact and interpretation to each other.

Norman Miller
Rodger Yeager

NOTE TO THE SECOND EDITION

Nearly ten turbulent years have elapsed since this book first went to press. So many changes have occurred and so many different actors have entered and exited the political stage that an entirely new edition was called for. Happily, Rodger Yeager, my long-standing friend and author of the Tanzania book in this series, agreed to coauthor the second edition. He has carried the lion's share of responsibility for researching and writing the chapters that follow. I also thank David Keith Jones and the editors and staff of the *Daily Nation* (Nairobi) for their generosity in providing photographs for this edition as they did for the first.

N. M.

KENYA

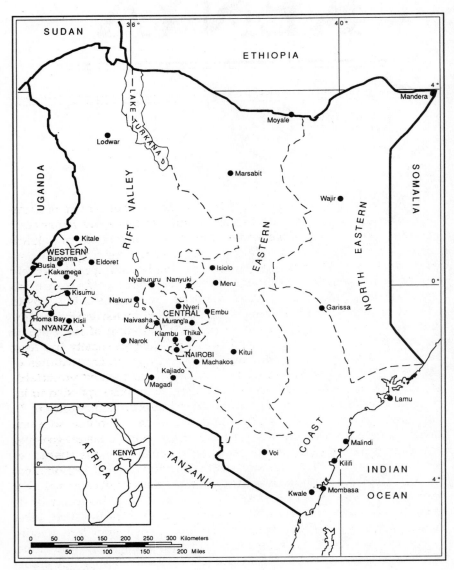

Republic of Kenya

Introduction

In comparison with the situation in Africa's other centers of European entrenchment, Kenya's transition to independence was remarkably orderly, free from racial strife, and sensitive to the importance of political rights and freedoms. Yet as democratic reforms are increasingly being secured elsewhere in Africa, these protections are becoming progressively eroded in Kenya. Again, although Kenya's economic performance has exceeded that of most other African countries, the benefits of this growth have been diluted by deepening elite corruption, increasing inequality, and a growing potential for class conflict. Consisting of forty ethnic groups dominated by three very large ones, Kenyan society has long been troubled by ethnic competition for land and other attributes of wealth, status, and power. Instead of remaining narrow and predictable over the years, however, the game of ethnic politics has expanded to include an ever-larger number of committed but insecure minor players. In human-ecological terms, few African countries have profited so much from so limited a resource base, but one of the world's fastest-growing populations is now causing serious resource depletion in the absence of effective measures to ameliorate relentless environmental exploitation. On the basis of its economic hegemony in eastern Africa, its commanding geopolitical location in that part of the continent, and the ability of its elites to manage foreign interests, Kenya has moved farther than most African states toward converting international dependency into a series of mutually beneficial relationships with other nations. At the same time, the very factors responsible for this success have made Kenya vulnerable to international forces that could soon overwhelm it.

To explain how Kenya came to be what it is today, the first two chapters of this book are devoted to the historical determinants of the country's modern quest for prosperity. These include early trade patterns and colonial experiences, important agreements reached at

1

independence, and the politics and policies of the first postcolonial government, led by President Jomo Kenyatta. The next four chapters focus on the contemporary period, beginning with the rise to power of President Daniel arap Moi in August 1978. These discussions approach Kenya from the perspectives of its current social, political, economic, and international realities. A concluding chapter projects the country into a twenty-first century full of dangers and opportunities.

The people of Kenya form an intricate mosaic of African societies with an admixture of Asian, Arab, and European influences. The population remains overwhelmingly rural, although voluntary and forced urbanization is rapidly altering this situation. Growing at an astounding annual rate of nearly 4 percent during the 1980s, the Kenyan population swelled from 19.5 million in 1984 (when the first edition of this book was published) to an estimated 27.5 million by 1993. This increase and the scarcity of arable land to accommodate it have created one of Kenya's most intractable problems of socioeconomic development. More than 80 percent of the population inhabits less than 20 percent of the land, producing demographic pressures that threaten agricultural carrying capacities in less well-endowed regions. High population densities in fertile zones have prompted movements of impoverished farmers to Kenya's vast but ecologically fragile arid and semiarid lands. Out-migration from heavily settled rural areas has produced annual urbanization rates of more than 8 percent. In 1965, 9 percent of the population lived in underemployed and food-dependent urban areas; by 1990 the urban proportion had risen to 24 percent.[1]

In this potentially Malthusian setting requiring urgent policy responses, the Kenyan governing system is dominated by hierarchically organized networks of patron-client relations. Power flows from the top, ultimately the office of the president, through formal and informal channels managed by ethnically and regionally oriented brokers and go-betweens. Kenya politics has a rough-and-tumble character that is observable in the brokerage process and in open contests for favor and position among individuals and ethnic cliques. Young politicians eagerly contend for influence in the ruling Kenya African National Union (KANU) political party, in the trade unions and government corporations, and in the private sector. For its part, the civil service functions as an elite technocracy, although informal economic and political maneuvering also permeates the bureaucratic ranks. Conflicts of interest are of little concern to the civil service, and consequently the administrative process can best be described as "disjointed incrementalism." Imbued with hidden agendas and somewhat casual about detail, this eclectic approach to public problem solving provides work incentives and distributes rewards in society, but it also leads to inefficiencies in daily operations, encourages a proliferation of ill-defined policies, and affords many opportunities for corruption and waste of resources.

Kenya has long served as the center of international capitalism in eastern Africa. Until the early 1980s, it was considered a model of economic opportunity and stability in the region. A 1982 military uprising cast doubt on this assessment, and issues of political and economic security have since preoccupied the domestic leadership and foreign investors as well. Some 350 multinational corporations are based in Nairobi, together with a host of development agencies and volunteer organizations. More than twenty thousand foreign residents belong to this community. Their presence contributes much-needed skills but also creates problems of coordination and control for Kenyan political and administrative elites.

Located astride the equator on the Indian Ocean, Kenya encompasses an area of 582,748 square kilometers (233,099 square miles), making it about as large as France and slightly larger than Texas. Eighty-three percent of the land is arid and semiarid, the remainder consisting of coastal and upland areas of medium to high potential for rain-fed agriculture. Annual rainfall depends on climatic patterns driven by dry winds blowing south from the Sahara Desert and meeting moist air masses from the Indian Ocean. During April and May, monsoon sea

Zebras with Mt. Kenya in background (photo by David Keith Jones/Images of Africa Photobank)

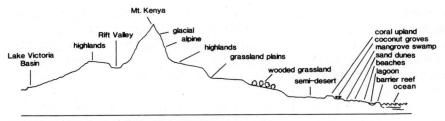

FIGURE 1   Selected ecological zones in Kenya

breezes change their northeasterly direction and become southwesterly trade winds. The pattern is reversed in November and December, completing a cycle that produces most of its rainfall in the April-May season.

Kenya's highest mountain, Mt. Kenya, is located in roughly the center of the country. From a high-altitude aerial perspective Kenya would look like an upside-down saucer. The eastern branch of Africa's Great Rift Valley slashes from north to south through the country, separating the Lake Victoria basin to the west from eastern hills that slide away into dry lowlands and coastal beaches (Figure 1). This complex topography is matched by an equally diverse ecology and pattern of human adaptation.[2]

Kenya can be divided into five ecological zones. Paralleling the Indian Ocean, the *coastal zone* consists of a lowland plain extending 16 to 64 kilometers (10 to 40 miles) inland. A barrier reef lies outside much of the 440-kilometer (275-mile) coastline, and several large islands, including Mombasa and Lamu, dot the offshore waters. The beach ecology of this zone incorporates mangrove swamps, communities of variegated dune vegetation, and brackish estuaries. Mombasa, Kenya's second-largest city and principal deep-water port, bustles on the southern coast. Nonurban settlement features small villages and dispersed homesteads situated a kilometer or more inland from the infertile coral sands nearest the ocean. Mixed agriculture, with maize and cassava predominating, is practiced in this hinterland. Sociologists have referred to the Kenya coast as a "shatter zone," in which a tradition of slaving, warfare, smuggling, and other disruptive activities has led to a permanent fragmentation of indigenous cultures. Coastal African society today is a loose ethnic assemblage, collectively termed the Mijikenda (nine villages).

Kenya's *arid zone* stretches in a great arc from the southeastern part of the country throughout the north and northwest. This expanse is characterized by low rainfall, frequent drought, and rock-strewn wasteland interspersed with hilly outcrops and low mountains. Soils are generally shallow, stony, and of recent geological origin. Despite its infertility and lack of rainfall, the arid zone offers sufficient vegetation and moisture to support widely dispersed human and wildlife populations. Groups such as the Boran, Gabbra, Rendille, Samburu, Somali, and Turkana persist in their time-honored tradition of seminomadic pastoralism despite attempts to settle them with a view to commercializing their livestock economies and providing their scattered communities with improved education, health care, and other amenities.

The Kenya *highland zone* was dubbed the "white highlands" in colonial times because its fertile soils, temperate climate, and relatively disease-free environment attracted the largest number of resident Europeans in British East Africa. Today Kenya's largest ethnic group, the Kikuyu, is concentrated in the central portion of the highlands. The highland zone is a region of rolling uplands characterized by cool weather, abundant rainfall, rich volcanic soils, and dense human settlement. Together with the eastern part of the Lake Victoria hinterland, it represents only about 10 percent of Kenya's total land area but contains over half its population. Here a plenitude of native flora and fauna is complemented by a wide variety of agricultural products. For example, under strong equatorial sunlight the upper reaches of Mt. Kenya support many varieties of bamboo, lichens, giant ferns, and other plants rare in eastern Africa. Lower on the mountain, a wide assortment of food and export crops is cultivated with high yields.

The highlands are divided into two sectors separated by the Rift Valley. The eastern highlands lie north of Nairobi and include Mt. Kenya, the Aberdare Mountains, and the high plateaus to the west. Here small and large farms, estates, settlement schemes, and ranches produce coffee, tea, wheat, maize, barley, dairy products, and cattle. The cities of Eldoret and Kitale serve as market centers for the western highlands, in which less-densely settled farming areas are planted in wheat, barley, and maize. The eastern and western highlands together generate the lion's share of agricultural output for Kenya's largely agricultural economy.

The *Lake Victoria basin zone* forms a crescent adjoining the northeastern corner of Lake Victoria. Here rolling, well-watered farmland is intersected by dry savannas rising to between 540 and 720 meters (1,800 to 2,400 feet) above sea level. Kisumu, the third-largest city in Kenya and the western region's major entrepôt, is situated on the lakeshore and functions as an important railhead and port. Sandy and loamy soils and a semitropical, often humid climate typify this zone. Exceeding 300 people per square kilometer in some places, average population densities in the Lake Victoria basin equal those of the crowded central highlands. Economic activities include commercial cotton and sugar production, intensive small farming in bananas and other food crops, and a substantial lake fishing industry. The Lake Victoria zone is home to Kenya's second- and third-largest ethnic communities, the Luo and the Abaluhya.

The *savanna zone* of south-central Kenya is a place of lush grasslands, majestic vistas, and plentiful wildlife. Varying in altitude from 750
to 1,800 meters (2,500 to 6,000 feet), the prairies of this zone separate the
western highland steppes and the Lake Victoria basin from the arid
reaches of the northeast. Some of Africa's best-known game preserves,
including Nairobi National Park, Maasai Mara National Reserve, and
Amboseli National Park, have been established here. (Islands of similar
grasslands in otherwise drier regions are likewise set aside for wildlife,
notably Samburu National Reserve and parts of Tsavo National Park.[3])
Roamed by the fabled Maasai, the open ranges of the savanna zone are
primarily given over to pastoralism, with some shifting cultivation of
food crops. This equilibrium will soon change, however, as the savanna
country is subjected to peasant migrations and elite land accumulations
from the densely settled and politically dominant north.

In a country still full of open spaces and frontier wilderness, it may
seem ironic that Kenyans have for so long been preoccupied with land
hunger, land struggle, and an unrelenting pursuit of territoriality. For
centuries, a central theme running through the Kenyan experience has
been intense competition for prime farming land, rights to grazing land,
access to hunting land, land to bequeath to kindred and to withhold from
strangers. Now as in the past, Kenya's quest for prosperity is intimately
linked with the land.

1

The Colonial Legacy

BEGINNINGS

Eastern Africa may very well be the birthplace of humanity.[1] Some of the earliest predecessors of *Homo sapiens* lived around the lakes and in the lush, game-filled savannas of the Great Rift Valley. During the late 1950s and 1960s, the remains of *Zinjanthropus boisei* and *Homo habilis* were discovered at Olduvai Gorge in northern Tanzania. These two species lived during the Lower Pleistocene epoch, between three million and one million years ago. More recently, a probable ancestor of these protohumans was uncovered near Lake Turkana in Kenya. Pioneered by the Leakey family of prehistorians, the search continues for still older evolutionary progenitors.

As far as can yet be determined, the human history of Kenya began about ten thousand years ago, when isolated communities of Khoi-San hunters and gatherers settled in the Rift Valley. These movements were followed in the first millennium B.C. by migrations of Cushitic-speaking pastoralists from southern Ethiopia and in the first millennium A.D. by a much larger influx of Bantu-speaking cultivators from western Africa. The initial settling of Kenya was completed between the tenth and the eighteenth century in a series of migrations from the Sudanic Nile region.[2]

By the beginning of the sixteenth century, many of the socioeconomic and cultural features of modern Kenya had taken basic shape. The dry reaches of the north were inhabited by widely scattered populations of seminomadic pastoralists. In the south, pastoralists and cultivators bartered goods and competed for land as long-distance caravan routes penetrated the territories of both from the Kenya coast to the kingdoms of what is now Uganda. A mixing of Arab, Shirazi, and coastal African cultures had given rise to an Islamic Swahili people trading in a variety of up-country commodities, including slaves. Networks of commerce linked inland societies with the coast. From their home territory in south-central Kenya, Kamba elephant hunters mounted long-distance expeditions in search of ivory. To the west, Kikuyu farmers overcame their hostility toward free-ranging herders in the interest of a sophisticated trade with the pastoral Maasai in cattle, iron goods, and items obtained from coastal merchants.[3] Commerce in the vicinity of Lake Victoria focused on skins and hides, salt, forged iron products, and beeswax.

Much of this early interaction among peoples was stimulated by the impact of Arab and Shirazi entrepôts including Kilwa Kisiwani, Pemba, Zanzibar, Gedi, Malindi, and Mombasa. Galleon-like dhows sailed with the monsoon winds to and from eastern Africa, transporting large varieties of imports and exports. Reaching Kenya were salt, metal goods, beads, furniture, tools, and cloth. Carried away were slaves, ivory, dried fish, tortoise shells, and building materials. As this traffic increased in the eleventh and twelfth centuries, key trading ports became self-governing city-states complete with merchant houses, military establishments, and civil administrations. Two important cultural nuances resulted from this activity. First, Kiswahili emerged as eastern Africa's major language of trade. Originating in a combination of Bantu and Arabic dialects, Kiswahili facilitated economic relations and, as a lingua franca, eventual European exploration, religious conversion, and colonization from the coast to Lake Victoria and beyond. Second, a rich coastal civilization—the Omani-Swahili—arose from the combination of African and Arabian Gulf traditions to form distinct patterns of architecture and art, poetry, cuisine, manners, and social customs.[4] Chief among the latter was a strong mercantile ethic.

In 1498, a new era began for coastal eastern Africa with the arrival of the Portuguese explorer Vasco da Gama. Trade and conquest were the twin objectives of the powerful Portuguese, and within a short time they dominated the western Indian Ocean littoral. Fort Jesus, with its imposing ramparts and turrets overlooking Mombasa harbor, was completed in 1593 to afford the Portuguese military control over the coast and to eliminate the commercial hegemony of the resident Omani Arabs. Intended primarily to establish and defend resupply points for ships en route to the Orient, Portuguese suzerainty was oppressive but relatively short. Under the command of the imam of Oman, Saif bin Sultan, Omanis took Mombasa in 1698 and captured Pemba and Kilwa a year later. By 1729 they had expelled the Portuguese from all settlements north of the Ruvuma River, which later formed the northern boundary of Portuguese Mozambique.

Although their tenure was brief and disruptive, the Portuguese contributed significantly to Kenya's food crops and coastal technologies. They probably brought the first maize, potatoes, and cassava root to eastern Africa.[5] They also exercised considerable influence over local naval design, navigation and sailing techniques, and modes of warfare. Still, the Kenya coast had nurtured an Islamic African-Arabian civilization before the Portuguese came, and when they left it returned to Islamic control. The interlopers represented an alien, Christian culture that subsequent Muslim rulers took particular care to eradicate.

Having expelled the Portuguese, Saif bin Sultan returned to Oman after appointing Arab governors over the coastal city-states. Several of these regimes later fell under the sway of the governor of Mombasa, Muhammed bin Uthman al-Mazrui, head of the powerful Mazrui dynasty. Appointees from this family soon gained dominion over much of the coast, ruling as independent sultans while offering ceremonial allegiance to the Omani imam and often quarreling among themselves for influence and wealth. These unstable arrangements persisted into the nineteenth century.

Trade and slavery characterized the second Islamic period in Kenya, extending from 1700 to 1880. Slaves were needed throughout the Arabian Peninsula to man Arab armies, to perform manual labor, and to serve as house servants and harem eunuchs. Europeans, particularly the French, also employed slaves in their newly acquired colonial outposts. The slave trade was controlled by Gulf merchants, who arranged orders and supplied dhow transport. Kenya-based Arabs organized expeditions and either led these forays themselves or relied on Swahili middlemen. Onslaughts of slave hunting tore apart indigenous coastal societies and spread enormous suffering as far west as the eastern Congo. Slaving continued throughout the 1700s, to be challenged only in 1807, when the British abolished slavery and initiated the long process of ending the trade.

A key personality in the Indian Ocean antislavery movement was Said bin Sultan, more commonly known as Sayyid Said, who became imam of Oman in 1806. Sayyid Said realized that he required British help to consolidate his rule in Oman and to reclaim Oman's eastern African territories. He was thus persuaded to accede to the Moresby Treaty of 1822, a European-Zanzibari agreement prohibiting the sale of slaves to Christian powers. Backed by the British, Sayyid Said traveled to Mombasa in 1828, expelled the Mazruis from Fort Jesus in 1836, and soon after moved his capital from Oman to Zanzibar. From there he extended his trading empire from Mogadishu to the Ruvuma, ruling both Oman and coastal eastern Africa until his death in 1856.

During the last twenty years of his reign, Sayyid Said displayed little enthusiasm for the antislavery movement and in fact lacked enforcement power over his acquisitive mainland and island subjects. Slavery continued and in some areas increased. It was not until a successor, Said Barghash, took stronger pro-British measures that the trade began significantly to diminish.[6] Said imposed a total ban in 1873, but because the measure was still extremely unpopular among traders and coastal merchants, clandestine slaving persisted. Trafficking in human beings provided a powerful incentive for Arab entrepreneurs and their Swahili agents. An equally compelling humanitarian concern for its abolition excited the interest of two other entrepreneurial groups. These introduced even more portentous alien forces, one religious and the other imperial, into eastern Africa.

THE EUROPEAN PENETRATION, 1880–1915

After "discovering" eastern Africa in the early to middle 1800s, Christian missionaries and missionary-explorers became preoccupied with two objectives: to stamp out the slave trade and domestic slavery and, through Protestant and Roman Catholic conversion, to confer a firm sense of Victorian morality on the indigenous societies thus saved. Given competing Islamic beliefs and economic practices along the coast and the potential resistance of myriad inland African societies, both tasks were formidable. Two such proselytizers, Johann Krapf and Yohannes Rebmann, established Mombasa's first mission station in 1846, but it was not until Said Barghash's banning of slavery in 1873 that missionaries felt free to speak out against the practice. Even then, there was widespread opposition; the resident Muslim population resented Christian teachings, and slavery was still a profitable business. General resistance was also encountered up-country until growing numbers of Africans began to associate religious conversion with the acquisition of colonial economic rewards.

Indeed, David Livingstone and those who followed him believed that commerce would pave the way for Christianity and that profit derived from a wage-labor system would put an end to all forms of servitude. From the 1870s on, European travelers and traders, particularly those involved in the Uganda caravans, came under strong moral pressure to pay fully for their porters and to avoid compulsory labor. Missionaries instructed their converts in the mechanical and agricultural arts and committed Kiswahili to the Roman alphabet so that it could serve future economic and administrative purposes as well as their own. In short, missionaries carried the related messages of Western religion, orderly progress, and commercial profit.[7] These lessons, especially the latter, were not lost on those who were to feel the full impact of colonial rule.

In contrast to the Portuguese, the second wave of eastern Africa's European invaders, led by explorers and missionaries, intended to move inland and, eventually, to settle. In the south, Germans occupied what later became Tanganyika Territory (plus present-day Rwanda and Burundi) and ultimately independent Tanzania (including Zanzibar). To the north, Britain claimed Kenya as its East Africa Protectorate in 1895 and in 1920 annexed all but the coastal strip as Kenya Colony. The coast remained under the nominal jurisdiction of Zanzibar, by now itself, like Uganda, a British protectorate.

The motives for this penetration were religious, economic, and political. By 1880, the missionary movement was bringing strong pressure on the British government to commit itself more fully to the antislavery campaign and to protect Victorian clergymen venturing up-country. The economic prospects of the entire region had been dramatically altered with the opening of the Suez Canal in 1869. Kenya was now closer to England, and Mombasa had suddenly become an important strategic port on the British trade route to India and the Far East. European industrialization had produced intense economic and political rivalries, allowing France and Germany to challenge Britain's technological dominance. In particular, new railroad technology facilitated communication from the sea to the African interior and stimulated the European demand for resources, markets, and the political prestige associated with empire.

For Kenya as for the rest of its African territories, Britain's initial colonial strategy was to permit commercial interests to take the lead and assume the attached risks. In 1888 a privately financed trading company, the Imperial British East Africa Company (IBEAC), was awarded a royal charter to develop commerce in the protectorate. IBEAC was structured like its British-African counterparts, the Royal Niger Company and the British South African Company, but unlike these enterprises it was not based on new mineral concessions or the prospect of quick agricultural profits. Seemingly without direction, the company drifted into financial straits, and this and the founding of the Uganda Protectorate in 1894 led the British government to assume direct control over Kenya in 1895.

According to a logic that today seems fanciful, British policy focused on Uganda as a key to its strategic interests in Africa. The reasoning was that unless Britain controlled Uganda, the headwaters of the White Nile might be dammed by another European power. This would disrupt the river, bring Egyptian agriculture to its knees, cause peasant uprisings in Egypt and the Anglo-Egyptian Sudan, threaten the Suez Canal, and prevent British entry to the Red Sea and beyond. India, the Pearl of the Empire, and the Far East trade could become virtually inaccessible. In reality, damming the Nile would have meant transporting heavy equipment to Uganda, 800 kilometers (500 miles) inland, through a territory with no improved roads or bridges, and thereafter building a structure that was technologically far beyond nineteenth-century capabilities. Nevertheless, Britain moved to safeguard its perceived interests and brought Uganda under its "protection." This action created the need for a supply line to link Uganda with the Indian Ocean, hence the need for an East Africa Protectorate. At first, the Kenyan interior was important not so much in its own right as because it happened to lie between Uganda and the sea and just to the north of suspicious activity in German East Africa.[8]

Begun in 1896, the Uganda Railway played a key role in creating the demographic, political, and socioeconomic configurations of modern Kenya. The immediate aims were to extend a line deep into the unmapped heartland of eastern Africa, to make it pay for itself through exports and by attracting settlers, and to safeguard an important source of the Nile. The ultimate consequences of the Uganda Railway were much more profound and far-reaching.

Construction problems were staggering. Little technical knowledge existed about the terrain that would have to be crossed. Because Africans were averse to the grueling work of railway building, more than thirty thousand indentured laborers had to be imported from India. These workers suffered in the sweltering heat, and some fell victim to man-eating lions in what is now Tsavo National Park. As unanticipated problems mounted, the enterprise quickly became a political issue in Britain. Skeptical of arguments defending the line's commercial potential, detrac-

First train to leave Mombasa for Voi, April 1898 (photo by David Keith Jones/Images of Africa Photobank)

tors dubbed the Uganda Railway the "lunatic line."[9] When the railway was completed, some seven thousand of the "Asian" (Hindu and Muslim Indian) work force elected to stay in Kenya. Mostly cooks, artisans, and suppliers, these immigrants swelled the ranks of an existing minority community that would eventually make a significant commercial impact on Kenya and add complexity to the country's ethnic and emerging class structures.[10]

The railway line followed older caravan tracks leading through dry coastal bush country and gradually climbing toward the 2,100-meter (7,000-foot) Rift Valley escarpment, 480 kilometers (300 miles) from Mombasa. At a place called Ngongo Bargas on the escarpment, forest-dwelling Kikuyu and grassland Maasai had long met to resupply and trade with passing caravans. It was near here that the railway built its repair shops and, after 1905, settlers attracted by the area's temperate climate and clear water established the commercial and administrative capital of Nairobi.[11]

Arriving at Ngongo Bargas as a young adventurer in 1890, Frederick Lugard lived for a time with the Kikuyu.[12] Despite the Kikuyu's reputation for violence, Lugard reported them peaceful, helpful, and eager to learn European ways. A different impression was left on Francis Hall, who served first as an IBEAC agent and then as a protectorate official. Siding with the Maasai in land disputes with the Kikuyu, Hall pressed farther north into present-day Murang'a District and encountered Kikuyu hostility. He proceeded to "pacify" the area with heavily armed Swahili troops. In 1894 Stuart Wall, central Kenya's first missionary, walked with his family from Mombasa to Ngongo Bargas and set up a mission station.

Following early contacts such as these, two developments occurred that facilitated the economic opening of central Kenya. First, the British were able to solicit the cooperation of two senior chiefs, Lenana, a Maasai, and Waiyaki, a Kikuyu. Lenana helped create a safe passage through Maasailand, an area that for decades had posed serious dangers to caravans. Although less powerful than the paramount rulers of Uganda, Waiyaki and some of the other Kikuyu chiefs mustered enough influence to control their immediate neighborhoods. Here the British established the foundations for their subsequent "indirect rule" approach to local administration. Colonial officers would manage the chiefs and the chiefs their people.[13]

A second advantage to European occupation and settlement was fortuitously supplied by nature. Beginning in 1897, drought combined with an epidemic of rinderpest to ravage south-central Kenya. Food crops and 95 percent of the region's cattle were destroyed, decimating both the Kikuyu and the Maasai. Surviving Maasai communities dispersed, and the Kikuyu retreated north to the heart of their territory near Mt. Kenya. When pioneering Europeans came to the south-central highlands, they encountered large tracts of uninhabited land. Here the settlers halted, believing (or wishing to believe) that they were the area's first inhabitants. Quite understandably, the Kikuyu viewed their withdrawal as only a temporary crisis response, and thus a land dispute was created that would plague Kenya for the next sixty-five years.

Part of the misunderstanding lay in the fact that, as settlers spread north and west into the fertile highlands, they were often welcomed by Africans. At first, the newcomers were not widely perceived as a threat. Like Arab caravans, supply expeditions bound for Uganda, and railroad construction crews, they were expected to move on. In any case, the number of Europeans was initially small compared with African populations. In 1900 only 480 Europeans resided in all of Kenya, including twenty farming families. Between 1903 and 1906, the arrival of 800 Boers from South Africa spearheaded a growth of from 790 to 1,800 Europeans. The ensuing eight years witnessed major increases, so that by 1914 the European community totaled 5,400, about 3,000 of them settlers.[14]

These trends seemed to justify the Marxist-Leninist critique of imperialism.[15] The argument was that advanced capitalism led to the formation of vast colonial empires from which alien usurpers extracted raw materials, cheap labor, and captive markets for themselves and their industrial metropoles. This proposition was to be debated and refined in Kenya over the next eight decades. It is doubtful, however, whether many Europeans of the period thought in such terms. Missionaries came to assume the Victorian "white man's burden"; public officials came to assist them and to pursue what they felt were legitimate political, economic, and security goals; individuals and families came in search of advancement; all came to find adventure. Most would have rejected the notion that the British Empire was exploitative and should be curtailed. Left at home were the isolationists, who believed that Britain would be better off attending to domestic society. While less-altruistic skeptics opposed imperialism on the grounds of the tax burden it imposed or the superiority of global "free trade," those who ventured to Kenya spoke of new opportunities for wealth and achievement.

What few Europeans acknowledged was that Kenya Africans had basically the same goals. Although precolonial Kenyan societies were generally small and relatively undifferentiated as to economic and political function, they were as dynamic and purposive as the kingdoms and interlacustrine states to the west. Their chief object of acquisition was land, for which they actively competed. Unfortunately for cultivators and pastoralists alike, the invading Europeans were after the same commodity, and they were the more powerful competitors.

Striking changes overtook Kenya between 1895 and 1915. A colonial bureaucratic hierarchy was structured, the lowest rung of which consisted of government chiefs and headmen grafted onto and supervising existing systems of age-grade and kinship authority. Missionaries built schools, clinics, and churches and assembled communities of African converts. Settlers flooded into the highlands, bringing with them European farming techniques that some younger African farmers began to emulate. Asian and European traders set up retail and wholesale businesses, spreading the practice of production for cash sale. Responsibility for the East Africa Protectorate shifted from the British Foreign Office to the Colonial Office, and the first advisory councils were established in Nairobi to serve the interests of European settlers and merchants. Further impetus was given to the cash economy through the imposition of taxes on all inhabitants of the protectorate. The final stone of colonial occupation was set in place by the East African (Land) Ordinance, which allowed Africans to occupy lands not held by Europeans but denied them titles of ownership in these "native reserves."

Perhaps the most profound and far-reaching change of the period was the rapid claiming by Europeans of Kenya's limited arable land.[16] In 1899, Britain decided that "wastelands and other unoccupied land and that occupied by savage tribes" should come under Crown control and be disposed of as the Crown saw fit. In 1902, the protectorate administration received authorization to lease Crown lands in parcels of between 64 and 256 hectares (160 and 640 acres). The original leases were for ninety-nine years, and this quickly became a bone of contention between settlers and government. In the Crown Land Ordinance of 1915, the administration relented and extended leases to 999 years—only 150 years fewer than had elapsed since the Norman invasion of England. Agrarian-based capitalism was the way of life projected for Kenya for the next thousand years, and white settlers were to be its vehicle. Access to land lay at the center of this dream as war broke out in eastern Africa.

WORLD WAR I IN EASTERN AFRICA

Tragically for the indigenous societies caught up in the struggle, Britain and Germany imported their bloody and, in the final analysis, purposeless European conflict to eastern Africa. At the outset, the Germans mounted a few raids on the rail line and supply dumps at Taveta, just inside the protectorate near the southeastern slope of Mt. Kilimanjaro. All subsequent fighting took place in German East Africa and in parts of Mozambique and Northern Rhodesia (now Zambia). For the survivors among the more than a quarter-million Kenya Africans pressed into service, the campaign provided a basis for long-term political and economic discontent.

At the beginning of the war, European morale was high in Kenya, and a quick, decisive victory over the outnumbered Germans was anticipated. Beginning with the November 1914 battle for Tanga, however, the British encountered one setback after another. At Tanga, a port city on the northern coast of German East Africa, British forces encountered their most decisive defeat since their annihilation at Kabul six decades before. Immediately after a rough crossing of the Indian Ocean, untried and seasick Asian troops were sent ashore to meet a withering hail of machine-gun fire from the *askari* (African soldiers) of the German colony's *Schutztruppe* (Protective Forces). The result was tersely recalled by the famed German East African commander, General Paul von Lettow-Vorbeck:

> The enemy felt himself completely defeated, and he was. His troops had fled in wild confusion and thrown themselves head over heels into the lighters. The possibility of renewing the attack was not even considered. From prisoners' statements and captured official English documents it was ascertained that the whole Anglo-Indian Expeditionary Force of 8,000 men had been thus decisively beaten by our force of little more than 1,000 men.[17]

So humiliating was the Tanga defeat that myths of German invincibility haunted the British and their *askari* for years to come. Assumptions about African cowardice and poor soldiery were put to rest. The British had been routed by a totally outnumbered complement of African regulars under the command of a handful of German officers. The German *askari* had proved themselves disciplined, courageous, and easily a match for the best the British could then muster.

Unlike the mass slaughters taking place in France and Belgium, the eastern African campaign took the form of small-scale guerrilla actions ranging over large expanses of territory. Lettow-Vorbeck had orders to tie up as many enemy troops as possible, thus keeping them out of the trenches in Europe. This he accomplished with hit-and-run tactics that relied on surprise and escape rather than on drawn lines and pitched battles. Eventually comprising Kenyan, Indian, South African, Belgian, and Portuguese elements, British colonial forces had still not caught up with Lettow-Vorbeck and his *Schutztruppe* when the European war ended in 1918.[18]

Given the relatively limited number of fighting men and support personnel committed to the struggle, casualties were high on both sides. At any given time, German forces never exceeded 3,000 Germans and 11,000 German *askari*. After Tanga, the British command grew to 300,000, about half of them seeing field action at the height of British troop strength. With Asian sepoys and African regulars from other colonies available for combat duty, the British employed Kenya Africans primarily as porters. Of the 250,000 men enlisted in the African Carrier Corps, between 45,000 and 50,000 fell—mostly to exhaustion and disease. Including 967 European officers, other Allied losses totaled about 10,000 killed, 7,800 wounded, and 1,000 missing or captured. The Germans counted 740 Europeans among an estimated 2,000 killed, 9,000 wounded, 7,000 missing or captured, and 6,000 to 7,000 carriers dead mainly, again, from fatigue and sickness.[19]

World War I affected mutual perceptions among all of Kenya's major racial and ethnic groups. Africans were newly respected by Europeans for their stoicism, valor, and discipline in both the Carrier Corps and the fighting ranks. For many African conscripts, the war's most profound and potentially empowering experience was to witness whites systematically hunting and destroying other whites. European and African contempt was reserved for the imported British-Indian troops and, by association, the local Asian minority. The Tanga engagement was followed by other instances of sepoys' breaking and running under fire. In spite of the spirit and courage displayed by Indian troops on other occasions, the stigma of Tanga reinforced European conceptions of Asian duplicity and inferiority and paved the way for African mistrust and discrimination in future years.

The war placed a significant strain on the political economy of the protectorate. Two-thirds of Kenya's male white settlers left their farms for the fight, and within months their fields and pastures had returned to bush.[20] African households suffered not only from an absence of men but also from the requisitioning of many of their livestock to feed the troops. The situation was worsened by a war-related shortage of veterinary personnel to combat a rinderpest outbreak in 1916 and by the drought and famine of 1918.

The struggle for German East Africa had political repercussions that the colonial government deemed equally threatening to European society. African soldiers and carriers came home with new perspectives on whites and on themselves as actors in the colonial milieu. Sensing the possibility of widespread discord and even insurrection, protectorate authorities urged London to encourage more European settlement. A new infusion of immigrants began in 1919 under a soldier-settler scheme that enabled British veterans of the European war to relocate in Kenya. Some 1,053 large farming tracts were sold to soldier-settler families at nominal prices, and another 257 were simply given away. Much of the land required for these farms was taken from Nandi reserves in the western highlands. The Nandi had stubbornly fought colonial expansion at the turn of the century, and the most recent imposition reopened old wounds. Soldier-settler land titles took fourteen years to adjudicate and administer.[21]

Although the seeds of anticolonial nationalism were sown by the returning Carrier Corps and British *askari* and by yet another European influx and loss of land, the postwar period also produced an expansion of African participation in Kenya's growing economy. Frustrated by a lack of opportunity in agriculture, many highlands inhabitants turned to a variety of alternative income-earning activities. They helped commit the country to a course of uneven capitalist development from which it has not departed.

THE INTERWAR YEARS

The Economy, 1920–1940

By the 1920s, a racially stratified private economy had become implanted in Kenya Colony. Europeans occupied owner-managerial positions, Africans worked primarily as servants, laborers, and petty traders, and Asians served as a buffer between these two groups in their roles as artisans, clerks, and merchants. Most important, Africans were inexorably drawn to the fringes of the formal economy, exposed to the advantages of Western materialism but excluded from most of its incentives and rewards.

The system was activated by sanctions employed by the colonial government to ensure a reliable African work force. Punitive hut taxes were imposed that could be worked off or paid from the proceeds of wage labor. A compulsory registration system installed in 1921 required adult African males to carry certified labor passes, or *vipande* (singular *kipande*). On each pass, successive European employers recorded the types of work assigned to the employee, wages earned, dates of employment, and evaluations of individual performance. The power to enter negative comments afforded white employers considerable control over their black workers. By 1928, an estimated 675,000 of the hated passes were in circulation.[22]

In order to obtain labor for the plantations, semifeudal squatterism was officially and privately encouraged. In the white highlands of central Kenya, Kikuyu farming families were restricted to native reserves and allocated plots too small to permit self-reliant subsistence. Thus forced into formal-sector employment, such families were allowed to build temporary huts and develop household gardens on European farms. This heavy-handed and deliberate manipulation of land tenure guaranteed white farmers a plentiful supply of cheap male labor, with women and children available nearby when extra hands were required. As squatter families became more numerous and dependent on their borrowed huts and gardens and as growing populations within fixed boundaries denied them return to the home reserves, a landless and increasingly restive rural proletariat became a permanent part of the economy of the highlands.[23]

Tension during the interwar years was not confined to European-African relations. As Kenya adjusted to the routines of colonial governance and economic extraction, differences between white public and private interests became more pronounced and openly contested. The bureaucracy in Nairobi was preoccupied with keeping the peace and maintaining a steady volume of exports so that career-enhancing profits could be remitted to Britain. Of equal importance to the government was making sure that Africans paid their taxes, the central source of the colony's domestic finances and thus its chief means of satisfying a Colonial Office requirement that British territories at least cover their own administrative costs. As altruists found their way into the Kenya colonial service, more discussion was heard about government's "trusteeship" obligations and about the need for "fair and proper treatment of the natives." For their part, European settlers were mainly concerned about their land, their superiority over Africans, and their continuing ability to acquire inexpensive, dependable farm workers. A basic rift could not help but develop between those who for various reasons were committed to colonial "law, order, and good government" and those who were just as determined to preserve Kenya as a "white man's country."

Much of the settlers' intransigence doubtless resulted from their precarious economic position. Despite the boom of the mid-1920s, European farming enterprises faced severe and largely self-induced investment and cash-flow problems. In 1930 the chronicler of British colonialism, Lord Hailey, reckoned that Kenya white settlers were actually cultivating less than 10 percent of the land under their control.[24] Notwithstanding the approaching global depression, the conclusion that the settler economy was not very well managed became inescapable. Liberally supplied with cheap African labor and with subsidized farm credit, official price supports, free extension services, and private wealth from home, the settlers' agriculture, like their early trading ventures, often remained inefficient and unprofitable.[25] Compounding a noticeable absence of business acumen within the settler community was a mentality common to plantation cultures. In one assessment,

> European settlers as a class more resembled a landed aristocracy than a capitalist entrepreneur group. Their concern with secure leisure, conspicuous display, and a generally gentlemanly status outweighed any tendencies toward maximum reinvestment of surpluses whenever such reinvestment was not essential to the very continuity of the plantation.[26]

By 1939, urgent questions were being raised in London about whether Kenya's evolving modes of production were conducive to the long-term development of the colony.[27]

Challenging the doubters were advocates who argued that Kenya was well on its way toward fiscal self-sufficiency, that the Royal Navy now had a strategically vital deep-water port on the Indian Ocean, and that Uganda, the Nile, the Suez Canal, and the passage to India were all securely protected. Other backers pointed to an agricultural experiment station whose presence would benefit the entire empire through its research into the improved production of coffee, tea, sisal, maize, cotton, tobacco, copra, fruits, vegetables, and livestock. British importers to Kenya especially appreciated the preferential treatment they received over local competition.[28]

On balance, a heavily subsidized, economically inefficient, and somewhat decadent settler society was effectively sheltered by British bias toward Kenya Colony. Until their edifice of support began to erode after World War II, Kenya settlers continued to be nurtured by this peculiar form of welfare capitalism.

African Protest and Colonial Response, 1920–1940

As early as 1920, Africans began opposing the inferior role assigned them in the settler-dominated economy and society. The first protests occurred in Kiambu, a coffee-producing district just north of Nairobi, where a Kikuyu rural association petitioned against the alienation of rich farming land to Europeans. District and central authorities pointedly ignored these expressions of discontent.

When petitions and letters of grievance failed to work, a more militant approach was selected by another group organized in 1921. Under the leadership of Harry Thuku, then a government telephone operator, the Young Kikuyu Association was formed to protest a number of colonial policies affecting central highlands Africans, including land confiscations and native reserves, hut taxes, and the reviled labor passes. To enlist support beyond central Kenya and the Kikuyu ethnic community, in 1922 Thuku traveled to Kisumu on Lake Victoria and there persuaded a small number of mission-educated Luo to form the Young Kavirondo Association. The Kisumu trip was politically successful, but it also led to Thuku's downfall. Soon after his return to Nairobi, a nervous colonial administration arrested and jailed him on charges of seditious activities. In what became Kenya's first political riot, Thuku supporters gathered outside the Nairobi central police station and were fired upon when they refused to disperse. Twenty-five Kikuyu were slain in the incident. Thuku's organizational triumphs and these martyrdoms established him as the colony's prototype African nationalist, but his political career had ended. Fearing Thuku's influence, the government exiled him for nine years to Kisimayu on the Somali coast. When he finally returned to Nairobi, he had been eclipsed by younger activists and a new protest movement.

In 1925 the Young Kikuyu Association was renamed the Kikuyu Central Association (KCA), which soon grew into a larger and more viable if still largely monoethnic interest group. KCA's issues—land scarcity, labor passes, regressive taxation, and inadequate educational and employment opportunities—had wide appeal among Kenya Africans. The protestors' major difficulty lay in organizing and coordinating political pressure on a colonywide basis. Travel was expensive, the registration system restricted movement, and ethnic animosities persisted. Ethnic suspicions presented a particularly thorny problem because mobilizing effective opposition to colonial policies demanded mutual trust, loyalty, and confidentiality. Early leaders such as Harry Thuku found it much easier to rally neighbors and kinsmen than to build alliances across ethnic lines.[29]

Three years after the KCA was founded, Johnstone (Jomo) Kenyatta became its general secretary. From this point until his death fifty years later, Kenyatta was the most important actor in Kenya's colonial and immediately postcolonial history. In 1929, the KCA sent him to London, where he presented a petition to the Colonial Office for the election of Africans to the Kenya Legislative Council, an advisory body representing mainly settler interests. In 1931 he returned to Britain, this time to bring grievances before Parliament concerning land alienation and work permits. He failed in both missions but remained in Europe until 1946. First traveling on the continent and to the Soviet Union and thereafter settling in London, Kenyatta married an Englishwoman and worked as a lobbyist for Kenyan and Pan-African concerns. He also studied at the London School of Economics under Bronislaw Malinowski and in 1938 published the now-classic anthropological study *Facing Mount Kenya: The Tribal Life of the Gikuyu*.[30]

Like Harry Thuku before him, Kenyatta was chiefly worried about the continuing loss of land claimed by the Kikuyu to European settlement. In 1900 the colonial government had begun relegating Africans to reserves that, as Kenyatta pointed out, were under serious population pressure merely twelve years later. The authorities had in fact calculated these excessive settlement densities into their employment strategy for the settler economy. Forced out-migration made about 12,000 Africans available for menial labor in 1912. The number rose to 152,000 by 1927 and more than 200,000 by 1939.[31]

In response to increasing African agitation and settler demands for heightened domestic security, the administration took steps during the interwar period to routinize official relations with the African majority. Decision-making power flowed directly from the governor and a council of ministers to provincial and district commissioners and finally to European district officers and government-appointed chiefs and headmen. Chiefs formed the cornerstone of local administration. Employed as colonial agents, few enjoyed traditional legitimacy, and most were perceived simply as local notables with authority to carry out public functions. Chiefs were assisted by headmen to collect taxes, to keep the peace and conduct civil courts, and to organize community development projects. Ostensibly to afford Africans experience in representative local government, native councils were established in 1924. As time passed it became apparent that the real (and finally futile) purpose of these bodies was to divert African political attention from the territorial to the village level of affairs.

Limited changes in land policy were also enacted during the interwar years. The Devonshire Declaration of 1923 provided the first indication of any flexibility toward non-Europeans by authorizing Asian, although not African, landownership. In 1932, the Kenya Land Commission (also referred to as the Carter Commission) conducted a firsthand investigation of African complaints in an extensive field survey of land use. Its findings led to the return of several large tracts to African hands but fell short of recommending abolition of the native reserves. Serious inequities in Kenya's land laws festered for two decades before an armed African revolt forced reform.

The 1930s world depression affected Kenya Africans in several ways. As demand for primary commodities and local consumer goods fell, so did employment. Workers who had become dependent on wage labor were thrown back onto the land, often to reserves that had already far exceeded their human carrying capacities. As Brett points out, the settler economy had proven highly effective in marginalizing African peoples:

> The settlers, although initially an exclusively agricultural community, accepted the need to industrialize partly in order to provide more secure markets for local agricultural products, partly out of a desire to see a viable modern economic system established on the lines of the others already under way in the white Dominions. Equally important, their presence had the effect of breaking down the self-sufficiency of the African economic systems much more rapidly than did the peasant systems based [more completely] on indirect rule. In the Kenyan case this had become evident by the mid-thirties, . . . taking the form of apparent rural impoverishment through overcrowding and worklessness.[32]

By 1939, the KCA had become the colony's main African protest organization. As white anxiety over Hitler grew, however, Africans fell victim to yet another European conflict. Declared a threat to the empire's wartime security, the KCA was banned in 1940 and its newspaper seized. Essentially the same fate overtook interest groups representing Asians and Arabs, as well as a series of ethnic associations formed by Kikuyu, Embu, Meru, Kamba, Taita, Luo, and Abaluhya converts to the European economy. These were mostly small protonationalist entities that mixed protest with millennial religious advocacy. All such fires of opposition were banked during the war years, legally by colonial decree but also with general African consent. In effect, blacks and whites declared a political truce for the duration of World War II.

WORLD WAR II AND THE MAU MAU PERIOD

Even before the Germans launched their attempted conquest of Europe and North Africa, the large military presence maintained by Germany's Italian ally in Ethiopia and Somalia caused great alarm in Kenya. British authorities feared that a quick Italian strike could cut off local and international communications, shut down the Uganda Railway and the port at Mombasa, and eliminate Kenya as a source of resupply for Allied African forces. To prevent this from happening, a contingent of King's African Rifles and settlers was dispatched to northern Kenya. Except for a successful invasion of British Somaliland, Italy's advance in eastern Africa was delayed. This hiatus enabled the Kenya garrison to be reinforced from Britain, with additional units from South Africa, Nigeria, Northern Rhodesia, and Gold Coast (now Ghana). The buildup of troops was so great that Prime Minister Winston Churchill ordered some of them redeployed north for the defense of Sudan and the Egyptian Nile delta. Still well protected, Kenya functioned as an important provider of food to soldiers fighting in the North African campaign and sent Africans and Europeans to oppose the Japanese in Burma.

For the remainder of what had now become a global conflict, land and employment issues continued to dominate Kenya's constrained political agenda. White farmers pressed into the war effort argued that, if they were to increase food output, they would need more land and African labor. As these demands were met, critics in Kenya and Britain renewed their complaint that the government was abandoning its trusteeship responsibilities and allowing African interests to be overrun. Labour Party members of Churchill's wartime coalition government expressed particular concern over alleged local abuses of imperial emergency powers.

A key question arising from this discussion became whether to permit Africans a voice in the affairs of Kenya Colony. The Colonial Office compromised in 1943 by authorizing a *European* to speak for Africans in the Kenya Legislative Council. The appointment fell to the Reverend L. J. Beecher, a noted political activist and defender of African rights. Beecher's first announcement in his new position must have stunned the conservative settler community. He looked forward, he said, to a time when blacks would sit alongside whites on the council and eventually replace them. This vision began to be fulfilled a year later, when former Oxford University student Eliud Mathu was appointed to the council. Thereafter pressure mounted for broader and more authoritative African participation in government.[33]

As these events suggest, World War II led to fundamental changes in Kenya politics. A new influx of missionaries, businessmen, colonial administrators, and discharged soldiers brought greater diversity to the European segment of society and reinforced the small liberal wing of the white-settler establishment. Like their elders after World War I, returning African troops brought home a new political sophistication resulting from their rejection of white-supremacy myths and their desire for a better future.

What most influenced postwar African politics, however, was the arrival of a single Kikuyu. Jomo Kenyatta returned to Nairobi in 1946 as the undisputed leader of the infant nationalist movement. He was soon elected president of the recently organized Kenya African Union (KAU) and by 1950 had built its membership to about 150,000. This rapid growth of support was made possible by considerable cross-ethnic agreement on land issues and on perceptions of socioeconomic inequity. India's achievement of independence from the British Empire in 1947 further inspired Kenya Africans to seek self-determination. Moreover, persistent unemployment and landlessness within the large Kikuyu population lent impetus to greater militancy than there had been before the war. Kikuyu leaders in the KAU, in the small trade union movement, in the vernacular press, and in other circles began openly calling for internal self-government by any means. Violence finally erupted in 1951 on the initiative of a Kikuyu secret society called the Mau Mau.

The Kikuyu Revolt

Mau Mau was much more than just another ethnic association. It represented an open rebellion of the landless, an uprising of Africans against European colonial authority, the white-settler society and economy, and a handful of landed Kikuyu loyalists condemned as traitors to their own people. The origins of the movement are clouded. The authorities at first convinced themselves that a fanatical religious current had been set loose upon the land, and rumors of oathings and other repugnant rituals quickly spread among Europeans. In all likelihood, Mau

Mau was formed from a coming together of several Kikuyu political forces, including the KCA and other banned organizations. Motivated by territorial complaints in the central highlands that extended back thirty years, Kikuyu dissidents recruited among Embu and Meru living near Mt. Kenya, but few others outside the central region became involved.

Mau Mau violence began with sporadic arson and cattle killing targeted at European and loyalist African farms. These persisted until a politically more serious incident prompted a decisive official reaction. In 1952 a senior native-authority chief and prominent British supporter, Kungu Waruhiu, was assassinated by Mau Mau rebels. The government responded by declaring a state of emergency, arresting Jomo Kenyatta, and calling in British troops to suppress the insurrection. The Mau Mau leadership countered with increasingly militarized attacks on African and European settlements. Over the next four years fighting ebbed and flowed across central Kenya. Most action consisted of surprise night attacks by Mau Mau guerrillas on police posts and isolated farms, matched with ongoing search-and-subdue missions by British troops. At the height of the campaign, nearly a hundred thousand Africans were being held in detention camps. Forced movements were not confined to the rural areas. As a result of a sweep in 1954, code-named Operation Anvil and designed to eliminate a suspected Mau Mau underground network, some twenty-seven thousand Kikuyu, Embu, and Meru residents of Nairobi were rounded up and repatriated to their home areas. Back in the countryside, more than a million Kikuyu were forced into stockaded villages. In a manner similar to what was then taking place in French Indochina and would later be repeated in Vietnam, thousands of existing homesteads and hundreds of unfortified villages were destroyed in order to deny them to the Mau Mau.

As British military superiority made itself felt, about 16,000 Mau Mau fighters fell back to the heavy bamboo forests of Mt. Kenya and the Aberdares. Here action ground to a halt, except for skirmishes between small foot patrols and air raids by Lancaster bombers that killed more wildlife than Mau Mau. When hostilities waned in 1956 and the human costs were calculated, the assumption that non-Africans had been the principal intended victims of Mau Mau was set aside. Official estimates indicated that 95 European, 29 Asian, and 1,920 loyalist African civilians and soldiers had been killed. Mau Mau losses were much higher, consisting of 11,503 killed, 1,035 wounded and captured, and 1,550 captured unwounded.[34]

As to financial costs, the colonial government spent £160 million (about $400 million) in putting down the rebellion, not including the expensive deployment of imported British ground and air forces. Within a short time after the cessation of hostilities, a Colonial Office white paper detailed the meaning and significance of Mau Mau from the British point of view. Although it failed to acknowledge the extent to which innocent Africans had suffered in the conflict, the report finally awarded official recognition to the root cause of the uprising—loss of African land to Europeans.[35]

Settler reactions to this finding ranged from hostile rejection to an acceptance of the need for interracial cooperation in binding up the country's political wounds. The state of emergency was not lifted until January 1960, but some Europeans began earlier to define their enlightened self-interest in terms of accommodating Africans within a de jure multiracial state. In this way, they reasoned, a black middle class would develop and join with whites to maintain a status quo beneficial to them all. On the other side of the debate, die-hard settlers attempted to use the fear generated by Mau Mau to shore up their essentially racist posture in defense of overwhelmingly white land rights. They failed in this last-ditch effort. As domestic and international pressure for land reform inexorably grew, colonial legislation that had protected the 43,420 square kilometers (16,700 square miles) of white highlands began to be struck down. This official turnabout prompted the first exodus of Kenya settlers, mainly to white-ruled South Africa.[36]

Broadly speaking, the Mau Mau experience triggered major policy changes concerning African land rights and representation in government. The reform process began as early as 1954, when a royal commission concluded that Kenya's racial basis for arable land allocation was no longer in keeping with the colony's best interests. This study led to the Swynnerton Plan of 1955, which among other innovations called for a modification of customary land rights in favor of individual freeholds based on plot demarcation and private registration. The plan was intended to consolidate small parcels of property previously held communally and to afford African landowners access to farm credit, agricultural extension services, and technical assistance, including the provision of improved water supplies. The overall objective was to bring profitable cash-crop agriculture to small farmers and thereby to create a yeoman class of rural capitalists fully integrated into the colonial economy.[37]

Implementation of the Swynnerton Plan was assisted by security measures undertaken during Mau Mau. The concentration of rural Kikuyu into fortified villages temporarily removed whole populations from the land and facilitated a rapid consolidation of farm holdings. By 1959 large numbers of freehold titles had been issued to former detainees, new farm supports had been put in place, and a campaign to settle and employ landless farm workers was well under way. The growth of an agrarian middle class had discernably accelerated.

Jomo Kenyatta was himself detained between 1952 and 1959. Arrested at the outset of Mau Mau, he was tried for complicity in the rebel-lion, found guilty, and sentenced to seven years' hard labor. Witnesses linked Kenyatta closely enough to early "seditious talk" to help the gov-ernment make its case. Kenyatta was probably not directly associated with the violent wing of the movement—indeed, he was imprisoned be-fore most of the killing began—but his unwillingness to speak out against it relegated him to exile. His incarceration, combined with his many pre-vious years in Europe, had the advantage of isolating him from the petty squabbles inherent in Kikuyu politics and rendering him attractive to many different factions. This advantage allowed him to be cast as a returning hero after 1959, providing him sufficient stature to become the undisputed leader of Kenya's final drive toward national independence and equality of economic opportunity.

Postwar African Entrepreneurship

Spurred by the wartime expansion of productive activity, a large number of Africans entered the formal economy, and some of these new arrivals soon struck out on their own. One option was trade in remote areas where communications were poor and Asian merchants had not yet penetrated. Peddling rural produce to Nairobi hotels, buying Tugen sheep at Lake Baringo for resale in highland towns, marketing vegetables among workers on settler farms, and undercutting Asians in the maize and millet trade also became profitable endeavors. Still other opportu-nities presented themselves in retail enterprises including shops, small hotels, maize mills, sugar presses, alcohol distilleries, and trucking firms. In many instances, traditional economic exchanges were simply modi-fied to take advantage of new possibilities. In central Kenya, for example, Kikuyu crop wealth continued to be traded for Maasai cattle wealth, now partly through middlemen who converted both groups' barter goods into cash and manufactured consumer products.[38]

African entrepreneurship often operated outside and at the edges of the regulated economy. This informal sector consisted of unlicensed, untaxed, and at times illegal ventures undertaken by local artisans, agents, and suppliers—some of them working part-time while holding jobs in the formal sector. Kenya's shadow economy grew considerably in the postwar years not only because it lay beyond government regulation but also because it afforded low-cost and highly flexible responses to an increasing demand for inexpensive, indigenously produced goods and services.

Countering these trends was the depressing influence of Mau Mau on local capitalism. The state of emergency virtually sealed off the rich central highlands, with the effect that the number of registered African companies dropped from 15 percent of Kenya's total in 1952 to 2 percent in 1953 and then to zero in 1954 and 1955. Even when Mau Mau subsided, African entrepreneurs suffered under government regulation and from shortages of capital, technical skills, and commercial networking. In closest competitive proximity to Africans, the Asian community enjoyed an exclusive mutual-support system reinforced by the Hindi and Gujarati languages. Africans had yet to forge their own patterns of economic trust and cooperation. By 1960, most formal economic power remained in Asian and European hands.[39]

Nevertheless, indigenous capitalism had taken root in the colonial economy, and a petite bourgeoisie of African trader-farmers and businessmen had accrued significant saving, investment, and purchasing power. An overabundance of African secondary-school leavers contributed to this trend. Some were absorbed into government service and into company posts, but many failed to find regular employment and instead turned to informal business activity. Career restrictions and constraints on indigenous entrepreneurship were relaxed somewhat as Kenya approached independence. Africans were admitted to the higher reaches of the colonial bureaucracy, government support of African firms increased, and new venture capital became generally easier to obtain. Since academic credentials opened doors to European-type jobs, the value of advanced education also rose.

By 1959, moreover, the structure of Kenyan industry was also changing. In their effort to establish local assembly plants and factory outlets, a growing number and variety of foreign investors began seeking out African employees, both for their skills and for the protection they would offer in an independent Kenya. The commercial sinecure previously enjoyed by British exporters was replaced by an import-substituting approach to the local marketplace. Foreign-financed firms such as East African Tobacco, East African Breweries, and Shell Oil began offering prospective African agents incentives to carry their products to the rural areas.[40] For their part, African businessmen formed joint-stock and wholly owned companies for the sale of basic commodities such as flour, charcoal, vegetables, and fuel oil. As the African merchant class grew in size and wealth, so did its bullish outlook. The mood was expressed by a wealthy trader: "Rich men of all races get on well together."[41]

The absorption of Africans into the Kenyan political economy was decisively influenced by key policy changes adopted between 1920 and 1960, especially those affecting land tenure and use. The Devonshire Declaration reaffirmed the standard colonial determination to deny Africans land rights, but the subsequent Carter Commission made some land available to the African community. A postwar African Land Development Organization created pilot settlement projects for African farmers

as part of its effort to rationalize land titles and to promote soil conservation, improved range management, and agricultural extension. Most
important, the Mau Mau rebellion gave rise to the Swynnerton Plan and
to land allocation on a nonracial basis. As Jomo Kenyatta's nationalist
movement gained momentum in the late 1950s, additional political pressures and legislative nuances created even brighter prospects for African
capitalism and state control.

THE TRANSITION TO INDEPENDENCE

The 1959–1963 period was as verbally turbulent as the Mau Mau
years were violent. A series of meetings had already been held to edge
Kenya toward a multiracial independence, but a new generation of
African influentials, led by Tom Mboya and Oginga Odinga, both Luo,
positioned itself close to the imprisoned Kenyatta by demanding his
release as a precondition to final negotiations for independence under
majority rule. Kenyatta continued to languish in jail, and the pace of
events quickened.

By 1954, the Lyttleton Constitution (named for the then-serving
secretary of state for the colonies) had opened the door to fuller African
participation in politics and government. Committed to an ultimate goal
of representational parity for all racial groups, this document authorized
eight Africans to sit on the Kenya Legislative Council and initiated a
multiracial civil service at all ranks. In 1958, the Lennox-Boyd Constitution raised the number of African council seats to fourteen and added
one ministerial position to the one already reserved for an African.
Mboya and Odinga were elected and offered ministries. Both refused
their portfolios in protest of an insufficient number of Africans in the prototype parliament.

Kenyatta's seven-year prison term ended in 1959, but he was detained once again for "security reasons" at Lodwar in northern Kenya.
Two other contentious issues were, however, resolved in that year. First,
the ban on political organizations in force during Mau Mau was lifted.
Second, sensing the inevitability of an African-ruled Kenya, the British
government announced a plan to subsidize the purchase of European
farms as a kind of graduation gift to the black majority. As the rebellious
1950s gave way to a new decade of African independence,[42] the first of
the colony's 2,750 settler farms were bought and held in reserve for final
disposition.

During 1960, there were complicated negotiations between the
colonial government and nationalist leaders on the specifics of the land
question. It was finally agreed that Europeans would be permitted to
expatriate their recovered investments, that land transfers would be con-

ducted in an orderly manner so that existing levels of agricultural production could be maintained and if possible increased, and that large
portions of the former white highlands would be subdivided and distributed among the landless rural poor and the unemployed.[43] Mean-
while, in London, the transitional MacLeod Constitution was concluded
at Lancaster House. Still formally requiring multiracial representation,
this latest compromise provided for a Legislative Council of sixty-five
seats with an effective African majority of thirty-three[44] and an African
majority of cabinet ministers. In one of the 1960 conference's most memo-
rable moments, Britain surprised the Kenyan delegation by declaring its
determination to move the colony swiftly through a phase of internal
self-government to full independence.

Almost immediately two political parties coalesced out of the constellation of political organizations, interest groups, and ethnic movements held in check during Mau Mau. With a core membership drawn
from the KAU, the Kenya African National Union (KANU) was formed
by Tom Mboya and Oginga Odinga in the name of Kenyatta. It received
most of its support from Kenya's two largest ethnic groups, the Kikuyu
and the Luo. A second party, the Kenya African Democratic Union
(KADU), was organized by Ronald Ngala, Daniel arap Moi, and others
to counter this Kikuyu-Luo coalition with a more diverse alliance of
ethnic minorities including the Kamba, Kalenjin, Maasai, Mijikenda, and
Somali.

In May 1960, KANU nominated Jomo Kenyatta as party president,
an action quickly disallowed by the colonial government. Undaunted,
KANU leaders insisted that Kenyatta was their undisputed head and demanded that he be released to lead the party following a general election
scheduled for February 1961. When the votes were tallied after a vigorous campaign, KANU had captured eighteen of the thirty-three available
African seats and KADU ten. The remaining five seats were distributed
among unofficial KANU and KADU candidates, independents, and
members of other parties.[45] The KANU majority refused to form a government while Kenyatta remained in detention, forcing the administration to violate its own majoritarian principle by inviting KADU
to form the government. Facing KANU's show of obstinate strength,
Governor Sir Patrick Renison finally agreed to Kenyatta's release. Set free
on August 14 and transported to his home at Gatundu, near Nairobi,
Kenyatta received a tumultuous welcome that was repeated in tours
through Nairobi and Mombasa. In October 1961, and with virtually
unanimous support from the party rank and file, Kenyatta became president of KANU.

Attempting to orchestrate a transition to independence on terms
favorable to themselves, British authorities and white private interests

bartered fundamental political and economic concessions for an informal promise of continuing influence in postcolonial Kenya. African nationalists committed themselves to maintaining and extending private land titles, a decision that would profoundly affect the country's future social and economic relations, its evolving class structure, and even its human ecology and physical environment. In a much broader sense, Kenyatta and his supporters accepted the blueprint offered them for a capitalistic, free-enterprise political economy based on the sanctity of private property. Accordingly, they assented to the buy-out of settler farms but not to a popular African demand that all such lands be redistributed among the dispossessed.[46] The KANU leadership further agreed to remain within the British Commonwealth of Nations, to encourage foreign investment and protect multinational corporations operating in Kenya, to favor British imports, and to emphasize Western partners in aid and trade relationships not involving Britain itself.

For its part, the imperial power consented to a speedy transfer of government and its symbols of authority. In the freewheeling bargaining environment of late-colonial Kenya, this quid pro quo favored an elite cadre of Africans that might later use its political leverage to accumulate land, businesses, and other accoutrements of material wealth at the expense of the poor majority. If its full potential were reached, the independence bargain stood a good chance of giving rise to increasingly unmanageable civil conflict as inequalities increased and disadvantaged Kenyans became more class-conscious. And this was not all. Despite their attempt to install constitutional checks and balances in the final two years before independence, the British were in fact handing over enormous power to one man. Jomo Kenyatta's unrivaled popularity and his skill at individual and group manipulation enabled him to move the system in virtually any direction he chose. He selected a populist and heavily rhetorical platform calling for national unity, centralism in government, "African socialism," and a nonaligned international stance. KADU responded with an independence agenda advocating explicit ethnic representation in a decentralized government, fiscal conservatism, and close ties with Britain.

With KADU in parliamentary control, Kenyatta and his party still lacked governmental authority. KADU had won merely 19 percent of the popular vote and 30 percent of African support in the 1961 election, but the party's parliamentary leadership gave it a false sense of political strength and negotiating power. The result was "two years of fruitless constitutional arguments and political maneuverings."[47] At KADU's insistence, the British experimented with a semifederal geographical distribution of power (the so-called *majimbo*, or "regionalism," arrangement) and a bicameral legislature—both intended to accommodate non-African racial groups and KADU's coalition of ethnic minorities. This contorted attempt at constitutional engineering may have been well-intentioned from a representational standpoint, but it succeeded only in worsening "tribal fears and suspicions over land and power to such an extent that it raised grave doubts over the stability of an independent Kenya."[48] It was not until the June 1963 election and the granting of internal self-government that Kenya attained majority rule under KANU and Kenyatta. Both African and non-African minorities remained uneasy throughout these proceedings, even though KADU and smaller splinter groups had gained twenty-three seats in the newly established forty-one-seat Senate and forty-seven seats to KANU's seventy seats in the House of Representatives. Ethnic Somalis went so far as to boycott the 1963 election, contending that their territory in the northeast should be ceded to Somalia. Notwithstanding such misgivings, a final constitutional agreement was reached at Lancaster House, and Kenya became fully independent on December 12, 1963. The Duke of Edinburgh and transitional Governor Malcolm MacDonald joined Prime Minister Jomo Kenyatta at the flag raising.

Preindependence ceremony, showing the Duke of Edinburgh (seated at left), Mayor Charles Rubia of Nairobi (speaking), Jomo Kenyatta (seated at right), and Governor Malcolm Mac-Donald (seated, far right) (courtesy the *Daily Nation*)

Jomo Kenyatta and Governor Malcolm MacDonald, Independence, 1963 (courtesy the *Daily Nation*)

Britain's Westminster style of parliamentary government lasted less than a year. Two constitutional amendments were adopted in 1964 to establish a Republic of Kenya and a presidency invested with wide-ranging powers.[49] Almost needless to say, Jomo Kenyatta stepped easily into this role. Further changes abrogated the bicameral and *majimbo* provisions of the independence constitution, making the republic a legislatively consolidated unitary state.[50]

CONCLUSIONS: REFLECTIONS ON AN AGE

Although the end of administrative colonialism constituted an important political break with the past, the transition from European to African capitalism in Kenya was so easy that critics were soon suggesting that a class of black compradores was now acting on behalf of a departed white elite and that Kenya had settled into a fixed orbit of dependency around Britain and the West.[51] More optimistic observers argued that Kenya might soon become a model for the rest of Africa, a black-ruled multiracial state simultaneously dedicated to social justice, individual rights, and economic growth. As is typical in such debates, the truth lay somewhere in between.

The roots of this controversy are deeply embedded in history. African and Arab traders had engaged in long-distance mercantilism for centuries before Europeans arrived in Kenya. Responding to the slave component of this trade, Christian missionaries endeavored to commercialize the African population by imparting European values of hard work, vocational education, individualism, and competition for profit. Colonial administrators were instructed to govern Kenya in such a way as to generate fiscal self-reliance and export revenue. These mandates required that a large number of colonial subjects be incorporated into a formal structure of local taxation and wage employment. White settlers kept most of their own profits to themselves but also introduced modern farming systems that Africans eventually adopted. Taking advantage of cheap labor and the availability of foreign venture capital, European corporate agents and domestic entrepreneurs established essential structures and key procedures including industrial rules and regulations, accounting systems, and administratively rational management techniques. Kenyans inherited all of these at independence.

Three aspects of Kenya's colonial experience promoted the considerably greater growth than elsewhere in British East Africa of an admittedly lopsided capitalist political economy. First, Britain's decision to encourage private European settlement colored all further developments in the colony by requiring the subjugation of African land, labor, and human dignity to enhance the wealth, status, and power of whites. Second, administrative policies designed to reinforce the settler economy actually encouraged a shift toward black economic independence. During the early colonial period, between 1900 and 1930, state support for the settlers carried with it an explicit discouragement of indigenous capitalism.[52] Beginning with the 1930s depression, however, the tide gradually changed, and Africans were slowly incorporated as essential participants into the colonial economy. The depression created a greater need for African export crops and tax payments. This shift in emphasis gave rise to an incipient African middle class that took on many of the values and goals of the economically more successful members of the settler community. In particular, an emerging, largely Kikuyu, petite bourgeoisie embraced capital accumulation and the individualistic, risk-taking attitude that attends it. Africans were prevented from accumulating real wealth until after independence, but a determination to do so was deeply internalized by the late 1930s, especially in the white highlands, where the positive and negative lessons of colonialism were most vividly taught and learned.

A third factor influencing the growth of Kenyan capitalism relates to land tenure issues as they emerged during the 1950s. After the fury of Mau Mau had subsided, African nationalist leaders accepted the principle of private landownership and demanded only a change in owners. British compliance was made possible by settlers' willingness, unique in African colonies with large white populations, to sell their farms and leave peacefully.[53] This agreement stands out as perhaps the most remarkable achievement of the final advance toward independence. It also committed Kenya to a potentially dangerous course of unbalanced and possibly unsustainable economic growth, to persistent ethnic and class-based inequality, and to increasingly destabilizing political elitism and personal rule. Today these remain the salient challenges to Kenya's quest for prosperity.

2

Independence: The Kenyatta Era

Anticolonial movements elicited new policy scenarios throughout eastern Africa, but Kenya's basic political and economic strategies remained essentially unchanged during and after the transition to independence. Along with their counterparts in Tanganyika, Uganda, and Zanzibar, Kenyan nationalists pondered and debated collective alternatives for the future. In contrast to what emerged from these other discussions, little real doubt was ever expressed in Kenya—except, notably, by Oginga Odinga—over ultimate goals and means to achieve them. As in colonial times, Kenya's modern quest for prosperity would be waged by competing and largely self-interested parties, each seeking access to domestic and foreign-based resources by capturing positions and/or patrons in the top echelons of state control. The major referee in this process, and its key participant as well, was Jomo Kenyatta.

Kenyatta's commanding presence dominated Kenya politics for the first fifteen years of independence. The period began with a series of constitutional pronouncements suggesting rule by law instead of by men[1] and a rhetorical commitment to socioeconomic equality through African socialism.[2] As Kenyatta consolidated his power, however, an informal system of nepotism and favoritism arose parallel to the legal and formally egalitarian governing system. The realpolitik of independent Kenya became fully apparent by the late 1960s, when Kenyatta and his associates had taken firm hold of the state and its conduits to local and international reservoirs of patronage. The Kenyatta era is important to understand not only because the political economy he set in place has survived his passing but also because Kenyatta's legitimation and extension of the new order's entrepreneurial legacy has lent special intensity to individual and group conflicts in the time since his death.

37

THE TRANSITION YEARS, 1963–1968

Barely had the heady celebrations of independence subsided when the regime was put to its first serious tests. Violence erupted on Kenya's northeastern border and quickly escalated into a major crisis. Ethnic Somalis had been demanding that their grazing lands be annexed to Somalia and, to demonstrate their displeasure, had boycotted the 1963 election. Now, with encouragement and material support from Somalia, *shifta* (bandit) guerrillas began attacking police posts and trading centers inside Kenya. Kenyatta finally declared a state of emergency in the north and began the tedious task of securing the area in a three-year military operation across a vast, arid frontier.

On January 12, 1964, in the midst of the Somali crisis, a mutiny occurred at the Nairobi-based headquarters of the Kenya African Rifles, and British regulars were called in to restore order. The mutiny was prompted in part by a command structure still dominated by British officers and unfulfilled expectations among enlisted men concerning increased wages and fringe benefits. In moves that would stabilize civil-military relations for the next eighteen years, Kenyatta quickly improved barracks conditions and promoted indigenous Kenyans into positions previously held by white expatriates. He also infiltrated all services with intelligence personnel and brought members of the KANU Youth League into military service, thus fostering a sense of partisan loyalty to himself and the party within the ranks. In short, his acquiescent but ominous responses to the mutiny were transparently intended to discourage any further military challenges to the civilian elite.

Kenyatta's ascendancy over real and imagined rivals was not limited to the armed forces. During 1964 most of the KADU membership, including its leaders, voluntarily left the party and joined KANU. KADU was later disbanded, leaving KANU in undisputed command of a de facto one-party state and its promising economy. Probably aggravated by this hegemony, a conflict came to a head between Kenya's ideological left and right wings. Vice President Oginga Odinga, an ally of Kenyatta in the independence struggle, became the self-designated spokesman for the KANU left—declaring at one point, "Communism is like food to me." In response, Kenyatta assumed an ostentatiously anticommunist stance, and a collision between the two became inevitable. In June 1965, Kenyatta publicly denounced "communist imperialism" and shortly thereafter reshuffled his cabinet to reduce Odinga's power.

More than on philosophical grounds, political differences between the two camps were based on practical disagreements as to which personalities should govern at levels immediately below the president. Also at issue was the ethnic and sectional distribution of patronage, especially managerial opportunities in the modernized sector of the economy. Partisan cleavages basically followed ethnic lines. Odinga gained most of his strength from the western Luo and Abaluhya, Kenyatta from the central-highlands Kikuyu, Meru, Embu, and Kamba. This is not to say that ideological and personal affinities played no role in the formation of competing alignments. Tom Mboya, for example, a Luo, remained one of Kenyatta's closest supporters. Also backing Kenyatta was a clique of local Kikuyu notables, many of them drawn from his home district of Kiambu. Odinga-led dissenters worried about what they perceived as an emerging "Kikuyuization" of the civil service and about Kenyatta's increasingly autocratic control over the economy. On a somewhat higher moral plane, Odinga called for domestic equality and international non-alignment, accusing Kenyatta of showing little concern for the poor and maintaining an elitist pro-Western bias in foreign investment and trade policy.

Continuous jockeying for position and trading of accusations preoccupied KANU throughout 1965 and into 1966. Exasperated with this situation, Kenyatta called a national party conference for March 1966 "to set the mischiefmakers straight." Dominating the meetings, he drove KANU's left wing out of the party. Even moderates who remained in KANU eventually lost their influence. Odinga reacted by resigning from the government and forming an opposition party, the Kenya People's Union (KPU). In the political maneuvering that followed, twenty-nine KANU members of parliament defected and joined the KPU. After tolerating formal opposition for two years, in 1968 Kenyatta ended it. Odinga was alleged to have received Eastern-bloc funds for use in fomenting national unrest. Subsequently Bildad Kaggia and other KPU leaders were arrested and detained for holding a public meeting without a permit. Despite widespread outcries against this obvious political harassment, the attack proceeded. KPU candidates were disqualified from running for parliament in 1968 for allegedly having filled out their registration forms incorrectly. After the election, the KPU was solemnly found to have won insufficient seats to form an official parliamentary opposition. In effect, the party had been driven from the scene through an act of sheer presidential will.

By this point the Kenyatta elite had fully consolidated its power. A single-party system was forced into reality under a constitution modified to provide for a highly centralized government. Organized opposition to KANU had been routed, potentially lucrative contacts with the West had been initiated, and a profit-oriented development strategy had been made explicit. At the center of this political monolith was Kenyatta, the master tactician—a man capable of flexibility and forgiveness but unbending and ruthless when he deemed these qualities more appropriate to his ends. He lacked deep philosophical intent or even ideological consistency and was not drawn into the great social debates swirling around him at the time. Unlike his Tanzanian counterpart, Julius Nyerere,[3] Kenyatta expressed no particular world view on domestic, Pan-African, or global issues. Both physically (because of his intense dislike of flying) and intellectually he preferred to remain at home tending the political machine he had created.

The Kenyatta style fascinated Henry Bienen and other political analysts of early independent Africa. Unlike most of his contemporaries, Kenyatta "ruled above [his] party by manipulating factions, working through a relatively strong civil service, operating in a rather narrow sphere of concerns, utilizing his ethnic base, but at the same time appealing to all Kenyans with the force of his historical position as 'He who suffered for the Kenya Nation,' as the spokesman for Kenya nationalism, as the *Mzee* or Elder of the nation."[4] Perhaps more than any other leader in eastern Africa, Kenyatta actively cultivated the "Father of the Nation" image and luxuriated in the aura of high public office. Whether his appeal can be termed charismatic remains debatable, but there was no doubt in the late 1960s about his mass following and ability to woo crowds. Doubts and disenchantment were still nearly a decade away.

During these early years of independence, Kenyatta's permanent agenda for Kenya became clear. The country would be guided on a capitalist course under the expert direction of a trusted civil service. In fact, the rapidly expanding bureaucracy remained loyal to the president because of the social status and material rewards conveyed by membership. African socialism soon became an empty vessel floating on a sea of pragmatism and ambition. Taking their cue from the top leadership, civil servants and private businessmen formed a new class that derived its power and resources from the government. The system was tied to society by an intricate network of patron-client relations operating through a combination of favoritism and repression to bolster and in some cases replace formal governing structures.[5]

Formal Governance

As time passed, it became apparent that a push-pull process was under way between constitutional governing arrangements partly inherited from the British and informal political alignments based on ethnic origin, patronage, and socioeconomic position. Some elements of the former colonial system, chief among them the central civil service, remained viable, employing nearly 80 percent of Kenya wage earners. Other organizations established to foster mass economic and political participation, including the trade unions and KANU itself, seemed nearly moribund. Still others, notably farmer cooperatives and local government councils, fell victim to corruption and poor fiscal management. Many of their functions were either assumed by the central government, abandoned, or carried on through private organizations such as local churches, the self-help movement, and indigenous interest groups. Nearly every constitutional and legal aspect of government was in some way altered to accommodate Kenyatta's determination to centralize power around himself.

Basic Constitutional Changes. Early amendments to Kenya's independence constitution had abandoned a bicameral and quasi-federal parliamentary system in favor of a unitary presidential state. Within this framework, the likelihood of highly personalized presidential rule was enhanced by the passage of a preventive detention act in 1966 and its incorporation as Section 83 of the constitution. This law provides that a person may be "restricted in his movements" if the Ministry of Home Affairs is satisfied that detention is required for the preservation of public security. In its original formulation, no time limits were imposed on a person's incarceration,[6] and even today the term "public security" remains ill-defined. Nor is the government compelled to reveal charges against detainees or permit them outside communication or automatic recourse to the courts. With a few important exceptions,[7] Kenyatta did not think it necessary to employ this infringement of basic rights in order to protect and extend his executive power.

Executive Prerogatives. By exploiting the official symbols of office and his own aura of paternal eminence, Kenyatta was able to adapt the Kenya presidency to serve his political goals and, at the same time, to protect his regime against internal challenges. By law, the office of the president was and remains vested with sweeping powers. The president serves as head of state, government, the civil service, the armed forces, and the governing party. Terms of office are five years, with unlimited opportunity for reelection. A serving president may appoint and dismiss any vice president he chooses, and Kenyatta appointed three.[8] He also initiated the unilateral presidential right of cabinet selection, the only limitation being that government ministers must be members of parliament. Kenyatta appointed some twenty ministers and twenty-five assistant ministers, and through them he manipulated the bureaucracy and the parliamentary leadership as well.

Civil Service Control. Kenyatta's pragmatism and leadership abilities were best revealed in his handling of the government administration. From the moment of independence, he acted decisively to create in the civil service a powerful bureaucracy that was at once highly professionalized and politically loyal. As titular head of the Public Service Commission, Kenyatta exercised pervasive influence over central appointments, pay scales, disciplinary actions, and dismissals.[9] He carried similar weight at the intermediate and local levels of Kenya administration. These jurisdictions include the Nairobi area, seven rural provinces, forty districts, and, within each district, divisions, locations, and sublocations. All of these units are staffed by centrally appointed civil servants,[10] although from the district level down the bureaucratic hierarchy is paralleled by a local government system based on elected councils. Throughout his rule Kenyatta maintained close personal control over the administrative apparatus.

Local Government Eclipse. At independence, Kenya's distinctly British local government system consisted of semiautonomous district and urban councils in the rural areas, towns, and cities. These structures were loosely regulated by the Ministry of Local Government in accordance with parliamentary law and functioned concurrently with the central administration. Councillors maintained permanent staffs to implement a variety of ordinances overseeing feeder-road maintenance, primary-school operations, sanitary inspection, trade and marketplace regulation, business licensing, and the like. Local taxes, license fees, and central government grants funded these activities. From the outset, many councils encountered their greatest difficulties in revenue and supply management, primarily involving inadequate bookkeeping, misappropriation, and outright theft. The Kenyatta government took advantage of these problems in the late 1960s to assume responsibility for the councils' budgets and reduce their authority.

Another embarrassment prompting Kenyatta to curtail council activity was the feuding that was taking place between councillors and members of parliament (MPs). Representing councillors' constituents in Nairobi, MPs tended to assume that their powers were supreme and freely exploited the patronage resources and central connections at their disposal to reinforce their power at home. Local politicians understandably resented these displays of grass-roots politicking and were further annoyed when MPs self-righteously criticized the locals' own often comparatively minor financial improprieties and nepotism. By 1969, this incessant squabbling had finally become intolerable to Kenyatta. Except in the larger cities, district and urban councils were reduced to little more than discussion groups. They were retained as a gesture toward democratic representation, but most of their public responsibilities and funding were transferred to the central bureaucracy.

Changes in KANU. Once the anticolonial goals of KANU had been achieved, Kenyatta relied on the party to organize elections, to rally support for causes he wanted to promote, to generate appropriate mass responses to regime-challenging events, and to focus popular and elite attention on Nairobi, all designed to help him shift power from the local areas to the center.[11] Save for these presidentially aggrandizing functions, the party was left to wither. It was cleared of its preindependence debts and provided a national office, an annual conference, and a district-level branch network. When not activated by Kenyatta, however, the structure fell dormant, and its local offices were vacated and padlocked.

The single-party philosophy meant to defend KANU stood in stark contrast to this reality. KANU was justified as a constructively unifying force in a country of great ethnic diversity and potential for mutually de-structive conflict. Political debate and economic competition were wel-comed only within nation-building and developmental limits set by the party. In fact, it was Kenyatta who established and enforced these rules. Cooperative societies and groups such as the Kenya Farmers' Associa-tion, the Central Organisation of Trade Unions, the Kenya National Chamber of Commerce, and the Federation of Kenya Employees were permitted to vie for political influence and private-sector rewards but were brought up short whenever their objectives conflicted with the president's personal agenda. Organizations offering modest political al-ternatives (e.g., KADU) or espousing irreconcilable differences (e.g., KPU) were either absorbed into KANU or destroyed.

Informal Political Processes

Partly in reaction to the curtailment of formal mechanisms for accommodating interests, informal channels of political and economic communication proliferated during the early Kenyatta period. In its postindependence incarnation, the informal system was at first evanes-cent and fragmented, with some of its elements officially encouraged, others merely tolerated, and yet others politely overlooked because of their sub-rosa and occasionally illegal patronage orientations. Gradually these alternative forms of expression evolved into permanent, although seldom fully visible and integrated, features of Kenya's political land-scape.

The Harambee movement continues to be the most overtly sup-ported parallel structure at the local level. *Harambee*, a Kikuyu exhor-tation to pull together, was chosen by Kenyatta as both a rallying cry and the name for a scheme to help finance village self-help activities, includ-ing the construction of schools, dispensaries, and community centers. Thousands of such projects, more than half of them involving primary education, had been completed before the Kenyatta era ended. Haram-bee ventures relied on voluntary contributions of money and work. In the intimidating atmosphere of local meetings, powerful "big men" were induced to provide public funding to match private labor commitments from community residents. Some communities were able to extract promises from government to staff their social-infrastructural enterprises once construction was finished. The movement was politically as well as socioeconomically significant in that it involved elites in local affairs, extracted funds from them for peasant use, and promoted elite/mass cooperation and consensus. Harambee projects also offered safe opportunities for local participation in an otherwise constricted political arena. In short, they were generally perceived as "good things" to do.[12]

In effect, Harambee schemes substituted for many of the mass-based structures that had been undermined by Kenyatta's drive toward centralization. The party, cooperative societies, trade unions, and local councils had all been brought under the central bureaucracy. Self-help remained local and locally popular, and politicians who needed backing were well advised to contribute. Harambee initially flourished because Kenyatta approved of it as a check on his political subordinates. With this encouragement, the process widened and became one of political brokerage, as villagers began projects and co-opted—often entrapped—leaders into postures of concern about specific improvements and other social issues. Kenyatta also used the Harambee movement as a mechanism for harnessing a sometimes unruly parliament, in essence telling MPs, "Go build the country, for it is in this way that the people will judge you." MPs, he argued, should stay out of national politics, spend less of their free time in Nairobi, and leave affairs of state to him. Ingeniously, Kenyatta turned a widely supported grass-roots campaign into an instrument of control over his last bastion of countervailing power at the top.[13]

Ethnic welfare unions provided additional opportunities for participation. The Akamba Union, the Luo Union, the Gikuyu, Embu, Meru Association (GEMA), and smaller organizations offered the protection of numbers in attempts to pry political favors and economic resources from higher authority. Kenya churches were similarly engaged, mainly as institutions of spiritual and social support during the Kenyatta years but later increasingly as political interest groups.[14]

The least visible political economy in Kenyatta's Kenya was that of the country's *sotto governo* (underground government), a loose network of politicians and private notables who operated at the outer limits of the administration, the party, and the formal private sector. The system incorporated local political figures and traditional leaders, well-off landowners, traders and shopkeepers, and young entrepreneurs for the purposes of mutual protection and advancement. These groups, operating defensively, may not have been able to engineer changes from the top, but they could usually either manipulate or block external initiatives from their vantage points below.

In Kikuyuland such arrangements had prevailed for decades, often according to boundaries set by *mbare* or clan-based patterns of human settlement along individual ridges in the central uplands. Here alliances were maintained between local establishments of older landholding families and younger, better-educated, and ambitious Kikuyu with ties to the new commercial economy. As the system spread to other ethnic groups and became more politically oriented, it began to look not unlike the Mexican camarilla (personal clique) system of hierarchically arranged client-patron relations linking lesser influentials with big men ever-closer to the Nairobi power base. The crucial element at each level was the availability to clients of their patrons' political and economic largess. At least to the extent that the Harambee movement allowed, rural communities shaped their own strategies of collective survival and improvement around these affiliations of local luminaries with those above them. Higher up the patronage chain, the informal political economy acquired a pervasive illegal dimension. Occasionally reaching public attention were cases of extortion, theft, influence buying, and favoritism. As Kenyatta's tenure passed into its middle years, MPs and other Nairobi elites were increasingly associated with nepotism and bribery in the letting of government contracts, subversion of the country's customs and excise laws, and serious conflicts of interest.[15]

THE MIDDLE YEARS, 1969–1974

Between 1969 and 1974, Kenya was subjected to severe drought, ongoing land-tenure controversies, and a recession brought on by unprecedented price increases for imported petroleum products. All of these difficulties were overshadowed by the country's worst political crisis since Mau Mau, stemming from the assassination of Tom Mboya. Mboya had emerged from the colonial period as Kenya's leading Luo nationalist and one of Kenyatta's closest political allies in the anti-Kikuyu western part of the country. Enjoying considerable cross-ethnic support, by 1969 Mboya headed the government's key economic planning ministry and further served Kenyatta as secretary-general of KANU. On the basis of his domestic and international trade union contacts and his exceptional persuasive abilities and organizational talents, Mboya projected himself as a possible candidate for the presidency after Kenyatta. As Kenyatta's health and age became more of an issue, so did the matter of presidential succession. In particular, senior Kikuyu politicians feared that the office might pass to a non-Kikuyu and, worse, to a non-Kikuyu representing one of the larger rival ethnic groups.

These anxieties fueled increasingly fierce struggles below Kenyatta for political favors and advantageous positions in the economic order. Following Odinga's ostracism and the informal banning of the KPU in 1968, a scramble ensued among aspirant Kikuyu to fill vacancies created by the discredited Luo opposition. Factions formed and reformed as tensions mounted in Kikuyuland and spilled onto the national scene. Mboya's genius lay in reducing such conflicts by weaving alliances among competing groups, and 1969 found him appealing for national unity within and across ethnic boundaries. His Luo heritage made Mboya an outsider among the Kikuyu, however, who perceived the planning minister as a singular threat if in taking the political high ground he was masking serious presidential ambitions.

Emerging from a downtown Nairobi shop on July 5, Tom Mboya was shot and killed by an African assassin. Within hours rioting broke out in pockets of Nairobi and in Kisumu, western Kenya's largest city and major Luo urban center. Four days later, when Kenyatta arrived at Nairobi Cathedral to attend a requiem mass for Mboya, his car was stoned by a mob shouting *"Dume!"*("Bull"), symbol of the ousted KPU. Police dispersed the crowd, but in the melee two persons were killed, sixty hospitalized, and three hundred arrested. The demonstration had grown into the largest display of public violence and official retaliation since independence. Sixteen days after Mboya's death a Kikuyu, Nahashon Njoroge, was arrested and charged with the murder. He was quickly tried, found guilty, and reportedly hanged[16] in an atmosphere of heightened ethnic unrest, particularly between the Luo and a Kikuyu elite now in total command of Kenya's political center stage.

Attempting to appease the Luo, Kenyatta traveled to Kisumu in November 1969 to preside over the opening of a new hospital. The event led to another violent confrontation. During his dedication speech, Kenyatta was repeatedly heckled by KPU youth. He reacted by delivering an impromptu and "angry, curse-laden personal attack on Odinga"—sitting a few feet away—that included the warning to the Luo, "We are going to crush you into the floor."[17] As the presidential convoy was leaving the area, young Luo agitators showered Kenyatta's vehicle with stones. His personal bodyguards fired into the crowd with automatic weapons, killing at least eleven and wounding seventy-eight or more. Rather than inciting the Luo to further antigovernment acts, the Kisumu shootings were followed by a period of shock and withdrawal throughout western Kenya.

An impending crisis was averted when Kenyatta authorized a reform aimed at accommodating the Luo. Nominations for the December 1969 parliamentary election were opened to all comers in a decree allowing candidates to be freely selected in local primary campaigns—but only after registering as members of KANU. Most of the detained KPU dissidents were released, permitted to join KANU, and allowed to stand for election. In a resounding affirmation of the electoral process, 700 candidates contested 158 parliamentary seats in a month of heated electioneering. The outcome purged the political leadership. More than 40 percent of incumbent MPs were defeated, including five cabinet ministers. The Luo opposition was now absorbed within, instead of excluded from the formal political process and its access to the rewards of office.

Kenya's post-Mboya ethnic reconciliation was never consummated.

Centrifugal forces persisted, some of them disrupting elite relations with a rising student generation and with the military. At root, the Kikuyu political and economic hegemony continued to disturb smaller and less-favored groups. In 1972, for example, 41 percent of senior bureaucratic offices were claimed by a Kikuyu minority representing 20 percent of the population. The Luo comprised 18 percent of population but controlled only 8.6 percent of these positions.[18] To use Victor Olorunsola's phrase, the "politics of cultural sub-nationalism" simply would not go away.[19]

Kenya's Asian community presented a distinctive ethnic dilemma. Originally favored by the British as a socioeconomic barrier separating whites from the African majority, Asians had become a culturally diversified but economically united merchant class that held itself aloof from African society and politics. As the postindependence drive to Kenyanize the country gained momentum, Asian merchants became prime targets for ambitious politicians at all levels. A main tool in the campaign was to exclude Asians not holding Kenya citizenship from renewals of trade licenses and credit card franchises. Wider restrictions were contemplated but not carried out, partly because the constitution protected citizens of all races from such discrimination[20] and partly because Kenyatta fully appreciated the substantial contributions to the Kenyan economy attributable to hardworking and internationally well-connected Asian entrepreneurs. Responding to populist complaints about Asians' relative wealth and social remoteness, the government did make clear that even citizens could be deprived of their civil rights and property (in effect, subjected to bills of attainder) if they proved disloyal to the nation. How disloyalty would be defined remained an ambiguity that effectively curtailed Asian political organization and expression.

University students rejected such conformity, and their relations with government became markedly more contentious after the Mboya assassination. In his role as chancellor of the University of Nairobi, Kenya's flagship higher-educational institution, Kenyatta was in a position not only to lecture students on politically correct behavior but also to deny them degrees and, if he felt it necessary, to close the university altogether. Additional controls were imposed on these idealistic and often politically naive future elites through the formation of a KANU student branch, the appointment of Kikuyu loyalists to higher academic posts, and the granting and withholding of jobs after graduation. Nevertheless, a series of student demonstrations, centering on an official decision not to permit Oginga Odinga to speak on campus, followed Mboya's death. Kenyatta promptly closed the university, sent the students home, and required the demonstrators to apologize for their behavior before being readmitted. These actions contained student protests for the moment.

Ethnic factors were also implicated in a disturbance of otherwise

placid civil-military relations. In March 1971, the government claimed
that it had foiled an attempted coup d'état by Luo, Kamba, and Kalenjin
members of the armed forces. Thirteen men were brought to trial, including three who had fled to Tanzania and had been extradited back to
Kenya. The trial also incriminated several senior officials, including the
chief justice and the army chief of staff. Neither was prosecuted, although both resigned. The alleged plotters were convicted and sentenced
amid long speeches lecturing the military on the importance of their political neutrality and loyalty to the state. Sensing the need to reinforce the
safeguards he had instituted after the 1964 army mutiny, Kenyatta took
steps to limit troop size and strength, to enhance his intelligence network
within the ranks, to increase military pay and fringe benefits, and to
maintain British personnel strategically placed as advisors.[21] These measures helped preserve regime security at the top, but seemingly less trac-
table issues had developed at a deeper level in the political economy.

A Decade of Land Politics

Kenyatta's greatest challenges in his first decade as president
involved land politics. An original plan for the transfer of 2,750 large
European farms had proceeded relatively smoothly and had been hailed
as an example of enlightened, socially responsible decolonization. The
British and Kenyan governments had indeed honored their commitments to buy out the settlers despite the high costs of the endeavor. Initial
purchases of European farms totaled $28 million, of which $25 million
left Kenya. An additional $30 million was expended in converting the es-
tates to African ownership, and the dislocations inherent in this process
caused temporary but financially significant declines in cash-crop production.[22] Nearly all of the former European holdings were located in
the highlands and were converted into four categories of enterprises according to their supposedly different productive and human carrying
capacities. High-density settlements, low-density farms, cooperative
farms and ranches, and state farms were envisioned under land-tenure
arrangements defining private freeholds, community leaseholds, and
publicly owned tracts.

Kenyatta's decision to subdivide and open large farms for resettle-
ment calculated political and economic risks. Popular resentment over
landlessness and central Kenya's large squatter population made reform
urgent. At the same time, sizable problems could be expected because of
production losses and the magnitude and complexity of the transfers
themselves. Abandoning customary tenure in favor of transferable and
presumably more rational land rights acquired from government meant
sacrificing the protections of that tenure, which guaranteed land to members of kinship groups on the basis of need. Property surveys, title regis-

tration, and litigation could take years. Because most settlers lacked investment capital and access to modern agricultural techniques, widespread indebtedness and defaulting on loans among the former landless were distinct possibilities. Kenyatta could anticipate further difficulties in addressing the claims of land-hungry Kikuyu influentials seeking merely to take over from the departed white settlers. Regardless of its dangers and uncertainties, the program was carried forward, and many of the new smallholders began to prosper.

In contrast to these grass-roots successes, by 1966 it had become apparent that larger farming schemes were not achieving financial viability. Unless default on their loans could somehow be reduced, the Kenya government would face severe investment and profit losses. One attempted solution lay in tighter fiscal control over the schemes. Another, economically questionable in light of the experience with larger holdings, was the promotion of large-scale state farms. Government managers were appointed to run these enterprises, employing landless farm families that were limited to household gardens averaging a hectare or less (usually between two and three acres).

The postindependence reorganization of land tenure eventually affected nearly 10 million hectares (25 million acres) of arable and grazing land. As the program neared completion in the early 1970s, 6.8 million hectares (17 million acres) were located in seven ethnic reserves, where the great majority of African small farmers held individual freehold titles. This left 2.96 million hectares (7.4 million acres) in the former white highlands, divided into settlement schemes (600,000 hectares or 1.5 million acres), mixed private farms (880,000 hectares or 2.2 million acres), and plantations (1.48 million hectares or 3.7 million acres). The policy was not without its detractors, but it could be judged a social and economic success in the context of the Kenyan approach to state-managed capitalism. As Colin Leys concluded:

> Land hunger, which was quite severe in central Kenya at independence, had been assuaged by the settlement schemes; smallholder incomes were increased; the white farmers had been bought out with over a third of their mixed farms retained for African-owned capitalist farming, to which large subsidies continued to be given; while the plantation and ranch sector was left undisturbed.[23]

From the perspectives of social equity and managerial efficiency, the record may have been somewhat less consistent than is implied in this summary evaluation. Agricultural output rose dramatically both because land was now widely available to hardworking peasants and because new and hybrid crop varieties, enhanced credit lines, and improved extension services were lavished upon larger, more "progressive"[24] farmers. Dealing with the less fortunate poor, settlement boards were forced to contend with incessant boundary disputes, loan defaulting, contract failures, and lawsuits—in addition to their own bookkeeping errors, petty thefts, and misuses of funds. The decision to set aside 640,000 hectares (1.6 million acres) for wealthy African landowners inspired charges of elitism and nepotism, critics pointing out that large farms enriched landlords at the expense of the landless, performed poorly as providers of rural employment, and produced less value per hectare than small farms. Historical parallels to the heavily subsidized settler community were inevitably drawn. In basic agreement with these views, the International Labour Office published a report recommending the further division of large holdings into more labor-intensive units with greater attention to the developmental needs of poor families.[25] The government's response was noncommittal.

In purely economic terms, some large farms were well run and some were not. Most were managed for their absentee owners by crop and livestock specialists who gradually registered productivity increases. At the other end of the scale, some 4.8 million hectares (12 million acres) were reorganized into more than 650,000 individual holdings, producing an explosion of pent-up human potential. Between 1958 and 1967, total cash revenues accruing to African smallholders grew from K£7.6 million ($21.7 million) to K£34.04 million ($97.2 million) in current prices and from K£7.4 million ($21.1 million) to K£23.8 million ($68.0 million) in constant 1956 prices.[26] Although these aggregate figures tell little about how incomes were actually distributed, many rural dwellers fared well and would have been even more successful under conditions of slower population growth. Political stability had also been maintained while more than half the land traditionally held communally was permanently switched to a system based on freehold titles. Most important, at least in the arable one-fifth of Kenya, a largely subsistence-oriented and significantly landless rural society was set well on its way toward becoming a society of independent yeoman farmers whose long-unrequited efforts were finally being rewarded. Compounding economic perturbations and misdirections of development policy, rapid population growth would eventually limit and threaten these gains. In the meantime, the political system had still to survive the internal machinations of a dying Kikuyu hegemony.

THE LATER YEARS: A TURBULENT MONARCHY

From 1974 until his death in 1978, Jomo Kenyatta appeared to be forging an economic aristocracy and, less successfully, a ruling dynasty drawn from his immediate and extended families and a political family of Kikuyu loyalists in his home district of Kiambu. Kenyatta had remarried after being released from British detention, and his second wife, Mama Ngina, had already acquired substantial wealth in her own right. Ngina's economic domain encompassed large tracts of uncultivated and agricultural land, as well as business ventures in road transport, the ivory and wildlife-trophy trade, and mining. In a setting in which high-level nepotism had become commonplace, both sides of the Kenyatta family and the Kiambu Kikuyu faction profited disproportionately from their connections with the aging patriarch.[27] Seeking to maintain his dominance over shifting coalitions of Kikuyu political in-fighters, the president refused even to hint at an heir or to display any open concern for what might happen to the country after his passing. He ignored his constitutional right to appoint a prime minister and thus perhaps to ease the turmoil that might engulf Kenya during a presidential succession.

Public criticism of Kenyatta and his Kiambu retainers intensified as increasing economic hardship made Kenyans of all ethnic affiliations less tolerant of the regime's political favoritism and corruption. The oil-based world recession of 1973 and a drought extending into 1974 weakened the economy and seriously compromised the government's ability to deliver on its often-repeated promise to better the lot of the common people. It is impossible to estimate how long average citizens and the non-Kikuyu shadow opposition would have endured this combination of economic reversal and official malfeasance, because another macabre assassination fixed the country's attention on an immediate crisis in the Kikuyu arena.

The Kariuki Affair

Whereas Tom Mboya had challenged Kenyatta's Kikuyu power base from without, Josiah Mwangi Kariuki posed a much greater threat from within. A flamboyant Kikuyu MP and outspoken critic of Kenyatta's Kiambu clique, Kariuki had become famous as a populist defender of the poor and powerless. In this role, the former presidential secretary had assumed leadership of an unofficial opposition in parliament and quickly acquired a sizable following in those parts of Kikuyuland where Kenyatta was least appreciated. In effect, Kariuki had positioned himself as a realistic alternative to Kenyatta and his Kiambu-based political clan, creating a situation that the regime could not tolerate.

In March 1975, senior police officers abducted Kariuki from a Nairobi hotel. When his body was later discovered under circumstances suggesting a governmental cover-up, student rioting broke out again, parliament railed against the administration, and deep political chasms opened within the Kikuyu community. Kenyatta hastened to form a blue-ribbon parliamentary commission to investigate the murder. This action averted further turmoil and bought time, but when the commission's report was presented three months later the crisis was rekindled. The document accused the police of a massive subterfuge and implicated the commander of the paramilitary Government Services Unit (GSU), a presidential praetorian guard, in the killing. The report called for the resignation of the commissioner of police and the director of its criminal investigation division because they had blocked the investigation by refusing the commission access to police files.

The report was tabled in parliament on June 3, 1975, and the ensuing debate, focused on Kenyatta, was met with strong countermeasures. Those critical of the government who also held administrative positions were dismissed or instructed to resign. Outspoken John Keen, the assistant minister for works, was among the first purged in this manner. Other MPs suffered harsher punishment. John Seroney and Deputy Speaker Martin Shikuku were arrested and detained. Mark Mwithaga was forced out of parliament altogether. Vice chairman of the Kariuki commission and an MP with strong support among the Nyeri and Nyandarua Kikuyu, Mwithaga was charged with a previous assault on his former wife, denied bail and appeal, and sentenced to two years' imprisonment just before the 1975 parliamentary election.[28]

As in the Kisumu incident following the Mboya murder, Kenyatta had responded to a threatening situation with an unambiguous display of personal power. The Shikuku and Seroney arrests were carried out in broad daylight and during a full legislative session. Police simply marched into the chamber, apprehended the MPs, and escorted them out. In a clear message to other dissenters, the president referred to recent events in his annual Kenyatta Day speech before a massive audience. He concluded with an ominous metaphor: "The hawk is in the sky. It is ready to descend on chickens who stray from the pathway." This warning stilled further overt opposition, but Kariuki's killing would haunt Kenyatta until his death.

Probably most damaging to Kenyatta's reputation was a trio of investigative reports published in the London *Sunday Times*.[29] On the basis of detailed inside information, the first of the series laid out the Kariuki affair, focusing on his threat to the Kiambu governing elite, the cover-up of his murder, and the naked power employed to contain the subsequent crisis. The extent of Kenyatta family landholdings was also exposed to illustrate inner-circle corruption. The article concluded that the assassination could not have happened without the concurrence of very highly placed persons. The second and third *Times* articles carried forward the attack on members of the Kikuyu "royal family." In particular, they accused Mama Ngina of profiteering at the expense of Kenya's wildlife and environment, citing examples of large-scale ivory poaching and the destruction of fragile ecosystems to make charcoal for export to the Arabian

Gulf region. Acceptance of bribes from European business interests was also alleged against the regime, which was held responsible for a growing disparity of wealth between a few well-connected Kenyans and the masses. In a parting shot, the series drew a straightforward lesson from the Kariuki killing and the circumstances under which it was perpetrated: Any opposition that got in the way of the Kenyatta clique would be ruthlessly eliminated.

In response to the *Times* disclosures, the British diplomatic mission was handed notes of protest, and the series was loudly denounced as a fabrication aimed at besmirching Kenya and its leadership. A flood of rhetoric to cleanse the presidential image flowed from government, and pleas were made for national reconciliation. Many Kenyans may have viewed this public-relations barrage as superfluous; even after the press revelations, few really doubted Kenyatta's ability to protect his central establishment.

A fortuitous external factor helped stabilize the country after the Kariuki crisis. A disastrous frost in Brazil drove up world prices for coffee in 1976 and 1977, bringing windfall profits to Kenya growers. A great many coffee barons were made in the middle 1970s, and others benefited indirectly from the boom. One lucrative option lay in the illegal transshipment of Ugandan coffee to the coast. So widespread was this

Coffee pickers and managers, Thika (photo by David Keith Jones/Images of Africa Photobank)

smuggling that in 1977 price quotations for Ugandan beans were readily available on the streets of Nairobi. Not even the simultaneous collapse of the East African Community (a regional common-market arrangement) served to dampen the economic enthusiasm of the coffee-boom years.

Economic Relations in the Late 1970s

As the Kenyatta era drew to a close, the strengths and weaknesses of the Kenyan political economy came into perspective. Postcolonial recovery had occurred, foreign investment freely entered the country, and international development assistance steadily increased.[30] Nevertheless, corruption, unemployment, income maldistribution, and land shortage persisted. The 1972 International Labour Office report had already confirmed these signs of major structural flaws. Recommending policy reforms that would "spread the wealth, benefit the poor, and open jobs in the rural and 'informal' manufacturing sectors,"[31] the report unequivocally stated that a prime target of such reforms had to be the working poor. Their economically deprived and politically explosive condition was reflected in massive inequalities among regions and ethnic groups and also between the sexes—disparities not only in earnings and employment but also in access to education, health care, and other vital social services.

The Kenya government accepted the ILO recommendations, but in practice only a few policies were changed. Licensing restrictions were eased to the advantage of petty traders and the informal manufacturing sector. The minimum wage was raised in 1974, and additional land was made available through an expansion of settlement schemes.[32] These measures reduced discontent among urban workers and farmers and contributed to the country's overall political stability. In a larger sense, however, the ILO recommendations for a more open economy would have called for greater selflessness than the elite deemed necessary.[33]

In a further ILO-sponsored investigation,[34] Crawford and Thorbecke discovered that an urban population of 12 percent produced 30 percent of the national income and that total income earned by the 17 percent of formal-sector workers almost equaled that of the 83 percent engaged in subsistence agriculture and informal business enterprises. The study also reported that 41 percent of rural incomes derived from off-farm activities, including migratory employment, casual local labor, and small business ventures. This finding raised the critical question of how capable the rural areas were of absorbing the effects of urban recessions, challenging the long-standing assumption that return to the land was a viable alternative for a mushrooming urban population.

There is little evidence that the leadership was prepared to treat these social and economic imbalances as politically significant. In the last

years of Kenyatta's life as before, a mercantile-capitalist fervor enrap-
tured the Kenyan elite. The national policy remained clear: encourage
new private enterprises, foster business expansion wherever possible,
and minimize state intervention to accommodate the inegalitarian side
effects of growth. Occasional nods were made to equality and the sharing
of wealth, but these goals were not taken very seriously. Major exceptions to the prevailing laissez-faire mentality were made mainly to make
possible state partnerships in foreign-owned companies and to provide
for the growth of parastatal corporations.

Notwithstanding this official lack of concern, heated debates on
class and social equity, begun in the early 1960s, continued into the late
Kenyatta era, especially at the University of Nairobi. These discussions
converged on the issue of how Kenya's class structure was evolving and
particularly on how wealth was being accumulated and what was happening to the masses of poor citizens in the meantime. Three basic
positions emerged. Argued in Marxist-Leninist terms, the first was that
Kenya's inescapable fate would be a violent confrontation between a
class of insatiably materialistic capitalists in temporary control of the
state and an increasingly desperate but vastly more numerous class of
impoverished workers and peasants. A second position was that a middle class of moderately successful farmers and traders was amassing sufficient economic and political influence to reduce class tensions by ex-
tracting distributional reforms from government. A third view was that
Kenya was still in a precapitalist stage of development and meaningful
socioeconomic class distinctions did not yet exist. According to this view,
the challenge for Kenyans was not class conflict but a downward-turning
economy that would inevitably work against everyone's self-interest.
Strong economic growth initiatives were therefore called for to minimize
the chances of developmental reversal.

As in the past, Kenyatta remained impassive to such speculations
except when they sparked opposition to his rule. In these instances, the
offending parties were simply labeled as radicals and silenced. One
reason he could safely behave in this manner was that, despite the best
efforts of agitators such as Odinga and Kariuki, no appreciable class
alignments had in fact formed. Instead, strong economic and political
linkages had evolved vertically along ethnic lines. At the all-important
Nairobi center of affairs, ethnic influentials were ranked according to
their educational accomplishments and their occupations, wealth, and
political connections. Here and deeper within society, communal alle-
giances were more important than potentially cross-cutting class identifications in the articulation and aggregation of private interests.[35] Factional
alliances formed and dissolved in response to changing signals from an
internally divided Kikuyu elite.

At the level of Kenyan high politics, nowhere was the dedication to this form of protocapitalist development more apparent than in the favored treatment received by multinational corporations and other foreign investors. Even before independence, Kenyatta had assured international sources of capital that Kenyans would "encourage investors to come to Kenya . . . to bring prosperity to this country."[36] Matching loans, equity participation arrangements, joint state-private undertakings, and direct subsidies were soon offered as inducements. The Foreign Investment Protection Act of 1964 guaranteed foreign nationals and firms the right to repatriate both capital investments and profits. The law was altered in 1976 to curtail corporate profit taking, but many of the new restraints were circumvented through fairly unsophisticated methods such as double invoicing and the manipulation of prices for imported manufacturing inputs in order to secure local sales and tax advantages.

Multinational involvement extended to plantation ownership and agricultural processing, mineral extraction, fuel distribution, road transport, advertising, banking and commerce, and manufacturing.[37] Among manufacturing enterprises employing more than fifty workers, multinationals dominated in such areas as leather and footwear, tobacco and cigarettes, soft drinks, petroleum refining, chemicals and paints, soaps, vehicle assembly, cement, and metal products. By 1972 multinational investment totaled about $364 million, or more than 20 percent of the Kenya's gross national product (GNP).[38] Overall, multinational corporations formed an essential part of the domestic elite's entrepreneurial strategies. A growing number of local businessmen, largely from Kikuyuland and including public servants, entered into affiliations with overseas interests and in the process "constructed the machinery through which to control foreign capital in the interests of indigenous accumulation."[39] Even as international investors were shaping the formal economy of independent Kenya, Kenyans were shaping international capital to serve their own interests. Expanding coteries of politically astute bargainers evolved on both sides of this relationship, and some of the wealth produced by their dealings accrued to Kenyans at lower levels in the system who otherwise would not have seen it.

In addition to encouraging foreign investment, Kenyatta sought to increase and diversify foreign aid and to entice United Nations and private philanthropic agencies to locate in Kenya. The donor-recipient relationship changed from a largely British-Kenyan affair to a much wider network of linkages, more than 90 percent of them with Western industrial countries and the World Bank. Total aid contributions grew as these ties were cemented. By 1976, for example, Kenya had become Africa's leading recipient of World Bank assistance, having obtained $333 million in loans and $146 million in soft credit facilities through the bank's International Development Association (IDA). In 1978 alone, $248 million in official development assistance reached the country from all sources.[40] In 1972 the UN Environment Programme established its world head-quarters in Nairobi, and the UN Centre for Human Settlements followed suit in 1978. Taking advantage of this open-door policy and the amenities offered by eastern Africa's largest and most prosperous city, private foundations and nonprofit organizations emulated multinational corpo-rations in choosing Nairobi as their headquarters for eastern and south-ern Africa.[41] As an added bonus, tourism increased significantly in the decade following independence. By 1972 the industry accounted for more than forty thousand jobs.

Growth occurred not only in the formal economy, where it could be tabulated, analyzed, and to a degree accounted for, but also in the infor-mal sector of cottage industries and unlicensed services, which em-ployed as many as two hundred thousand by the time of Kenyatta's death. The informal sector was, of course, only part of a larger, hidden economic order that incorporated legal and illegal, public and private, and large-scale as well as small-scale activities—all operating outside the officially reported economy. At the apex was the Kenyatta family and its wider circle of Kiambu Kikuyu, which used presidential influence to ob-tain business contracts, trading privileges, and private property. Wealthy Kenyans speculated in land, and senior civil servants extracted favors in return for confidential information and preferential treatment regarding government employment and contracts. Multinational and domestic companies engaged in their own influence buying—paying extra for protective services, import licenses, and work permits and bribing bureaucrats to sabotage competitors by denying or delaying crucial clearances. Illegal accounting practices and tax evasions proliferated. Election campaign irregularities, smuggling, and wildlife poaching be-came entrenched.[42]

The effect of these developments was to restrict control over wealth to the governing elite, to redirect public revenues into private channels, to nourish the political clientage system, and to establish a parallel set of rules governing the acquisition and disposition of resources. The under-ground economy remained firmly in Kenyatta's hands until his death. It then became decentralized and was more heavily criticized in the press, in parliament, and throughout Kenya. Even then, corruption was not widely condemned unless money left the country or local Asians were involved. As long as it remained within the African community, illicit wealth could be employed to dispense largess in return for votes, to cre-ate employment, and to support camarillas of relatives and followers. At the grass-roots level of everyday commerce, informal family-based busi-nesses continued to serve the income and consumer needs of ordinary people through their low operating costs and unregulated markets, their lack of formal training requirements for employment, and their improvising technologies and reliance on indigenous resources.[43] Even more than in the sometimes illegal maneuverings of the larger hidden economy, the frenzied entrepreneurial dynamism of modern Kenyan society is still best revealed in the workings of these ubiquitous small enterprises.

CONCLUSIONS: THE KENYATTA ERA
IN PERSPECTIVE

The death of Jomo Kenyatta on August 23, 1978, marked a turning point in Kenyan history. There followed an outpouring of emotion throughout the country, eulogies from around the world, and a great display of funereal ceremony. Personal tributes, hymns, and Christian pronouncements were beamed by radio to all corners of Kenya. The corruption and heavy-handed rule that had marred Kenyatta's last years seemed forgotten. In death he was again the Father of the Nation, the Mzee, the honored national elder. He was buried with dignity and solemnity, and a massive statue of him gazing toward parliament buildings was soon erected.

To appreciate Kenyatta's era fully, one must understand its central mission. Individual and familial advancement formed the main concerns of Kenyans throughout society. Landless peasants, productive farmers, and city dwellers alike defined prosperity in terms of material rewards, security of land tenure, employment opportunities, and education for the next generation. The mass of people at first applauded and then tolerated the Kenyatta regime because it espoused these goals. In a context of accord that transcended—even as it exacerbated—ethnic and regional animosities, all major decisions came down from on high, emanating either from the president himself or from his clan of family members and close political advisors. Any real or suspected connection with this coterie was negotiable in the currency of influence and power, and a large share of the nation's business was conducted according to "the wishes of Mzee." To enter the game for high economic stakes, both Kenyan and foreign capitalists needed entrée to the clan with their proposals and promises. Contrary to the suppositions of international dependency theorists,[44] the Kenyatta elite manipulated individuals, groups, and organizations at all levels in what it considered its own and the country's best interests.

As the 1960s gave way to the 1970s, Kenyatta became at once more autocratic and less willing or able to curb the political and economic excesses of those around him. He either authorized or shut his eyes to the assassination of J. M. Kariuki and thereafter assisted in its cover-up.

While accumulating great personal and family wealth, he lent his name to dozens of business and land schemes of questionable legality. His presidency finally assumed the guise of a rather unstable monarchy, its court full of sycophancy and favoritism, nepotism, and the buzz of high intrigue around a fading king.

In terms of their freedoms, rights, and opportunities for self-advancement, Kenyans were probably better off than most other people in early independent Africa. With a few important lapses, the leadership tolerated public criticism. Journalists remained basically unfettered, members of parliament were usually allowed to debate and at times modify executive policy, and students did not hesitate to demonstrate over political issues. Human rights were generally protected, and occasional instances of preventive detention and police intimidation typically met with pointed condemnation in the press. The darkest days for rights and freedoms followed the Kariuki murder. Kariuki had threatened from within to dismantle the regime's Kikuyu power base, and Kenyatta had responded by muzzling criticism and shutting down a relatively open political process. The Kariuki episode had, however, challenged his hegemony only at the top; the majority of Kenyans approved of a system that delivered on its pledges and offered a reasonable expectation of benefits in the future.

Political stability under Kenyatta was based on his adroit balancing of rewards and punishments. He built a political force field around himself that either absorbed or eliminated disruptive elements. Showdowns with parliament, the journalistic community, students, and organized opposition groups were consistently won by the regime, partly because of its centralized structure and monopolistic control over the country's assets and partly because of the implicit support it received from Kenya's proto–middle class. Ethnic and subethnic factionalism was nearly always managed through the dispensation of advantages to cabinet officers and members of parliament[45] and thence to networks of patrons and clients extending downward into society. Among the machine's staunchest local agents were traditional leaders and provincial and district commissioners (many of these Kikuyu) who backed the central establishment from the security of their communal and bureaucratic fiefdoms. Rather than on an abstract sense of nationhood and a dedication to political harmony through social compromise, independent Kenya was founded on an effective patronage system welding disparate ethnic, sectional, and nascent class components into a coherent whole. By 1978, the system was even reaching out to influence the aspirations and behavior of physically isolated and culturally aloof pastoralists such as the Maasai, the Turkana, and the Boran.

On balance, one must underscore the pragmatic, ideologically unimpeded character of the Kenyatta era. Inequity and corruption were part of it. Aggressive black capitalism victimized many as the penetration of international capital created windfalls of wealth, status, and power for the governing elite. Simultaneously, however, economic growth occurred, many people improved their material conditions of life, and one of Africa's few truly multiracial societies evolved out of a racist colonial order. Military rule was avoided, and in most instances political freedoms and human rights were protected. The policy mistakes made did not arise from any rigid adherence to such idealistic notions as *ujamaa* (familyhood) in Tanzania and the "move to the left" in Uganda.[46] In a modern situation of widening social, economic, and ecological imbalances, Kenya's developmental policy problems are attributable less to ideologically motivated errors of commission than to difficult and necessary decisions not taken.

3

Ecology and Society in Modern Kenya

Kenya's highly differentiated and fragmented society has been shaped by the dynamics of its history and the advantages and limitations of its physical environment. The country's rich human mosaic is divided in several ways. Among the African majority, 40 major ethnic groups have produced some 120 dialectically distinct subgroups.[1] Regional differences in values and customs parallel and cut across these distinctions. Further complicating this mix, Asians, Arabs, Europeans, and Africans from other parts of the continent have all established small but influential communities in Kenya.

For rural dwellers, ethnic and clan membership, age, and gender remain paramount indicators of social identity, but one's place in modern society is also determined by education, occupation, family economic status, and often religious affiliation and home location. Secondary group memberships are also important, in organizations ranging from churches to secret societies, sports and recreational clubs, hunting and threshing societies, self-help associations, and welfare unions. As Kenya becomes urbanized at an average annual rate of over 8 percent, nuclear families and special-purpose secondary groups will assume even greater significance in determining the country's social configurations.

Capitalism has had both integrative and disintegrative implications for Kenyan society. Wealth has been generated, economic growth has occurred, and many people have attained a far higher standard of living than was thought possible three decades ago. At the same time, the entrepreneurial spirit has imposed penalties such as nascent class barriers, socioeconomic cleavages among ethnic groups and between rural and urban residents, new forms of discrimination against women and ethnic (notably pastoral) minorities, and serious disparities in the distribution of health, education, and other vital human services. A freewheeling system of material accumulation has created a kind of "we versus they" mentality. The "we" are those in the upper economic echelons, who are well-placed to enjoy the fruits of the state-managed economy; the "they" are those on the lower rungs of the ladder and those who have not yet begun their climb.

Less concrete but equally compelling disjunctures arise from the effects of rapid culture change. Many Kenyans lament the passing of traditional ways, and some blame this loss on an alien invasion of Western materialism. Similarly, religious diversity creates tensions not only between Muslims and Christians but also between orthodox and radical factions within these faiths, for example, between Sunni and Shi'ite Muslims and between organized churches and millennial movements combining traditional beliefs with Christian tenets. Somewhat mitigating these rivalries, major denominations are now finding common ground in pursuit of secular causes involving political reform, human rights, and environmental conservation.

Demographic and land issues are intimately linked with social mores and cultural values and represent the greatest sources of future conflict. In a disturbingly immediate sense, Kenyans face three critical threats to economic growth, social harmony, and political stability:

1. An average annual population growth rate that, despite a decline from nearly 4 percent during the 1980s to about 3.7 percent today, will still result in the addition of up to ten million people to society by the year 2000.
2. An environmental and ecological setting for this increase in which 83 percent of the land area and 94 percent of the land open for new settlement is either arid or semiarid.
3. The potentially catastrophic impact of Africa's most recent human scourge, the Human Immunodeficiency Virus (HIV)/ Acquired Immunodeficiency Syndrome (AIDS) pandemic, one of whose epicenters is very close to Kenya's main east-west transportation networks and major urban centers.

DEMOGRAPHIC AND ENVIRONMENTAL DILEMMAS

Population Trends and Problems

During the late 1970s and early 1980s, Kenyans may have experienced the world's highest annual rate of natural increase. The country absorbed more than eleven million surviving children between 1979 and 1993, augmenting the population by 72 percent. Kenya's total fertility rate[2] has fallen from 7.7 in 1984 to about 6.5 at present, however, and overall population growth will likely decline from 3.96 percent in 1979 to less than 3.5 percent by the end of the century (Table 3.1).[3]

TABLE 3.1 Trends in Kenyan Population Growth, 1979-2000

Years	Midyear Populations	Growth Rate (%)
1979/80	16,044,710/16,693,138	3.962
1984/85	19,535,645/20,314,786	3.911
1989/90	23,718,052/24,639,261	3.810
1994/95	28,565,356/29,608,532	3.587
1999/2000	33,997,084/35,141,795	3.312

Source: U.S. Census Bureau estimates (1989).

Several factors seem responsible for these reversals. Kenya has received large amounts of family planning assistance, and since 1984 the government has accepted family planning as a necessary component of its national health and development plans.[4] Immunization programs have helped reduce infant and child mortality, thus lowering rural dwellers' need for additional children to attain the necessary numbers of family workers and old-age providers. Urbanization has also exerted a negative influence on desired and achieved family sizes, as have higher levels of education and income. Especially for the poor, rising parental aspirations and educational expenses may promote a desire for fewer children by increasing the opportunity costs of raising multiple school-age dependents. In short, socioeconomic changes and the improving effectiveness of family planning services appear to be moving Kenya toward a vital "demographic turning point."[5]

Still, the Kenyan population will grow from more than 27 million in 1993 to probably more than 35 million by 2000, representing a net growth for this seven-year period of between 27 and 30 percent. Moreover, the proportion of persons entering or soon to enter their child-bearing years is expected to decrease only slightly, from about 62 percent of the population to somewhat more than 57 percent.[6] Compounding this high natural increase, a 1980s exodus from the rural areas at an average rate of 8.2 percent has raised the ratio of economically dependent urban dwellers from 14 percent of the national total to 23 percent. Nairobi's 1993 population stood at approximately 1.74 million, 111 percent more than in 1979.[7] Similar influxes have affected other towns and cities, as is reflected in a recent World Bank estimate that Nairobi's share of urban residents fell from 57 percent to 26 percent during the 1980s.[8]

These trends have certain unavoidable consequences. First, a minority of the current generation must work to support the majority, a situation that imposes severe socioeconomic strains on individuals and their families and bodes ill for national economic growth.[9] All indications point to the conclusion that Kenya is outstripping its ability to create jobs.

Of the 6.6 million economically active Kenyans in 1979, only 1.9 million were wage earners. The remainder were engaged in nonwage rural work. Two million additional persons joined the work force between 1979 and 1989 and an estimated 2 million more between 1989 and 1993. The 1989–1993 development plan reckoned that an annual economic growth rate of 5.4 percent would be necessary to accommodate the most recent intake, requiring a problematic 1.2 percent increase over the 4.2 percent average growth rate achieved in the 1980s.[10]

Perhaps the most portentous set of demographic factors relates to population distributions and differential rates of natural and migratory increase between rural and urban areas and by region. Kenya's population is heavily concentrated in the south-central and southwestern portions of the country, creating a pattern that accounts for and reinforces a similar concentration here of commercial agriculture, industry, and modern infrastructure, including water supply, electric power, and communications. All major cities and the bulk of rail, road, and air traffic are compressed into a 992-kilometer (620-mile) southern corridor extending from Mombasa through Nairobi and Nakuru to Kisumu, Kitale, and the Uganda border. In 1979, Kenya's cities and towns accounted for 2.2 million people; by 1989, this number had mushroomed to 5.4 million. To a degree fortunate for those concerned with urban planning, employment, and the provision of social amenities, total fertility is lower in towns and cities than in the countryside—4.8 as opposed to 7.7. In regional terms, average fertility ranges from more than 7.0 in Central, Rift Valley, Nyanza, and Western Provinces to less than 6.0 in Coast and North-Eastern Provinces.[11] High fertility rates in the rural areas of south-central and southwestern Kenya are especially ominous, involving not only forced urban migration that far outstrips any ready means to absorb it but also excessive rural settlement densities (some themselves caused by movement from still more overcrowded farming areas) that threaten the human carrying capacity of the land and the country's ability to feed itself.

The Crisis in Rural Carrying Capacity

With its foreign assistance to Kenya focused on agricultural commercialization through environmentally sustainable land use, the British Overseas Development Administration (ODA) has endeavored to ascertain the productive potentials of the country's major agro-ecological zones. The results suggest that even at average population densities as they stood in the mid-1980s the ability of Kenya's land resources to accommodate more people was severely limited (Table 3.2). With a rural population increase of more than 25 percent since that time, such remains the case today. The vast arid lowlands of Eastern and North-Eastern provinces, comprising 69 percent of total land area, are environmentally

TABLE 3.2 Agricultural Carrying Capacities in Kenya

Land Resource Zone	Province(s)	Percentage Area	Persons/km²[a]	Agricultural Potential per Technology Level		
				Low[b]	Medium[c]	High[d]
Lake Victoria basin	Nyanza, Western	4	275	Poor	Fair	Good
Western highlands	Western	2	6	Very poor	Poor	Fair
Upland plateau	Western, Rift Valley	3	90	Poor	Good	Good
Central highlands	Rift Valley, Central, Eastern	4	280	Very poor	Fair	Good
Coast	Coast	6	30	Fair	Fair	Poor
Northern semiarid uplands	Rift Valley	3	20	Very poor	Poor	Fair
Southern semiarid uplands	Rift Valley	4	10	Very poor	Poor/fair	Fair
Eastern semiarid uplands	Eastern	5	40	Very poor	Poor	Fair
Arid lowlands	Eastern, North-Eastern	69	2	Very poor	Poor	Poor

[a]Based on extrapolations from Kenya's 1979 census.
[b]Mostly manual labor employing few modern inputs.
[c]Some modern inputs such as fertilizer, hybrid crop varieties, and extension services.
[d]Heavy capital investment in technologies such as irrigation, drainage, mechanization, and processing.

Source: Adapted from Land Development Resources Centre, Kenya: Profile of Agricultural Potential (Surbiton, U.K.: British Overseas Development Administration, 1986), pp. 4-5.

unfit for new settlement on any large scale. Another 14 percent, which is either forested on steep slopes or consists of semiarid uplands, offers potential for additional agricultural production if high-technology methods are employed. Eleven percent of rural Kenya, extending from the Lake Victoria basin to the central highlands, is suitable for further agricultural intensification through high technology, leaving a mere 6 percent in the coastal region available for expanded cultivation by small farmers employing essentially manual techniques.

The ODA study warns:

> Everywhere there is competition for limited land and water resources, the potential for further gains in production being limited in many areas to yield increases derived from more intensive use of farm inputs and improved management. As the population increases . . . highland farms are increasingly fragmented and people are forced into the semi-arid margins, where cropping is precarious and where successful pastoralism depends on maintaining livestock numbers in equilibrium with range potential.[12]

These economically and ecologically destabilizing processes are now well under way. Arable tracts in Central, Nyanza, and Western Provinces form Kenya's overcrowded agricultural core area. In 1985, per capita arable land in these provinces averaged 0.26 hectares (0.65 acres) and average population densities had increased by 18.6 percent since 1979, from 237 to 281 per square kilometer. A less congested subsistence periphery is found in Rift Valley, Eastern, Coast, and North-Eastern Provinces. In these regions, per capita arable land averaged 1.5 hectares (3.75 acres) in 1985, but average population densities had grown by 92.8 percent, from 14 to 27 per square kilometer, since 1979. By 2000, per capita arable land is expected to decrease to an average of 0.15 hectares (0.37 acres) in the core areas and 0.60 hectares (1.5 acres) at the periphery, representing further losses to rural dwellers of between 42 and 60 percent.[13]

Statistical averages identify part but not all of an unfolding crisis in carrying capacity driven by rural population growth and dispersal in a milieu of limited land resources and mounting urban dependency. If allowed to persist, ecological imbalances of the magnitudes experienced in Kenya will soon jeopardize human survival and much of the country's resource base and environment. The first and periodically most visible of these threats arises from a failure to maintain national food security. Despite a continuous and environmentally risky commitment of semiarid pastoral lands to cultivation, Kenya has experienced periodic shortfalls in per capita food production. Kenyans have managed to keep abreast of their food requirements only at considerable cost in terms of financial outlay and foreign-aid dependency. Purchased cereal imports increased from 15,000 metric tons in 1974 to 188,000 metric tons in 1990, and cereal food aid grew by nearly three times as much, from 2,000 metric tons in 1974/75 to 62,000 metric tons in 1989/90.[14]

Although maize is a staple, Kenya fell short of maize self-sufficiency in 1978. In order to regain lost output, the government estimated that more than 900,000 hectares of new land would have to be brought under cultivation. As an inducement to farmers, in 1983 the government raised the official price for maize by 30 percent. This incentive led to a record planting made possible in part by an accelerated opening up of arid and semiarid lands (ASAL). Unfortunately, insufficient rain fell in 1983 and even less in 1984, leading to an·approximate 45 percent decline in maize yields. By late 1984, donor agencies estimated that 1.5 million metric tons of grain might have to be imported before the next harvest at a cost, if purchased, of about $250 million. This sum equaled Kenya's total reserves of foreign exchange. A local consulting firm had already projected that, even under conditions of moderate rainfall, by 2000 Kenya could suffer a domestic maize deficit of nearly 1 million metric tons, representing an almost fivefold increase since 1980.[15]

In addition to a bias toward export crops in high-potential farming areas, much of the domestic food problem arises from Kenya's marked susceptibility to drought. An extended dry spell between 1979 and 1982

Boran children in the arid and semiarid lands of northern Kenya (photo by Norman Miller)

forced more than eighty thousand Turkana pastoralists in the northwest
to abandon their desiccated rangelands for famine relief camps. Full-
scale drought returned in 1984 and 1985, making Kenya one of five African countries facing life-threatening food shortages.[16] The government
responded with a surprisingly effective program of emergency food
solicitation and distribution[17] but continued to ignore the larger issues
surrounding the movement of land-hungry farmers into drylands best
suited to limited numbers of highly mobile herders and their livestock.

Six multisectoral pilot projects begun in the 1970s aimed at diversi-
fying economic activities in selected ASAL locations and upgrading their
physical infrastructures and social services. The administration of each
project was centralized and divided among several individual ministries,
however, and each was implemented almost entirely with funding and
technical services contributed by a different foreign donor.[18] Both of these
factors reflected the relatively low priority assigned by government to
population-growth management through a centrally coordinated and locally flexible long-term commitment to ASAL development. As one aid
official observed,

> Problems of slow and cumbersome planning and mobilization, a lack of
> community involvement in planning, too few technical successes, and re-
> mote prospects for institutionalizing the programmes if and when expatri-
> ate support is withdrawn are apparent. Behind these problems lie a num-
> ber of basic obstacles, including the structure and orientation of the
> government's lack of support for the drylands among politicians [as op-
> posed to their keen interest in Kenya's agricultural core areas], and the
> technical difficulties of raising dryland production. Faced with these obsta-
> cles, ASAL programmes look set to run into continuing problems. Over-
> coming them will depend on both the success of recent government moves
> to deconcentrate, and patient support both from the government and the
> donors. Historically the prospects for such support are poor.[19]

It was not until the late 1980s that government began seriously to address
these issues, even then continuing to rely on uncertain foreign-aid allocations.[20]

Unaccommodated population pressures affect virtually every aspect of Kenya's biosphere, including not only its lands but also its forest,
energy, and water resources,[21] its treasure of wildlife and wildlife-
protected areas,[22] and perhaps even its weather patterns and climate.[23]
This situation persists in the face of the perennial attention paid to environmental issues by the nation's press and public-interest community[24]
and the presence in Kenya of Africa's largest concentration of official,
private, and foreign-assistance agencies dedicated to sustainable socioeconomic development through natural resource conservation.[25] At root,

much if not most of Kenya's crisis in human carrying capacity lies in the realm of perceived interests and priorities.

Section 75 of the Kenya Constitution requires that "no property of any description shall be compulsorily taken possession of, and no interest in or right over property of any description shall be compulsorily acquired except where [specified] conditions are satisfied."[26] This provision is in keeping with the country's dominant social and economic values both before colonialism and since. Applied to the land and its resources, the principle of private ownership has produced mixed blessings. It has fueled the inherent dynamism of Kenyan society and economy that the historian John Lonsdale finds deeply embedded in Kikuyu culture:

> Kikuyu virtue lay in the labour of agrarian civilisation, directed by household heads. Honour lay in wealth, the proud fruit of burning back the forest and taming the wild, clearing a cultivated space in which industrious dependents too might establish themselves in self-respecting independence; the possibility of working one's own salvation was the subject of more Kikuyu proverbs than any other.[27]

By the late 1980s, Kenya was still the first and only country in tropical Africa to have a countrywide system of land registration, and no fewer than five laws had been enacted to protect and advance rights of property ownership.

The ethic motivating these guarantees has given rise to a dual approach toward natural resources: that which is owned carries permanent value and should be nurtured, that which is not may contain transient value and can be freely exploited by anyone on the basis of need or desire. As a result, the delivery of agricultural extension and other economic inputs is highly skewed in favor of the export-oriented highlands and against the subsistence-oriented drylands, where communal land use still prevails.[28] Tree planting and afforestation are actively pursued on privately held tracts, but the semiarid uplands of Eastern Province are subjected to widespread commercial bush stripping so that charcoal can be manufactured for sale to Arabian Gulf countries. Only as the prospect of falling tourist revenues became apparent were steps taken to ban hunting, to intensify antipoaching campaigns, to prevent criminal attacks on visitors to the national parks and game reserves, and—most significant—to assist peasants crowded into the fringes of these preserves.[29] By presidential decree, ivory trading was finally ended in 1989,[30] but the threat to inland waters and water users is still not calculated into lucrative contracts for the construction of hydroelectric facilities.

Kenya is basically facing what Hardin has termed a "tragedy of the commons"[31]—a situation in which, out of choice and necessity, people overexploit their common environmental heritage in their immediate self-interests, thereby causing irreversible damage to their resource base and bringing disaster to them all. Evidence abounds that customary land-tenure and land-use practices included mechanisms for allowing both food security and resource conservation through controlled exploi- tation of the land and an equitable sharing and constant renewal of its physical assets.[32] Today these coping mechanisms no longer work. Devel- opment in western Kenya mainly benefits a small landowning class that looks down upon food crops as a poor source of income. Growing num- bers of landless food producers are forced east into low-rainfall zones on the central plateau, where they receive little help in dealing with the con- ditions they encounter. In the east, large blocks of land have been accu- mulated by private interests engaged in ranching, tourism, irrigated export horticulture, and charcoal production. To make room for these en- terprises, displaced dryland farmers are pushed west toward other ASAL locations that, to the dismay of the drought-prone peoples already living there, they quickly deplete.

The damage is no longer confined to the neglected communal dry- lands but extends to officially protected areas. As early as 1986, the Rift Valley provincial commissioner announced that three thousand illegal squatters had already been taken to court for destroying trees in order to obtain land for cultivation. Similar incursions were reported in the Irangi and Chogoria forests of Eastern Province.[33] At stake here are pressing is- sues of rural overpopulation at existing levels of agrarian development, forced urban drift and vanishing food self-sufficiency, and resource ex- haustion followed by advancing environmental degradation. Unless these conditions are soon eased, they will rob the leadership of politically stabilizing patronage benefits associated with land. They will also men- ace the foundations of rural life and profoundly disrupt Kenya's emerg- ing urban culture.[34]

Resource imbalances are not the only problems challenging human welfare and survival. Sweeping east from central Africa, HIV/AIDS now threatens to erase Kenya's steady improvement in health-care availability and quality of life and its reduction of maternal, infant, and childhood mortality[35] for many urban dwellers in the vanguard of the drive toward modernization and perhaps also for the farmers and pastoralists who still form the bedrock of Kenyan society.

The Specter of HIV/AIDS

Rates of HIV seroprevalence and AIDS–related diseases have quickly reached crisis proportions throughout eastern Africa. The region reported its first full-fledged AIDS cases between 1982 and 1984, and the virus has since spread widely within selected populations. Kenya stands somewhere between Uganda and Tanzania in these grim statistics. According to recent medical estimates, in 1990 HIV seroprevalence afflicted 86 percent of urban dwellers practicing high-risk behaviors in Uganda, 59.2 percent in Kenya, and 38.7 percent in Tanzania. HIV was much less prevalent among the three countries' urban majorities, affecting 24.3 percent, 7.8 percent, and 8.9 percent, respectively.[36] The disease is mainly transmitted through casual heterosexual relations involving prostitutes, truck drivers, traders, soldiers, and transient laborers. It first took hold in towns and cities linked by roads such as the Trans-African Highway, which passes from Uganda through Eldoret, Nakuru, and Nairobi to its terminus at Mombasa. Rural seroprevalence remains virtually undetected in Kenya but has become ominously widespread in parts of Uganda and Tanzania.[37]

Until recently at least, the government has been reluctant to emphasize measures to combat HIV/AIDS. Fearing domestic unrest and the loss of tourist and other foreign revenues, offended at what it considered to be inflated foreign estimates of the pandemic's extent, and unwilling to share the public agenda-setting process on this politically sensitive issue, policy makers at first sought to curtail the interventions of international health experts, nongovernmental organizations (NGOs), and aid agencies. A National AIDS Control Committee was incorporated into the Ministry of Health, but its NGO representatives were dismissed until donors insisted on their reinstatement. In spite of this concession, the mandate of the committee continued to be described cautiously and with some detachment. The 1989–1993 development plan states: "To the extent that AIDS has become an issue of international concern, the Committee will work closely with relevant regional and international agencies to control the spread of AIDS and in furthering research on its possible cure."[38]

Even this rather bland commitment reflects an easing of earlier fears about domination by highly vocal foreign researchers, health workers, and donors. The new position is well-conceived with regard to NGOs, which have proven efficient agents of HIV/AIDS education and prevention. Not unlike its approach to ASAL development, however, the Kenya government's latest stance assigns heavy financial responsibility for these activities to aid agencies whose contributions may fall far short of what is required for an effective effort.[39]

Kenya has no time to waste in mounting a workable campaign against HIV/AIDS. Recent mathematical projections suggest that, across Africa, HIV seroprevalence may rise from less than 4 percent of urban dwellers in 1990 to more than 40 percent by 2015 and that the total number of HIV carriers could grow from less than 10 million to more than 70 million during the same period.[40] Left unchecked, increases of these magnitudes will not only ravage Kenya's urban centers but also destroy their vital links with the countryside and may eventually reduce the ability of rural communities to produce food.[41] Health-care systems will be overwhelmed, and heavy losses of life within the country's most productive age-groups will leave an unmanageable number of younger and older dependents. Fearful consequences are likely unless a full range of resources—domestic and international, public and private, human and financial—is permanently mobilized and specifically targeted at a large number of variably receptive groups. An effective response will require that policy elites overtly legitimate HIV/AIDS prevention and fully incorporate it into the normal workings of government. They must utilize but also match NGO contributions and avoid treating program funding as an add-on responsibility of foreign aid. Above all, they must be willing to convert what amount to power relations in a highly sensitive area of human behavior into problem-solving relations, relying on local institutions that have considerable potential for behavior modification but currently lack the freedom, guidance, and financial resources to realize it.[42] Until these changes are effected, a common Kiswahili interpretation of the AIDS acronym will become tragically applicable to increasing numbers: "*Aibu imeingia dunia sasa*" ("Shame has fallen on the earth now").

ISSUES OF ETHNICITY, CLASS, AND GENDER

Indigenous ethnic groups account for 98 percent of Kenya's population, with Asians, Arabs, Europeans, and non-Kenyan Africans comprising the other 2 percent. In general, ethnic labels denote formerly independent societies once characterized by common patterns of kinship, language, and custom, distinctive types of economic and political systems, and some sense of collective identity. Today ethnicity is largely based on one's geographic origins, extended family ties, and cross-kinship affiliations. Confusion frequently arises in ethnic labeling because some groups, such as the Kalenjin, the Mijikenda, and the Abaluhya, are in fact clusters of constituent units that at times are carefully differentiated by their members. As is apparent from the discussion of Kenyatta-era politics, subethnic distinctions are also very important to the dominant Kikuyu minority.

Many ethnic agglomerations are the historical products of constant flux, with segments breaking away and reforming according to modified regional, socioeconomic, and political criteria. Ethnic categories are often artificial designations rather than authentic names for original Kenyan societies. Some labels simply mean "the people," others derive from changing kinship and territorial affinities frozen in time by colonialism, and still others have been attached to resident communities by outsiders, including coastal Arabs and early European explorers and missionaries.[43]

Kenya's three largest ethnic entities make up approximately 44 percent of the total population. Not surprisingly, these groups predominate in the agricultural core areas of Central, Nyanza, and Western Provinces. Representing slightly more than 19 percent of society, the Kikuyu of the central highlands grew in number from 3.2 million in 1979 to about 5.3 million by 1993. While under British rule, these Bantu-speaking agriculturalists experienced the European presence at close range through contacts with missionaries and settlers and proximity to the Nairobi center of administration and commerce.

Today as in the past, the Kikuyu are considered the most aggressive and acquisitive of Kenyans. Their hegemony became entrenched in the late colonial period and waned only after the death of Jomo Kenyatta. Until then, a Kikuyu elite controlled many of the highest governmental and military posts and dominated the postcolonial business establishment. Especially advantaged were Kikuyu drawn from Kenyatta's home district of Kiambu, and as a result there was serious friction between the Kiambu faction and aspirants from the other Kikuyu districts of Kirinyaga, Murang'a, Nyandarua, and Nyeri. Measured in terms of land, the local stakes of this competition remain high. With the exception of Nyandarua, Kikuyuland contains some of the highest population densities recorded for Kenya. Rivalry over land rights likewise continues with the pastoral Maasai, although cordial relations are maintained with ethnically related Meru and Embu communities east of Mt. Kenya and to some extent with the Kamba of Machakos and Kitui Districts in Eastern Province. Numbering about 2.8 million in 1993, the Kamba form Kenya's fourth-largest ethnic group.

At 3.5 million, the Abaluhya of Nyanza Province constitute nearly 13 percent of the population. They are a society of Bantu-speaking cultivators partly surrounded by Nilotic farmers and pastoralists and are divided into sixteen main branches.[44] Large parts of Abaluhya country, in the highlands northeast of Lake Victoria, are even more densely settled than the central highlands, prompting many people to seek employment in Nairobi and other cities.

More than 3 million Luo live to the south, in the equally crowded Lake Victoria basin. Nilotic in origin, this once-warlike people represents 12 percent of Kenyan society and is commercially diversified into cash-crop agriculture, ranching, fishing, and retail business. Protected at home by exclusive land rights based on clan membership, Luo migrants range far afield in search of education, jobs, and trade. They make up at least 13 percent of the population of Nairobi and have created substantial enclaves in northwestern Tanzania and eastern Uganda.

Since independence, few ethnic groups have approached the socioeconomic and political significance of the Kikuyu, the Abaluhya, and the Luo. An important recent exception is the Kalenjin alliance of Rift Valley farmers and stock owners, totaling about 2.7 million people. President Daniel arap Moi belongs to one of these groups, the Tugen of Baringo District, and he has taken pains to seed the country's upper political and economic echelons with Tugen and other Kalenjin since his rise to power in 1978.[45] The Meru, the Kamba, and the Gusii of Nyanza Province have also made a political and economic impact on the national scene. Notably absent are physically and culturally isolated herding societies, including the Rift Valley Samburu and the northern Boran, Gabbra, and Rendille. Even the more numerous Maasai, Turkana, and Kenya Somali have yet to establish a strong collective presence in the modern political economy.[46]

Problems of Ethnic Identity and Conflict

Kenyan society is deeply divided according to ethnicity and location, education and income, and age, welfare, and gender. Differences in religious and other basic values underlie and help to perpetuate these cleavages. In the first instance, deep-seated ethnic, subethnic, and sectional animosities always lie close to the surface of social relations and at times erupt into open conflict and violence. Such factors were implicated in the assassinations of Tom Mboya and J. M. Kariuki and may also have played a role in the February 1990 murder of the foreign minister and prominent Luo leader Dr. Robert Ouko.[47] Ethnic hostilities reflect a weakness inherent in Kenya's civic culture; primordial fears and mistrust permeate society.

A dramatic illustration of these tensions may be found in the events following the 1986 death of a distinguished Luo trial lawyer, Silvanus Melea Otieno, who had rejected many of the strictures of Luo tradition. Having married into a leading Kikuyu family, Otieno had refused to teach Luo customs and the Luo language to his children. When he died of a heart attack, his widow announced that she would bury him on the family farm on the outskirts of Nairobi instead of in his ancestral homeland, as Luo custom required. When Otieno's brother and clanmates pressed for custody of the body, Mrs. Otieno ejected them from her house and asked the Nairobi morgue to keep them away from the remains.

The widow and her Luo adversaries both retained legal counsel and filed for injunctions against moving the body until the case was resolved. The ensuing trial filled the news media and became a cause célèbre throughout Kenya. Siding with his mother, one of Otieno's sons faced his uncle and the Otieno family's clan chairman and accused the Luo of being lazy and uncivilized. The Luo partisans who packed the courtroom were shocked and angered at this gratuitous display of disrespect for one's elders. The presiding judge seemed to agree in his ruling of February 13, 1987. Arguing that customs governing such sensitive matters should be changed only gradually, he ordered that Otieno be laid

Fishing boats, Lake Victoria, western Kenya (photo by David Keith Jones/Images of Africa Photobank)

to rest in western Kenya.[48] The dead man's brother and clan leader were carried in triumph from the court, and riot police were called in to halt a crowd of jubilant Luo descending on the city morgue to claim the body. Mrs. Otieno appealed the decision to the Kenya high court but again lost. In May, thousands of Luo took part in traditional ceremonies near Kisumu to banish evil spirits when Otieno was returned to the home ground of his ancestors.

Ethnic instability extends far beyond the personal tragedies of individual elites. The Moi government was widely suspected of inciting communal violence in west-central Kenya as a ploy to prevent, for "security reasons," the holding of a national election in either 1991 or 1992. Earlier, during the 1980s, an increasingly insecure regime had employed force to suppress Islamic fundamentalism among Arabized residents of Mombasa and other coastal towns. It had also renewed Kenyatta's attack on real and imagined revanchists within Kenya's Somali community. In 1984, local councillors and members of parliament from North-Eastern Province charged that security forces had killed at least three hundred villagers in one township near Wajir, another thousand Somalis remaining missing. A program to identify and deport illegal aliens was launched in 1987 and soon degenerated into a campaign of police harassment against Kenya citizens and political refugees of foreign ethnic origin. Somalis were the first among several targets of this persecution, apparently in retaliation for a rise in *shifta* bandit attacks from Somalia into Kenya.[49] Later objects of police intimidation included documented refugees and other immigrants from Uganda and Rwanda.

In his October 1990 Kenyatta Day speech, President Moi told Ugandans and Rwandese, "I am going to tighten all the screws and even those who have businesses here should know that this Kenya is for nationals. If they do not want to go back to their countries, let them go elsewhere."[50] A cartoon character in the newspaper article carrying the speech mused, "I wonder whether they are using flashlights to flush them out." However the roundup was accomplished, more than a thousand Ugandans and Rwandese were reportedly expelled from Kenya by the end of the year.[51]

In a futile attempt to prevent further immigration from strife-torn Somalia, the government ordered that no visas should be granted for Somalis to enter or pass through Kenya. Although Kenya is bound by international law to accept and protect political refugees, Somali applications for refugee status were purposely stalled in official red tape, and the local Somali community remained in a state of disarray.[52]

Since early colonial times, private associations had been formed within Kenya's larger ethnic populations to combat discrimination and promote communal self-improvement. The Kikuyu Association was founded in 1919. In succeeding decades, the constellation of ethnic interest groups expanded to include the Young Kikuyu Association (1921), the Young Kavirondo Association (1922), the Kavirondo Taxpayers' Association (1923), the Luo Union (1925), the Kikuyu Central Association (1925), the North Kavirondo Central Association (1932), the Akamba Union (1948), the Abaluhya Association (1954), and the New Akamba Union (1961).

The movement culminated in the Gikuyu, Embu, Meru Association (GEMA), organized in 1971 to encourage economic cooperation among these three peoples and to preserve their joint cultural heritage.[53] GEMA quickly became one of Kenya's most influential ethnic associations. It created GEMA Ltd., which amassed extensive business holdings in wholesale and retail trade, banking, manufacturing and processing, shipping and airline transport, land acquisition, and hotels. The company's ultimate goal was full or part ownership of the local branches of multinational enterprises doing business in Kenya. To this end it provided scholarships and other support for the educational and job advancement of its members and their families. Counting wealthy businessmen, senior civil servants, and cabinet ministers among its leaders, GEMA urged other ethnic groups to create similar organizations and helped them raise funds for the purpose.

GEMA prospered until 1980 when the Moi government, unwilling to share control over affairs with a variety of well-organized communal interests and alarmed at recent trends in this direction, banned all ethnic associations in the name of national unity. One credulous commentary on this decision speculated that "the government appears to be adopting assimilationist and 'melting pot' models of national integration and development . . . in order to pave the way for the gradual disappearance of indigenous heritages, languages and cultures."[54] This may eventually prove an accurate assessment, but at present appointments to the cabinet and the senior civil service are carefully calculated according to ethnic criteria—with a bias toward the selection of Kalenjin evident from the outset of the Moi presidency. The ethnic center of gravity in leading private-sector posts has similarly shifted from the central highlands to the Rift Valley.

On a wider scale, subcultural distinctions have become firmly institutionalized in parliament, whose constituencies continue to reflect the particular ethnic compositions of individual provinces. As a group, MPs stand quite apart from society at large. In spite of a growing tendency toward the election of younger politicians, the typical MP remains a middle-aged, well-educated male who occupies a senior and highly remunerative position in business, KANU, and/or government. At the same time, "the one characteristic that [MPs] share with their constituents is ethnicity. With elections still decided in the main at the local level, communities want to be sure that a candidate will represent their interests, and this is most likely if voters feel that he is one of 'us.'"[55] Strong communal linkages may speak fairly well for patronage-oriented interest representation in parliament and the national executive, but they extend inequalities and intensify local enmities and resentments as developmental investments, educational and other social services, and Harambee project finances are inevitably diverted to the districts of the Nairobi ethnic elite. In modern Kenya, wealth creates power, power generates wealth, and both are uncertainly grounded in the shifting sands of ethnic competition.

Problems of Rural and Urban Stratification

Kenya is very much a low-income country. In 1990, the Kenyan economy was tied with Haiti's and China's as the 26th poorest among 182 economies surveyed by the World Bank.[56] According to another estimate, Kenya's 1989 per capita gross domestic product (GDP) was only 5.2 percent that of the United States.[57] These averages are not meant to imply that poverty is evenly distributed throughout society. In modern Kenya, extreme ethnic fragmentation is exacerbated by exaggerated differences in access to socioeconomic rewards. This situation is giving rise to a small but growing middle class of farmers and urban wage earners, but it is also preserving a sharp distinction between the few who have obtained exceptional advantages and the many who remain exceptionally disadvantaged.

At the apex of this hierarchy is a wealthy and internally competitive African elite that governs the country. Most of its founding members are educated, self-made individuals who have attained wealth and position within one generation. They include large landowners and urban professionals, businessmen, physicians, high-ranking politicians and civil servants, and senior Kenyan associates in resident multinational corporations. Although separated by disparate communal backgrounds and loyalties, those who belong to this informal aristocracy share a desire for the best that modernity has to offer for themselves and their children. They are sometimes called *wabenzi* ("Mercedes-Benz people"), as opposed to *wananchi*, or common folk, and are now represented by a second generation whose approach to life is a natural extension of that of its predecessor:

> The elite began to regard themselves as a cohesive group that deserved prestige and economic well-being. There were variations in income, but members of this elite were clearly distinguished from the poor and the lower middle class not only in income but in style. They adopted British standards in clothing, housing, furniture, and entertainment. They lived in red brick tiled bungalows with well-tended gardens in Nairobi's residen-

tial sections. They played tennis, drank whiskey, and owned high-priced cars. In fact the new African elite who had joined or replaced the white elite not only copied their life-style but often adopted their outlook. They would still help their poor relatives, in conformity with traditional African values, but many of them tended to keep aloof from less favored citizens. They were accused, especially by university students, of perpetuating the dualistic social system of colonial days and of favoring a system of mutual accommodation with the remaining whites. They did not yet constitute a hereditary upper class, although their children might one day do so. Most had been born of poor parents in simple country dwellings, and their achievements were the result of their own efforts.[58]

At a lower level on the social scale is an increasingly cohesive urban grouping of small businessmen, lesser government employees, nurses and teachers, artisans and mechanics, plant supervisors, and skilled factory workers. Most in this incipient middle class are highly ambitious and hardworking and are willing to exert great effort to advance their fortunes. Very little political dissent emerges from the urban middle stratum, leading conventional wisdom to suggest that the *wabenzi* and these would-be *wabenzi* together act as a stabilizing force in Kenya because of their stake in the existing system.

By contrast, the potential for discontent among the least fortunate urban dwellers poses a distinct threat to political stability. These people include underemployed laborers, drivers, clerks, cooks, waiters, and scrubbers, who rarely earn more than KShs.1,000 ($50) per month.[59] Below them, the poorest of the poor consist of casual day workers and the outright unemployed, who may form more than 15 percent of Kenya's adult urban population.[60] Many are landless recent migrants to Nairobi and other cities. Others have lived for many years under abject conditions on the urban fringe and have never been effectively reached by public services and welfare agencies. These have-nots often become street hawkers and beggars, with a portion of the young drifting into petty crime and prostitution. The government has been unable to deal with their swelling numbers in Nairobi and has resorted to destroying their shanty villages and driving them from the city center into encampments away from the view of tourists and better-off residents. In late 1990, up to thirty thousand squatters were evicted from Kibagare, a collection of makeshift huts at the edge of a fashionable Nairobi suburb. The shacks were then bulldozed, causing a Kenyan Roman Catholic nun and relief worker to complain that the authorities intended to move Africans out of the area so that it could be converted into a high-income residential neighborhood for Europeans.[61]

A landed gentry predominates in the rural areas, whose large farms of more than 200 hectares (500 acres) accounted for 33 percent of registered landholdings in the late 1980s.[62] A middle-level yeomanry of surplus-producing commercial farmers has also emerged. Emulating the landed gentry, the rural bourgeoisie frequently combines farming with off-farm business enterprises and government employment, which may produce as much as half of family income. Typically ranging in size from 20 to 100 hectares (50 to 250 acres), the farms of this minority total about 43 percent of registered holdings. Most rural dwellers, and therefore most Kenyans in general, form the agricultural poor. To the extent that they own land, members of this sizable majority control less than 24 percent of registered landholdings. Other elements include subsistence farmers and pastoralists eking out a living on communally held arid and semiarid lands, together with landless, near-destitute peasants from arable farming regions who are pushed into ASAL locations and into towns and cities where they become the urban disenfranchised. Both socially and economically, the masses of people who belong to this potential underclass are Kenya's least mobile and most alienated citizens. They are also, at least until they enter the urban milieu, the least politically organized and active.

Nairobi is the hub of the nation and of eastern Africa, but for rural

Nairobi city center (photo by David Keith Jones/Images of Africa Photobank)

Kenyans seeking jobs the chance of employment is less than one in ten and the realities of survival are harsh. An inexpensive room in one of the city's transient hotels will bring with it problems of water, sanitation, and security. Even for the new arrival who finds work, life is not easy. The workplace may be some distance from where one can afford to live. Beginning at the low end of the wage scale and virtually without employment security, the former rural dweller becomes a magnet attracting relatives to the city who need food, shelter, and hospitality. The requirements of traditional etiquette come into direct conflict with the imperatives of urban survival, and if drought has devastated the migrant's home area the human flow from there increases. The new job seeker is automatically placed in competition with workers from other ethnic groups who may profit from better contacts derived from longer traditions of urban migration. Luo, Kikuyu, Abaluhya, and Kamba migrants enjoy a decided advantage in this regard. Lacking the support of a city-wise ethnic community, arrivals from the coast, the north, and parts of the Rift Valley face bewildering obstacles in coping with an urban environment.[63]

Newcomers to Nairobi of all socioeconomic levels, ethnic identities, and races encounter a city whose neighborhoods are well defined according to these criteria. Radiating from the city center in roughly concentric circles are the apartments and maisonettes of Asian and African middle-income groups, followed by the larger homes and gardens of the elite. Farther out lie African low-income housing projects and beyond them the shantytowns of the impoverished. Segregation is economic rather than racial, although some Nairobi neighborhoods retain distinctive Asian and European atmospheres created by colonial-era housing precedents—Parklands for Asians; Karen, Lower Kabete, and Langatta for Europeans; Muthaiga for Europeans, the diplomatic community, and other expatriates; and Mathare Valley and Kawangware for poorer Africans and squatters. As might be expected, the African elite has chosen Karen, Langatta, and Muthaiga as favored places of residence.

In Nairobi and in other urban and rural areas, relations among Asians, Europeans, coastal Arabs, and the larger African population are congenial enough on matters of business and commerce but remain rigid, episodic, and occasionally hostile along social lines. Arab and Swahili Muslims are actively engaged in trade and shipping, export-import businesses, and ship supply. Otherwise, a kind of three-tiered system of mercantile capitalism prevails. Asian shopkeepers and investors, African traders, and a blending of European and African professionals and corporate representatives conduct business together in the multiracial manner envisioned by the British and by many early nationalists. Outside the strictly economic sphere, however, exchanges remain highly stratified. Asians stay close to their particular communities and rarely marry out-

side them. Long-term European residents follow British social customs
and tend toward clubs established during the colonial period. Other foreigners, usually in Kenya only temporarily, form social contacts largely
by nationality. Arabs are constrained by Islamic tenets that to varying degrees isolate them from the rest of society. As in the countryside, African
social linkages in Nairobi and other cities remain communally biased.
Within discrete ethnic categories, informal relations are further differentiated according to class-producing factors such as education, income,
and occupation. One long-standing prejudice that to some degree unites
all local groups is revealed in the expressions of envy and mistrust directed against the Asian merchant establishment.

Women are conspicuously underrepresented on all but the lowest
rungs of the socioeconomic ladder. In a country that is still predominantly rural, agricultural, and patriarchal, women perform most of the
work and must also see to the reproduction of society. Nevertheless, they
have yet to be awarded or to secure for themselves a status commensurate with their vital place in Kenya's present and future.

The Central Role and Uncertain Status of Women

Women serve as the chief productive force in the local economies of
rural Kenya, and gross disparities in female versus male labor contributions impose heavy annual penalties in lost working hours and food
output. Women perform most routine farm chores, including the ar-
duous tasks of hoeing and weeding. They are also held responsible for
gathering firewood and water, sometimes from considerable distances;
for managing the household hearth; for tending babies, children, and the
elderly; and for carrying planting materials and harvested crops to and
from the family *shambas* (production fields). Men are primarily committed to animal husbandry, hunting, and beekeeping and to occasional
heavy labor such as the opening of new fields and the construction of
roads and waterways. Men also oversee the cultivation of export crops,
often with the advice of agricultural extension specialists, while women
are assigned to food crops without such assistance. In this manner, men
maintain control over family earnings.[64]

Economic gender inequality is reinforced by social customs, some
of which pervert former rights and obligations. Bridewealth is a system
wherein a groom's family compensates a bride's family for marriage
privileges. Commonly found in societies with agnatic (male only) descent rules, the bridewealth exchange traditionally "provides a means of
attaching children to lineages, as its payment is the test of the validity of
a marriage and its refund the mechanism of establishing divorce."[65] Legal
nullification has widely replaced the return of bridewealth as a means of

formalizing divorce. Originally transacted in livestock and other commodities, moreover, many bride-wealth transfers have degenerated into simple cash payments of the type that Tom Mboya once criticized as inimical to a woman's constitutional right of free choice. In addition to the personal hardships they imply, de facto wife purchases and the persistence within some groups of female circumcision offer powerful testimony to the inferior and dependent roles allotted women throughout rural Kenya.

Among the most disadvantaged are uneducated rural women in the transitional age-group born between 1963 and 1973. In a rapidly changing society, they remain subservient to male interests and enjoy little in the way of individual freedoms and economic opportunities. Impoverished townswomen share the lot of the urban poor and often fare worse than men, but at least they command a degree of independence that would be withheld in their home locations. Times are indeed changing, and for most women a future of continuing marginalization or increasing self-determination hangs in the balance.

In the mid-1980s, 70 percent of Kenya's female population was rural, and about the same percentage was functionally illiterate. Although urbanization and new educational openings are now altering these ratios,[66] women remain constrained by a combination of customary, statutory, and religious obligations governing marriage and divorce—all legally binding—that either favor men or are honored by them only when it suits them. Women still constitute less than 20 percent of urban job holders and are limited mainly to the lower pay scales. In the countryside, they confront a perception of dependency barring their participation in extension programs and development projects, as well as a circularity of practical obstacles preventing them from obtaining and employing the major factors of agricultural production. Private ownership places women in a situation in which their traditional rights to land are no longer recognized. Without land to use as collateral, they cannot obtain farm credit to buy fertilizers, seeds, and other inputs.

Rural Kenyan women have challenged this discrimination by coming together in a variety of self-improvement associations, but even here male priorities seem to intrude. In 1989, 32 percent of 410 officially funded women's groups were located in Rift Valley Province, home to Kenya's president and ascendant ethnic elite. Heavily populated Central, Nyanza, and Western Provinces claimed only 29 percent of these government-subsidized organizations.[67] Urban women have been aided mainly by domestic and international agencies whose activities are not dependent on direct government support. In 1989, a group of women in Nairobi's Mathare Valley was awarded a grant to build and operate a tile factory by the African Housing Fund, an endowment supported by twenty-three African governments, in an attempt to facilitate the entry of poor urban women into Kenya's formal industrial economy.

In 1977, a women's association was formed that quickly swept through the rural areas, captured the imagination of educated and uneducated women alike, earned the lasting respect of the international environmental and developmental communities, and was at first applauded and then condemned by the Moi regime. Green Belt was conceived by Wangarí Maathai, a biologist and two-term president of the National Council of Women of Kenya, under whose auspices it was initiated. Maathai had challenged Kenya's marriage laws in 1981 and had been jailed for contempt. She and Green Belt have since promoted both environmental and women's causes and, in the process, have come to oppose Kenya's male-dominated political establishment.

Green Belt is a grass-roots environmental organization encouraging tree planting by women and children. Its members have planted millions of seedlings since the late 1970s, and the concept has spread to other countries including Tanzania, Rwanda, Sudan, and Zimbabwe. Green Belt volunteers also promote environmental education in Kenyan primary schools. Both nationally and regionally, the movement's impetus derives from the dynamism of Maathai and from the specter of desertification, drought, and famine raised in the early 1980s. Despite its

Wangarí Maathai of the Kenya Green Belt movement (courtesy the *Daily Nation*)

common-interest goals and the support it once received from the government, Green Belt has been inexorably drawn into political controversy. Speaking for its thousands of formerly apolitical members, Maathai has argued:

> I think the Green Belt movement appears threatening because it is organizing ordinary people, poor people, and it is empowering them—telling them that they can cause positive change to their environment and that they can do it on their own. African governments do not encourage and have not yet accepted the fact that the people can direct their own destiny. They want to guide them and they want to be followed blindly. They do not want their people informed or organized because organized groups threaten their position.[68]

During his Independence Day speech of December 12, 1989, President Moi singled out Maathai and Green Belt in a wide-ranging attack on critics of his record on political practices, human rights, and environmental issues. In question was the construction of a sixty-story commercial building in Nairobi's Uhuru Park, the central city's only extensive green space. To be financed mainly by government-guaranteed foreign loans, the $200-million Kenya Times Media Trust tower would have been the tallest structure in Africa and was intended to house the headquarters of KANU and several ancillary organizations, including the party newspaper and Kenya's second television station. It was also to feature as its centerpiece a large statue of President Moi. Some criticized the proposal for its excessive cost and for the questionable connection it created between KANU and the British press magnate Robert Maxwell. Maathai protested it on environmental grounds, pointing to the loss of Uhuru Park and to the shadow the structure would cast over its immediate vicinity.

On behalf of Green Belt, Maathai filed suit to halt construction pending the completion of an environmental impact statement. When this motion was thrown out of court, she approached the attorney general, who declined to respond. Maathai was then denounced in parliament, and one day after the president's speech Green Belt was given two weeks to vacate its offices. On the following day this deadline was reduced to twenty-four hours. Moi had accused Maathai of urging Kenyan women to show disrespect for their men, and on December 15 the KANU women's organization Maendeleo ya Wanawake called on the party to revoke her membership. An assistant minister in the president's office had already complained that he did not appreciate such criticism coming from what he described as a group of disaffected divorcees.[69] The member of parliament for Mt. Elgon went so far as to ban her from his constituency.

Green Belt probably suffered under this assault, which may have frightened many women away. In something of an anticlimax, the project was indefinitely postponed and apparently shelved for quite different reasons. In February 1990, donors announced that the Times Media Trust project entailed greater expense than Kenya could afford to incur and still expect to receive foreign financial credits and aid. For Wangarí Maathai and Green Belt, however, this incident demonstrated the dangers of public protest against the will of Daniel arap Moi and his one-party state.[70]

Insofar as educated women are concerned, these limits may not be as narrow as one might infer from the skyscraper episode. The new television station freely airs foreign criticisms of the government and sometimes even ignores the movements and pronouncements of President Moi—a practice previously almost unheard of in the Kenya news media. A woman, Kathleen Openda, has become one of the station's most popular reporters and has covered stories on a number of highly sensitive topics, such as the razing of Nairobi shantytowns and rioting by opponents of single-party politics.

Nevertheless, female participation in public affairs is almost entirely confined to the tiny minority belonging to one or more of Kenya's elite women's associations.[71] Even within this select group, the impact of women on public policy is strictly limited. In the parliament formed after the 1988 general election, only 2 of the 171 elected and appointed MPs were women. No women were named to cabinet positions, although one was appointed to serve as a ministerial permanent secretary. Only two female judges sat on the Kenya high court, and the KANU leadership continued to be characterized as an exclusive male club.[72] Clearly, Kenyan women face a long road ahead in achieving equality with men. To a large extent, the success or failure of any such endeavor will hinge on the quality of life offered to Kenyans of both sexes.

ISSUES OF SOCIAL INFRASTRUCTURE AND VALUE CHANGE

Education for What and for Whom?

Most of Kenya's formal education is organized under the central government, in a highly centralized bureaucratic operation employing more than two hundred thousand teachers (about 86 percent of whom are primary teachers) at various levels of qualification. They serve more than six million primary students and approximately one million secondary students in the country's more than seventeen thousand schools. Advanced educational opportunities are offered in a variety of technical, teacher-training, and polytechnic institutes, as well as in the country's four public universities (Nairobi, Moi, Kenyatta, and Egerton).

Education is the largest single item in the central government budget, consuming up to 23 percent of annual expenditures. Half of this funding is allocated to the primary schools and less than 20 percent to secondary programs. During the 1980s, an effort was begun simultaneously to emphasize higher education and to satisfy communal interests through the opening of new universities and university campuses in densely populated and ethnically significant regions. By 1989, over 60 percent of the educational development budget and slightly less than 20 percent of recurrent spending were committed to these purposes.[73] The result has been a dramatic rise in the number of university students, from under 9,000 in 1981 to nearly 30,000 by the early 1990s. Primary enrollments increased by 35 percent during the 1980s, secondary enrollments by 38 percent, and university enrollments by 200 percent. To keep pace with entry-level demand created by population growth, primary teacher-training colleges expanded their intakes by 22.4 percent in the last half of the 1980s, from 25,248 to 30,912 students.[74]

With independence, Kenya inherited an elitist British educational sequence involving seven, four, two, and then three years of mainly generalized primary, secondary, and postsecondary study. In 1985, this system was replaced by an American-style progression of eight, four, and four years of formal education and training. Curricula were revised to incorporate vocational courses "designed to make the graduates at each level properly oriented to face realities in agriculture, small-scale enterprises and other forms of self-employment that most of them will inevitably have to be engaged in, as opportunities for rapid generation of jobs in the modern non-agricultural sector will be critically limited."[75] Despite the government's determination to "instil realistic attitudes and aspirations regarding employment in both the parents and school leavers," competition for perceived educational advantages continues to overwhelm available teaching facilities and personnel. Because education is so closely tied to position and wealth, its provision raises particularly contentious issues of education for what and for whom.

For the generation of students entering Kenya's labor market in the 1990s, the educational investment has all but lost its earlier automatic returns. The national economy is growing much too slowly to accommodate the annual outflow of holders of higher-level certificates, diplomas, and degrees, let alone the yearly flood of primary and secondary graduates. There is a bitter irony in this imbalance. Lacking alternative career prospects, many of the better-educated add to the surplus of jobless school leavers by becoming teachers. Qualitatively speaking, the enlightenment gained through formal education leaves students with unrealistic job aspirations and life-style expectations. Compounding the divisive influences of these misperceptions is an entrenched pattern of educational

discrimination against girls and young women, against pastoral minorities, and against the poor and ethnically uninfluential. For the economic
and political elite, education is a tool to be used less in the development
of problem-solving abilities than in the struggle to maintain control and
to transfer privilege to the next generation. Education is staggeringly expensive in modern Kenya not only in terms of its increasingly uncompen-
sated drain on the public budget but also in terms of the social discontent
and unrest that it triggers with its unfulfilled promises.[76]

Using the Harambee self-help movement, government has attempted to address some of these inequities. During the 1960s and 1970s,
the Kenyatta administration encouraged Harambee school construction
as a way of both reducing shortages in primary and secondary educational space and encouraging cooperation between ordinary citizens and
their political leaders. Once completed with voluntary labor and financial contributions from local notables, Harambee schools became eligible
for official staffing and maintenance assistance. By the time Daniel arap
Moi came to power, more schools had been built than Nairobi could support. Even so, public and private spending for Harambee education rose
by a current value of nearly 400 percent between 1979 and 1985, from
K£5.05 million to K£24.48 million.[77] This increase attests to the high priority education receives throughout Kenya, but it also reflects a continu-

Primary school teacher, Marsabit (photo by Norman Miller)

Secondary school classroom, Marsabit (photo by Norman Miller)

ation of educational elitism in that Harambee school graduates are out-distanced by conventionally educated applicants in the limited job market.

Against all odds, education has not lost its central place in the competitive ethos of Kenyan society. As long as officially certified learning is viewed as the key to opportunity, it will serve as a kind of socioeconomic and political cement for a rising meritocracy of the few. The fundamental problem is that Kenya can no longer afford to extend educational benefits in the absence of economic gains that, for now at least, seem unattainable.

The Political Economy of Health

In reality, health is related to wealth.
Those who have wealth, have health.

—Missionary doctor, Marsabit, 1983

Another major social issue is the health sector's ability to deliver on its pledge of "health for all by the year 2000."[78] The ratio of persons per physician fell only slightly during the years of explosive population growth, from 7,890 to 1 in 1980 to 7,262 to 1 in 1989. Hospital beds and cots per hundred thousand Kenyans declined from 158 in 1984 to 138 five years later.[79] A legacy of high fertility has combined with the geographical remoteness of many communities and high medical costs to ensure that the provision of modern health care remains sporadic in the 1990s. Traditional healers still form the first line of defense against illness for an estimated 68 percent of the population.[80]

Kenya's health system includes eastern Africa's largest number of private practices operating on a fee-for-services basis. The public component is organized in a manner similar to the structuring of formal education, hierarchically upward from more than 1,500 health subcenters and dispensaries through nearly 300 health centers and to more than 260 hospitals emphasizing high-technology Western medicine. Mission-sponsored and secular volunteer care facilities operate within this framework under government supervision. Although barely maintaining parity with population growth, the supply of registered physicians has increased substantially in recent years, from eighteen hundred in 1980 to more than four thousand today.[81]

Kenyans who are relatively wealthy can afford treatment in higher-level referral hospitals. Those who are not must rely on local dispensaries and traditional healers. Western-trained doctors tend to disparage customary herbalists, diviners, psychological counselors, and general practitioners, often dismissing them as "bush healers." Once sharing this view, the government has since acknowledged the need for an informal health network to service the poor. The 1989–1993 national development plan encourages the formation of "professional associations for traditional medicine practitioners [to] facilitate the gathering of necessary information for the use, development and appropriate adaptation of traditional diagnostic, therapeutic and rehabilitative control technologies that will become part and parcel of formal medical research and of the Primary Health Care Programme."[82] With this change in attitude, policy makers and medical specialists may learn useful lessons from the past and, at the same time, alleviate income-related disparities in health care by elevating the traditional healer to the level of an auxiliary health worker. If the new approach works, it may also help in some small way to narrow the dangerously wide gap in social values that currently isolates society's privileged minority from its underprivileged majority.

Values in Flux

Although political repression has mounted under the rule of Daniel arap Moi and KANU, since independence Kenya has become a far more open economy and society. The new freedoms have produced benefits in terms of material acquisitions and mobility, but the accompanying rapid change in social values has also exacted a price. The drive toward modernization has created unattainable standards for amenities such as water supply, sanitation, and housing. Standards governing the behavior of individuals, families, and communities have simultaneously eroded, to the extent that problems of private security and public safety have become matters of deep concern to politicians and planners alike.[83] Urban street crime and rural banditry have increased in frequency and level of violence; juvenile delinquency and promiscuity threaten to shatter domestic authority patterns;[84] male absenteeism for employment purposes attacks family cohesiveness in the rural areas and encourages a normless "bachelor town" atmosphere in the cities; alcoholism affects families in both places. In short, anomie and loss of identity have overtaken a large portion of Kenyan society.

Kenyan writers have argued that colonialism and a post-colonial commitment to Western materialism lie at the root of a cultural malaise afflicting society. According to Ben Kipkorir, colonialism deprived Kenyans of meaningful values through a process of social, economic, and political emasculation that depersonalized them, crippled their mechanisms for resource sharing and mutual support, misinterpreted their histories, and eulogized European culture at the expense of their own.[85] Few leaders found it possible to adapt the positive, essentially technological aspects of imperial rule to an African heritage, and the result was an elite value structure alienated from its historical roots and incapable of generating a coherent substitute for the whole of society. This legacy further increased the social distance between rich and poor.

Politically, the independence movement rushed Kenya to statehood without creating a unifying sense of nationhood. Early nationalists eschewed traditional values in the interest of cross-ethnic harmony. Despite rhetorical support for African traditions, Jomo Kenyatta, Tom Mboya, J. M. Kariuki, and others worked toward their replacement with European forms. The practice continues and now plays a significant role in socioeconomic and political class formation. Modern politicians not only shrink from indigenous values but use Western dress and mannerisms, consumer durables, modes of entertainment, and codes of behavior to distinguish themselves from the mass of citizens.

As secular values have changed, so have religious conceptions and practices. Modern Kenya is a meeting ground for Christianity, Islam, Hinduism, and traditional belief systems, each with its devout followers. More than 50 percent of the population professes some form of Christian faith, but this estimate is somewhat speculative. Although diluted by education and conversion to Christianity and Islam, indigenous religions still carry weight for many Africans, particularly those of the older generation. A mixing of beliefs has led to an array of messianic churches, prophet movements, and breakaway sects that freely borrow ideas and adherents from each other. Perhaps less so now than during colonial times, a certain amount of opportunism has entered into the choice of the more conventional denominations, conversions often being motivated by educational and occupational opportunities directly and indirectly associated with church membership.

This is not to say that organized religion is not a strong and independent force in contemporary Kenya. President Moi is a devout Christian, and biblical messages are embedded in his oratorical repertoire. Through their leading African clergy, the Anglican Church of the Province of Kenya (CPK), the Presbyterian Church of East Africa (PCEA), and the Roman Catholic church exert powerful moral and political influence. Missionary support of hospitals, clinics, schools, and nongovernmental voluntary organizations affords the expatriate religious community an important if limited voice on broader social issues.

Until the 1980s, Kenya's main Christian denominations served as effective agents of social control and acceptable political expression. Since then, the KANU government's increasing concentration of power, suppression of dissent, abuse of political and human rights, and tolerance of high-level corruption have provoked a vigorous debate within church circles on the proper role of religious groups in politics. Between 1980 and 1988, dissident clergymen and KANU politicians traded dire warnings and threats culminating in a declaration by the party's general secretary, Moses Mudavadi, that parliament might very well enact a constitutional amendment to abolish freedom of religion.

Individual church leaders singled out for attack in these exchanges included PCEA Reverend Dr. Timothy Njoya and CPK Bishop and Archbishop David Gitari and Manasses Kuria. Njoya had complained that, under strong political pressure and also because of jealousy within the church over his popular following, the PCEA hierarchy had excluded him from both of its two top posts. In 1987 he was ordered by the PCEA General Assembly to transfer his ministry from St. Andrew's parish in Nairobi to his home presbytery in Nyeri District. Njoya had gained press notoriety at St. Andrew's for his highly controversial sermons.[86] In response to the transfer directive, he announced that he would exercise his option to retire with benefits rather than suffer the humiliation of being forced from his Nairobi pulpit. The PCEA leadership countered by declaring that his only option would be to resign without benefits and be defrocked. Njoya acquiesced and was placed on probation in Nyeri. This action removed him from political center stage, but it failed to halt his verbal assaults on the Moi regime.

Njoya was not alone in his opposition. Bishop Gitari characterized KANU's 1988 annual conference as a blatant example of undemocratic one-party rule. The conference had lasted for only one day and had been limited to the uncritical ratification of resolutions previously adopted by the party's national executive committee. In late 1990 the Roman Catholic cardinal of Kenya, Maurice Michael Otunga, condemned the cruelty of shantytown bulldozings in the Muoroto and Kibagare suburbs of Nairobi. Until then the Roman Catholic clergy had mainly confined its public criticism to the government's family planning initiatives. Protests of these kinds persisted well into the 1990s.

Not surprisingly for Kenya, communal factors often enter into religious affairs. For example, the 1990 death of CPK Bishop Alexander Muge, also an outspoken critic of the KANU elite, in a mysterious automobile accident led to conflict within the CPK over his replacement. Part of this dispute involved competition between Nandi and Pokot factions of the Kalenjin ethnic complex. Similar leadership quarrels have erupted among Kikuyu cliques in the African Independent Pentecostal Church of Africa and between the Kikuyu/Embu and Nandi/Tugen segments of President Moi's own church, the African Inland Mission. For both ethnic and other reasons, religion has become a highly politicized part of Kenya's fragile common culture.

As a countervailing tendency to the social divisiveness associated with changing values, cultural homogenization is also occurring in Kenya and is facilitated by rapidly expanding literacy and by a steady growth in heavily Westernized mass communications. During the last half of the 1980s, English-language newspaper circulation rose by 38 percent to more than 500,000 copies, while sales of dailies and weeklies in Kiswahili fell by 29 percent to just over 100,000 copies. In the same period, the number of purchased and licensed radios multiplied by 75 percent, from 128,000 to 224,000, and television set ownership increased by nearly the same rate, from 11,800 to 25,500.[87]

Purveyors of news, art, and entertainment are subjected to official censorship, but restraints vary in impact because they are imposed sporadically and sometimes almost whimsically. Kenya's best-known novelist, Ngugi wa Thiong'o, was detained during the late 1970s for speaking out against the infant Moi government. Forced to relinquish his professorship of English at the University of Nairobi, he went into voluntary exile in Europe. Some of his writings, principally works with political themes that he published in vernacular Kikuyu for consumption by the less well-educated, are still banned in Kenya. Included in this proscribed list is the profeminist play *Ngahika Ndenda* (*I Will Marry When I Want*). Curiously, two books by Thiong'o published in English are readily available in Nairobi bookshops. One is a personal account of his prison experiences and the other a novel whose protagonist is overcome by the evils of capitalism. Both volumes contain strong antigovernment messages.[88]

Official sensitivities on matters of artistic expression sometimes seem to border on paranoia. In 1991, a theater group attempted to present a Kiswahili version of George Orwell's *Animal Farm*, a satire on totalitarian society. Because the story featured farm animals in human roles, the troupe thought that it would amuse Kenyans of rural origins. Before it could open in the Nairobi slum of Kangemi, *Shamba la Wanyama* was banned because of its supposedly inflammatory nature. Kangemi had recently been caught up in violent prodemocracy demonstrations during which twenty-three protestors had been killed by police. In its determination to prevent future outbursts, the regime has also taken to outlawing popular music that laments familiar urban miseries such as homelessness and unemployment.

Such attempts to expunge reality from the public mind may be abating. Kenyans noticed an apparent relaxation of press censorship soon after the December 1991 decision to restore party competition to the country's political process. The new mood was epitomized in a banner headline carried by Nairobi's leading newspaper, the *Daily Nation*, proclaiming the call by a newly legalized opposition for President Moi's resignation. In this setting of sweeping social change and political uncertainty, one cultural value remains constant—the value that Kenyans still attach to the land.

CONCLUSIONS: THE SIGNIFICANCE OF LAND

Kenya has scarcely developed a permanent urban culture and a self-consciously articulated urban class structure. Although growing numbers are falling short in the attempt, most city dwellers hope someday to return to the comfort and security of individual family *shambas* in their ethnic home areas. This means that being landed ranks very high among Kenyans' social and economic priorities and will figure centrally in personal aspirations for years to come. A kind of land fever grips society and affects people of all stations. No other topic is so engrossing and controversial. Who has land, who inherits land, who buys and sells land—and how much and for what price—are perennial topics of discussion at all socioeconomic levels. This preoccupation is bred by land shortages and inequalities of ownership in a country where land still represents a critical linkage to welfare, wealth, and survival itself. Land is welfare where there is no alternative welfare system. Land is wealth when no other forms of wealth are available. Land is the key to survival in an insecure world.

Status and honor also derive from the land. The qualities that distinguish one person and group from another are closely related to the earth. It is honorable to possess a large *shamba*, to manage it well, and to make the soil yield a bountiful harvest. To own land and be its "father" gives a man status among his peers. To cultivate skillfully and productively still affords a woman special distinction. In small communities these differences are important. People struggle to own and master the land; without it a person is of less consequence.

The problem is that Kenya has run out of arable land to distribute in established ways, and economic growth is proceeding too slowly to hasten the transition to a more fully urbanized society. Human fertility will continue to trouble economic planners into the next century, but natural population increase is only part of Kenya's social-ecological dilemma. Other elements are the accumulation of large baronial tracts by an acquisitive elite at the expense of an ever-larger proportion of agrarian society; the relegation of surplus rural populations to arid and semiarid wilderness areas that they quickly degrade; the shackling of women to the land, which they are expected to work, often alone, without the protection of legal tenure; and the tendency for cash-crop agriculture to reward the few and sentence the many to impoverishment at the periphery of rural and urban life. Poverty results not only from population growth but also from an inequality of opportunity deeply rooted in social practice and public policy. The majority of Kenyans will soon have lost the ability simply to fall back on the land,[89] but this is still what most people, if all else fails, long for. Issues of land and inequality are the driving forces behind the daily perturbations of modern Kenyan politics and government.

4

Modern Politics:
The Moi Era

Although recent years have witnessed a resurgence of democratic forces in some African states, most of the political rights that nationalists demanded and won at independence have since been seriously compromised or lost. Rights to a free press, a free parliament, and an independent judiciary, rights to organize politically, to form interest groups, and to criticize government openly have all given way to closed authoritarian, often military, rule. Avenues of conflict resolution through the interaction of political parties and other formal organizations have been blocked and replaced by channels of centralized—and usually highly personalized—command. Political relations have been forced into alternative conduits of interest expression and demand satisfaction involving exile parties, thinly veiled protest movements, opposition churches, and grass-roots alliances tied to the informal patronage networks of those in power.

Until the middle 1980s, Kenya remained fairly free of what has been termed the politics of "departicipation" in modern Africa. Repression occurred periodically, and governmental actions taken just before and after the 1982 coup attempt further eroded some freedoms. In that year, the country was also declared a one-party state. In general, however, the basic rights of citizens, parliament, and the press were protected. In comparison with neighboring Ethiopia, Somalia, and Uganda, Kenya was still remarkably free and stable. By 1987, however, serious problems of civil-liberties and human-rights violations had developed. As political protest escalated, detentions multiplied and press freedom was curtailed. Criticism of the Moi government began to be voiced by Western nations, particularly the United States. In 1990, Foreign Minister Robert Ouko was murdered, and Kenya entered a period of even greater unrest and repression. The slow and reluctant investigation of Ouko's murder, its outcome, and persistent accusations of Kalenjin corruption at higher levels fueled political discord as the very survival of the Moi regime came into question. Responding to growing pressure from within and without, the government celebrated Kenya's thirtieth year of independence by reluctantly opening the system to multiparty competition for an election in 1992.

The movement away from single-party rule was accompanied by a frantic attempt on the part of the regime to retain power, intense competition for dominance among and within rival opposition parties, and an upsurge in political violence and intimidation throughout the more populous parts of the country. As 1992 wore on, President Moi continued to delay announcement of the national election date in an effort to keep the opposition confused and fragmented. The constitution required an election by no later than 1993, and a series of proposed amendments, if adopted, would provide for choice of a president from a wide range of candidates.[1] This prospect was regarded with a mixture of anticipation and apprehension, and when a December 1992 election date was suddenly announced political tensions came to a head.

THE FIRST FIVE YEARS, 1978–1982

Although the structure of government remained in place when Daniel arap Moi became Kenya's second president, in fact a new political era had begun.[2] The Kenyatta years had created the mold; executive and legislative structures were well established, the constitutional rules were known if not always followed, and the problems were recognized. Kenya was still overwhelmingly rural, land-poor, and dependent on cash-crop exports and Western economic assistance. As Moi rose to preeminence, so did a new set of problems: a worsening energy crisis, scarcity of foreign currency, rising interest and inflation rates, and a faltering ability of Kenyans even to feed themselves. Not least disturbing, within months of Moi's taking office the 1979 census confirmed that Kenya's population growth rate was now the highest in the world and would continue for the foreseeable future to overwhelm human services and opportunities for productive employment.

The first five years of the Moi presidency encompassed a period of relative goodwill (1978–1979), a time of economic decline and political unrest (1980–1981), and an upheaval surrounding the attempted coup d'état of August 1982. As vice president, Moi had automatically assumed the presidency for a three-month interregnum after Kenyatta's death. A Kikuyu plot to unseat him never fully developed, and before the end of the three months it was obvious that he had marshaled enough support to win KANU's nomination. Part of the reason for Moi's success was that he had moved swiftly to consolidate his position by bringing two Kikuyu leaders—Charles Njonjo, the attorney general, and Mwai Kibaki, the finance minister—into his close confidence. By the time of the KANU nominating convention there was no effective opposition to the Kalenjin outsider and a peaceful succession ensued. Moi's election in November 1978 was thus more of a national expression of relief than a contest of power. The parliamentary election of the next year ousted most of the Kenyatta old guard, brought into office many candidates sympathetic to Moi, and effectively awarded him a sweeping mandate to proceed with his own agenda.[3] The president had already selected Mwai Kibaki as his vice president.

Because he had himself served as vice president for eleven years, Moi was already well known in governmental and diplomatic circles. He was born in 1924 at Sacho Location in Rift Valley Province's Baringo District, to one of Kenya's smallest ethnic groups, the Tugen of the Kalenjin ethnic cluster. Educated at an American mission school in his home area, he turned first to teaching. In 1950 he entered politics, first as a member of the Baringo District Council and in 1957 as one of the first eight Africans elected to the colonial Legislative Council. Moi split from his Luo and Kikuyu colleagues in 1960 to help lead KADU, rejoining KANU in 1964 when KADU was disbanded. Between 1961 and 1967 he successively served as minister for education, for local government, and for home affairs, becoming Kenya's third vice president in 1967.[4]

After Moi assumed the presidency, nearly every political faction in Kenya joined the new order. During this unifying phase of his regime, the

Daniel arap Moi, second president of Kenya 1978– (courtesy the *Daily Nation*)

president vowed to end political factionalism and corruption. As he toured the country to build support for his program, he developed a distinctive leadership style—that of an avuncular yet energetic school teacher, an abstemious man who neither drank nor smoked, a person given to homilies and biblical pronouncements.[5] To gain public backing, he released a dozen detainees who had been held by Kenyatta, abolished school fees, initiated a national literacy campaign, and went to the hustings on the corruption issue. He denounced smugglers, hoarders, and bribe takers in several open meetings and moved behind the scenes to purge the bureaucracy.

On the international front, Moi assumed an openly pro-Western stance. Following the United States's lead, Kenya withdrew from the Moscow Olympic Games in protest over the Soviet invasion of Afghanistan and went on to denounce the Soviet Union as a threat to the Indian Ocean "zone of peace." In domestic affairs, a new five-year development plan was launched that called for an economic growth rate of over 6 percent and a campaign against poverty. The plan's objectives reflected Moi's enthusiasm for free enterprise, even though the economic realities of the time were not encouraging. Coffee and tea prices on the world market were falling, manufacturing and tourism had slowed, and a maize shortage had developed.[6]

During the early Moi years, the entrepreneurial ethic that drove Kenya's ongoing quest for prosperity became a double-edged sword. Sustaining the regime were wealthy and rising elites that wanted to preserve the economic and political status quo. Support also came from the West through multinational corporations and through large infusions of foreign aid. Partly from resources filtering down from this assistance, Kenya's patron-client system continued to function, but it had its destabilizing aspects. As the 1978–1979 recession deepened, illicit economic activity became commonplace and official corruption proliferated. With shortages beginning to appear at the lower levels of patron-client exchanges, mass withdrawal and discontent increased. '

Kenya's economic decline continued into 1980 and 1981. The country experienced a series of strikes and threatened strikes by doctors, students, bank employees, and even professional musicians. Widespread concern arose over the national food supply with revelations about thefts of grain reserves and evidence of serious mismanagement in the provision of agricultural credit, storage, and transport. During 1980 the country registered an economic growth rate of less than 4 percent. In 1981 the economic picture grew still worse as retail prices rose dramatically for fuel, sugar, rice, milk, and meat.[7] Political instability paralleled the economic slide. Splinter groups, some led by candidates who had lost in the 1979 parliamentary election, appeared on the scene. These were publicly denounced by the president, and a wave of loyalty pledges to him and the government followed. Student riots attributed to poor food and inadequate academic services broke out at the University of Nairobi in early 1980, and in May university students went on a destructive street rampage in support of a threatened nationwide doctors' strike. Student demonstrations and destruction of property also occurred in outlying secondary schools.

Searching for ways to keep ahead of political dissent at the top, in 1981 Moi reshuffled his chief lieutenants by elevating loyalists G. G. Kariuki and Nicholas Biwott to cabinet posts. Further to bolster the regime, he expanded the army from 12,400 to 14,750 troops, increased military salaries, and formed a new infantry unit named the "Moi Battalion." To underscore Kenya's military readiness and regional significance, Moi entertained Mengistu Haile Mariam, the Soviet-backed Ethiopian leader. During a convivial four-day visit, the two heads of government jointly condemned Somali military irredentism. In the course of this two-year period the president became sterner, more paternalistic, and less flexible. He lectured against social disobedience and repeatedly called for loyalty to the government. The question was whether his more rigid demeanor originated in a belief that he was in control and could act accordingly or in fear that control was slipping away and an authoritarian rod was needed to sustain it.[8] The attempted coup d'état of August 1982 seemed to supply an answer.

During 1982, fear of plots against the regime led to increasing harassment of writers, lecturers, and students and to fundamental uncertainty about the government's short-term stability. This apprehension arose in the context of tensions created by the effects on Kenya of a world economic recession, mounting lawlessness along the country's borders, discipline problems in the universities and secondary schools, and unsustainable levels of official spending in the health and defense sectors. Kenya's bloodiest postcolonial uprising and most serious threat to civilian rule overshadowed all of these difficulties. At 3:30 A.M. on August 1, 1982, Kenya air force personnel seized Nairobi's radio station, main post office, air bases, international airport, and several other strategic points around the city. The first message from the "People's Redemption Council" was "Rampant corruption and nepotism have made life almost intolerable in our society. The economy is in a shambles, and the people cannot afford food, housing, or transport."[9] Army troops loyal to the government counterattacked rebel positions just after dawn, and by noon the government announced an end to the rebellion. This was an accurate claim for Nairobi, but fighting continued for several days at the Nanyuki air base near Mt. Kenya. Back in Nairobi, already well-organized looters began breaking into shops, and for the next two days there was indiscriminate pillaging and vandalism. To end the disorder, the army was instructed to shoot looters on sight. After civil order had been restored, official tallies reported 159 killed, $3 million in merchandise lost, and extensive property damage. Unofficial estimates put the death toll at between 600 and 1,800, including a Japanese tourist, an Asian United Nations employee, and many other innocent bystanders. A number of Asian women were raped.

In the immediate aftermath of the disturbance, some detatchments of loyalist troops began a protracted search for rebels while others returned truckloads of looted goods to Nairobi's Kenyatta Conference Center to be reclaimed. President Moi reassured the nation by radio and asked everyone to resume work. All air force personnel were arrested, and their branch of the armed forces was disbanded. Two enlisted men believed to be key instigators fled to Tanzania, where they were offered asylum. The University of Nairobi was closed, several students were arrested, and a detailed investigation of the uprising was begun. In the ensuing months, military tribunals imposed prison sentences of up to twenty-five years on several hundred airmen. Six officers and two enlisted men were sentenced to death. In civilian courts, charges against all but a few student leaders and other civilians were dropped.

Three explanations soon emerged for the coup attempt. The least likely was that the uprising was a whimsical, episodic event without deep roots in protest, largely the work of malcontents on a binge. Advo-

Kenyatta Conference Center tower, downtown Nairobi, viewed from Uhuru Gardens (photo by David Keith Jones/Images of Africa Photobank)

cates of this view pointed to air force personnel across Africa, depicting them as jaunty, arrogant, and highly trained professionals who often believe that they can do anything with their awesome military power. A more probable interpretion linked the uprising to social issues, including Kenya's general economic distress, falling producer prices for tea and coffee, high energy costs, rising unemployment, and urban food shortages. The rebels' initial statement that "people cannot afford food, housing, or transport" seemed at least partly to confirm this thesis. Others who took essentially the same position specifically pointed to political issues. The journalist Smith Hempstone concluded that the rebels had charged the Moi regime "with imposing a one-party state, censoring the press, violating human rights, indulging in corruption and nepotism, and mismanaging the economy. In effect, the have-nots were rising against the haves, and there was more than a little truth in the charges."[10] A final and possibly related explanation portrayed the coup attempt as a series of failed plots. The central theme of this argument was that the air force plot was only one among several—that conspirators existed in the air force, army, and police but the air force group, fearing exposure, had attacked prematurely. It was suggested that many soldiers, airmen, and police officers had known of these plans two weeks before the event and that Kenyan intelligence officers had been aware of the plot but had chosen not to inform President Moi.[11]

Whatever the internal machinations behind the episode, the regime was deeply shaken. The president moved quickly to reward those who had been loyal and set in motion measures to placate the military. As 1982 drew to a close, it became clear that he had barely survived a very serious threat to his rule—and not only from the military. The behavior of civilians during the disturbance pointed to deep discontent. Organized gangs may well have been part of the conspiracy, but the nearly instantaneous looting by thousands of city dwellers spoke of a malaise lying just below the surface of Kenyan urban society. Unbridled attacks on Asians and their shops underscored the resentment that many low-income Africans still harbored against this non-African trading class. More broadly, the uprising and its aftermath had challenged Kenya's entire system of governance. The main political question in late 1982 was whether the Moi regime would be able to ease the stress by addressing the country's most pressing socioeconomic issues and allowing the return of some open dissent.

YEARS OF TURBULENCE, 1983–1987

Moi was easily reelected in 1983, but as time passed the weakened economy sagged even further and the political climate darkened. Fully a dozen purported coup leaders were reportedly hanged in 1985, and increasingly open complaints were voiced in Kenya about human-rights abuses and of high-level malfeasance.

The Njonjo Affair and the 1983 Election

The 1983 fall from power of Charles Njonjo is an instructive example of the workings of Kenyan politics. As a leading Kikuyu politician, Njonjo had helped Moi to consolidate his position in the transition from the Kenyatta period. Having already demonstrated his prowess at gaining and dispensing political and economic influence, "he became . . . the regime's 'gray eminence' without at first appearing to rival Moi."[12] Lacking a strong local constituency, he had still built a powerful following at the national level and eventually emerged as one of the few possible challengers to Moi's increasingly endangered presidency.[13] Factional infighting among Njonjo's supporters, several Kikuyu cliques, and Moi loyalists had apparently begun before the 1982 coup attempt.

The means of Njonjo's removal was unique for independent Kenya. Whereas Mboya and Kariuki, the only other leaders to command large national followings and threaten the central establishment, had been assassinated, Njonjo was simply forced from office. When President Moi announced that a "traitor" was plotting with a foreign country to overthrow the government, he became the immediate focus of speculation. Moi made it clear that Mwai Kibaki was not suspect, and it was not long before several MPs attacked Njonjo in open parliamentary session. The "informal" charges against him included supposed connections with South Africa, possession of large foreign bank accounts, and collusion with several governments wishing to see him replace Moi. After an official commission of inquiry had condemned him as an *msaliti* (a betrayer), he resigned from parliament, and rejoicing broke out in the chamber. The president then silenced further talk about the affair, quoting the biblical passage "Let him among you who is without sin cast the first stone."

The Njonjo affair turned public attention to the national election set for September 1983 (a year earlier than necessary). Standing unopposed for both his Baringo parliamentary seat and the presidency, Moi quickly won the party's nomination. All but 4 of more than 900 other applicants were cleared by KANU to contest the 156 available legislative seats. Moi reemphasized that the "traitor" issue should not enter into the campaign, but in fact the fate of Njonjo's supporters had become one of the key issues. Great interest was focused on whether Moi would try to use the vote to oust Njonjo's partisans from parliament. The results of the balloting were inconclusive. Some of Njonjo's supporters lost, but others were returned, and a few of Njonjo's critics were also defeated. More decisive was Moi's prompt appointment of a twenty-three-member cabinet made up of politicians loyal to him. His hold on power was now reestablished and Kikuyu influence in the national political arena further eclipsed.

Aftershocks from the 1982 coup attempt continued to be felt throughout 1984. General P. M. Kariuki was sentenced to "four years and twenty-one months" on charges that he had failed to prevent the insurrection. In 1985, according to diplomatic sources, twelve airmen who had been convicted as ringleaders were hanged at Kamati Prison in Nairobi. The government refused to confirm or deny the reports, but all of the men except one were thought to have been Luo.

The Mwakenya Movement

In 1986 a shadow political organization called Mwakenya (a Kiswahili acronym for "Union of Nationalists to Liberate Kenya") became the object of great security concern. In March, six activists including Ogangi Mbaja, an associate of the aging opposition leader Oginga Odinga, were detained on a charge of publishing subversive documents. Although many accused Moi of fabricating a conspiracy to rally support for his regime, there was little doubt that covert political activity was taking place. Most alarming to the government, it seemed to be geographically broadbased and cross-ethnic, apparently led by Kikuyu and Luo dissidents. Moi charged Mwakenya with masterminding the 1982 coup attempt, and by early 1987 more than a hundred persons had been detained for subversive behavior, including arms smuggling along Kenya's western border. Rising from relative obscurity, Oginga Odinga vigorously criticized the government for its actions. The regime did not react directly against Odinga, but it did accuse two prominent church leaders of Mwakenya involvement.

International criticism of Moi's methods of dealing with political opponents became increasingly frequent. Complaints were largely ignored, but the president did order the dismissal of several senior police officers for corruption and brutality. Muslims in Mombasa rioted in protest of bans on Islamic public meetings. Overall, the late 1980s were clouded by increasing paranoia in government, periodic prohibitions and detentions, and a growing public conviction that high-level corruption and arbitrary uses of power were out of control.

REPRESSION AND RENEWAL, 1988–1992

Kenya's passage into the 1990s was eventful if not definitive in terms of resolving the political problems of the 1980s. Government repression and sporadic violence continued, and churches and voluntary associations increased their political opposition. Incumbents of senior offices were frequently reshuffled, and people who had been demoted or dismissed from cabinet positions were occasionally reappointed. In the midst of these events, the foreign minister fell victim to a political assassination, triggering charges of a political cover-up, months of antigovernment protest, and increasingly widespread demands for an end to single-party rule.

The 1988 parliamentary election began with open-air queue-voting to select candidates; party members were required to line up behind their favorite candidates. This procedure seriously compromised free choice in the ensuing general election not only because all final contestants had to be members of KANU but also because the primary election had been marred by voter intimidation, ballot rigging, and blocking of candidates deemed undesirable by the party leadership. After his own reelection, Moi again rearranged the government by demoting Mwai Kibaki from vice president to health minister and naming another Kikuyu, Josephat Karanja, in his place. The move was widely perceived as the president's way of containing Kibaki's political aspirations and those of the Kikuyu factions he represented without alienating the restive Kikuyu counter-elite. Having served this purpose, Karanja was soon discarded and replaced by George Saitoti, a Maasai and a former professor and parastatal manager.

Heretofore suppressed, Mwakenya resurfaced in March 1988, ac-

George Saitoti, vice president of Kenya
1990–   (courtesy the *Daily Nation*)

cusing the government of corruption and vote manipulation in the February election. Never far below the surface, anger and mistrust increased
within the Luo, Kikuyu, and other larger ethnic communities, and the
regime blamed Mwakenya for inciting them. Responding to unabated international criticism of his human-rights record, Moi released all political
prisoners detained without trial and offered amnesty to dissidents in exile. Although some foreign observers praised these gestures, university
students and other elements of the domestic opposition pointed to the
many Kenyans still unjustly imprisoned. Before the end of the year the
University of Nairobi was once again closed because of student unrest.

The Ouko Murder and an End
to Single-Party Politics

In February 1990, Kenya's minister for foreign affairs, Dr. Robert
Ouko, was murdered near his home in western Kenya. Immediate
press allegations of government involvement led to riots in Nairobi and
Kisumu. President Moi promised a full inquiry, reluctantly appointed a
commission to conduct it, and invited help from Britain's Scotland Yard.
A year later the commission was still taking testimony, and in November
1991, at the government's request, the senior British detective assigned to
the case, John Troon, presented his team's evidence. He testified that
Ouko's efforts to curtail high-level corruption provided a strong motive
for his murder and that two senior officials, Industry Minister Nicholas
Biwott and Director of Internal Security Hezekiah Oyugi, had probably
planned it.[14] Moi promptly dismissed Oyugi and Biwott, both frequently
named for their tendencies toward graft and disrespect for the law, and
later ordered their arrest in connection with the murder. The president
then dismissed the commission of inquiry. Like Moi a Kalenjin, Biwott
had been the president's closest confidant and thus the second-most-
powerful politician in Kenya. Despite his arrest, the Ouko assassination
cast a pall over the regime as critics quickly drew parallels to the political
killings of Tom Mboya in 1969 and J. M. Kariuki in 1975. It was suggested
that Moi had mistrusted and envied the foreign minister, who had been
very highly regarded in Western diplomatic circles.

Ouko's murder further galvanized Kenya's rising opposition movements. The government used the crisis as an excuse to clamp down on
the largest of these, a loose affiliation of Moi opponents named the
Forum for the Restoration of Democracy (FORD). On November 16, police fired tear gas into a crowd of several thousand FORD supporters
who had assembled in the Nairobi slum of Kamukunji, and the entire
FORD leadership was arrested. The dissidents were flown to their home
districts and detained until an international outcry prompted their release. Led by Oginga Odinga, Paul Muite, and Gitobu Imanyara, they

resumed their attacks on the government and eventually managed to register FORD as a formal opposition party. As chairman of the Kenya Law Society and editor of the *Nairobi Law Monthly*, respectively, Muite and Imanyara were outspoken critics of the Moi regime. Two former MPs, Henry Masinde Muliro and Martin Shikuku, soon joined another ex-detainee and former cabinet minister, Kenneth Matiba, among the FORD leadership. In reference to Ouko's demise, the human-rights organization Africa Watch sagely observed that "the events of 1990 proved to be a watershed in Kenyan politics."[15]

The affair came at a bad time for Moi's presidency. During 1990, the regime had come under intense international pressure to liberalize its economic policies, to reinstate a de jure multiparty system, and to halt its abuse of civil liberties and rights. Rights abuses had become the key domestic issue as well; peaceful protests and occasional violence were followed by seemingly indiscriminate arrests and detentions. Pressures for change rose to a crescendo toward the end of 1991, when key donors met in Paris and announced that Kenya's foreign aid would be held in abeyance for six months pending the initiation of political and economic reforms. Moi capitulated in December, asking parliament to authorize multiparty competition by rescinding the 1982 constitutional amendment (the now-infamous Section 2[a]) that had legalized the single-party state. Donors also pressed Moi to initiate repeal of constitutional provisions that permitted political detentions without trial and to privatize large segments of a parastatal system that was considered to encourage rampant corruption. One day after parliament eliminated KANU's political monopoly, new political parties began registering for an election anticipated to be held in late 1992 or early 1993. In addition to FORD, these unstable coalitions of competing opposition leaders included the Democratic Party (DP), the Kenya National Democratic Alliance (KENDA), the Social Democratic Party (SDP), and the Kenya National Congress (KNC). Polling its readers in May, a local news and opposition-opinion magazine found that nearly 80 percent preferred FORD and somewhat less than 16 percent the DP. In this admittedly biased sampling of Kenyan public sentiment, KANU received 1.29 percent of subscribers' support.[16]

FORD disintegrated into a three-way leadership struggle among Oginga Odinga (supported by Paul Muite and Gitobu Imanyara), Henry Muliro, and a coalition of Kenneth Matiba and Martin Shikuku.[17] Former vice president Mwai Kibaki came to head the DP, Jonestone Makau the SDP, and Mukaru Ng'ang'a the KENDA. The only positions upon which the opposition could agree were a demand for an independent electoral commission to supervise voter registration and a plea that government release an election timetable. Factional divisions within FORD were particularly advantageous to Moi. Matiba had suffered a stroke while in de-

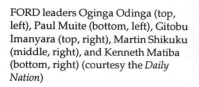

FORD leaders Oginga Odinga (top, left), Paul Muite (bottom, left), Gitobu Imanyara (top, right), Martin Shikuku (middle, right), and Kenneth Matiba (bottom, right) (courtesy the *Daily Nation*)

tention and had spent nearly a year recovering in Britain. A wealthy Kikuyu businessman as well as a former cabinet officer, he enjoyed strong support only in Central Province. Shikuku, although serving as FORD's secretary-general, was similarly disadvantaged by a narrow base of support within the Abaluhya community. Odinga was the only FORD politician to enjoy a national following, and he was thought to be over eighty years of age. Most serious, it was likely that the vital Kikuyu vote would be decisively split among Matiba, Muite, and Kibaki.

Despite this display of self-destruction in the ranks of the opposition, Moi launched a vigorous attack on all of his opponents. In a February 25 speech at Kitale, he declared that "the DP . . . was formed by a very few, very rich leaders. FORD on the other hand is a party of rich Luos and a few Kikuyus who have failed in politics."[18] Hastening to match rhetoric with action, the regime declined to announce an election date, blocked attempts to register opposition parties in several parts of the country, and barred opposition leaders from addressing their partisans. Moi himself decreed Rift Valley Province an exclusive "KANU zone," and the U.S. embassy was outraged to see Matiba prevented from speaking in Wajir and Embu Districts. The government refused to register the Islamic Party of Kenya (IPK) on the grounds that it involved "religious inclinations" and thus did not qualify as a political party. The president went farther, claiming that Muslims did not deserve such representation because they were "behind the slave trade during which thousands of Africans were sold outside the continent."[19] The IPK's Sheikh Salim Balala was arrested for having threatened the KANU national chairman and the KANU district vice chairman for Mombasa, fellow Muslims Shariff Nassir and Said Hemed.

Political Violence and Electoral Politics

The regime's struggle to preserve its hegemony was not limited to recriminations, harassment, and arrests. Politically motivated ethnic violence once again tarnished and endangered the country's halting steps toward truly representative government. During the first half of 1992, 240 persons were officially reported killed in Rift Valley, Nyanza, and Western Provinces. Informal estimates raised the number slain and wounded into the thousands. The fighting included Kalenjin attacking Luo, whom they claimed were stealing Kalenjin cattle, and Nandi assaulting Abaluhya farmers in long-festering land disputes. Kalenjin attacks on Kisii tea growers disrupted production of Kenya's second-largest foreign-exchange earner.

The opposition in Nairobi promptly accused the Moi government of fomenting or at least tolerating this violence to justify declaring a national state of emergency before the March 1993 constitutional deadline for a new election. In May, an assistant minister, Noor Abdi Ogle, lamely counptercharged that FORD was planning to assassinate the leaders of rival opposition parties and blame these murders on the government. Odinga shot back that Moi-supported terrorists had established seven paramilitary training camps in Rift Valley's Maasai Mara Game Reserve. Whether or not this allegation was correct, it was clear that an armed gang calling itself the Kalenjin Warriors had emerged in the struggle. According to the DP leadership, powerful Kalenjin politicians were in the process of organizing a second such group, code-named "Tanganyika."

At conferences in March and May, the National Christian Council of Kenya (NCCK) stepped into the fray by condemning the violence and appointing a task force to investigate the Moi regime's culpability. In an emergency meeting of May 21, a group of Catholic bishops pleaded with the government to stop the killings, "if for no other reason [than] to save itself from collapse."[20] The government responded to all of this with a strong denial of involvement and a thinly veiled threat:

> In the past, the government has assured Kenyans that its commitment to maintain the peace is paramount and that any person, however important, will not be spared if he or she is suspected to be a threat to security. In the same vein, the government will not spare anybody bent on spreading rumours aimed at causing fear and despondency among the peace-loving *wananchi* [citizens]. Every Kenyan should, therefore, ignore rumours.[21]

As if in response, the two-hundred-thousand-member Kenya National Union of Teachers (KNUT) threatened to strike unless the government ended its "political thuggery."

Kenya's descent into violent confrontation was not limited to ethnic clashes. In January 1992, between one hundred thousand and two hundred thousand people participated in an antigovernment demonstration in the Kamukunji area of Nairobi. Odinga addressed the crowd, accusing Moi of using security forces to terrorize ordinary citizens and urging that he and KANU be voted out of office. In contrast to a similar rally in 1990, in which twenty people were killed, and another in November 1991, which was forcefully broken up by police, the January protest concluded without incident. In March, however, a two-day riot broke out in Nairobi. Bands of unemployed youths threw stones at passing vehicles, smashed shop windows, and engaged in minor looting. As police dispersed these gangs, some reformed elsewhere and continued their rampage. Many of the rioters who were caught were beaten by police before being herded off to jail. These disturbances had been triggered by an incident in which police had violently dispersed a crowd gathered to support a group of women fasting in protest over political detentions. One of the hunger strikers was the environmental activist Wangari Maathai, who was tear-gassed and beaten in the melee but from her hospital bed announced that the fast would resume on church grounds. Maathai urged the international community to prevent Kenya from disintegrating into chaos. Similar demonstrations against the government were taking place in the western towns of Kisumu and Homa Bay, and on March 18 President Moi banned all political rallies until further notice. Amidst this confusion, voter registration with a target of ten million voters began in June.

Initially, the opposition boycotted the registration drive, charging the electoral commission with pro-KANU bias. At the urging of church leaders and the U.S. embassy, however, the boycott was abandoned. Acknowledging that KANU was still far better-organized and financed throughout the countryside than the fledgling opposition parties, FORD leaders resorted to opposing the government's proposed electoral amendments to the constitution and a bill that would make newspapers and magazines convicted of publishing "defamatory and criminal materials" liable to fines of not less than K£50,000 ($30,000) and remove the KShs.40,000 ($1,200) limit on campaign spending.

In spite of its show of unity on these issues, FORD soon found itself hopelessly split into two competing camps. The leader of the third earlier faction, Henry Muliro, had collapsed and died at Jomo Kenyatta International Airport upon his return home from Britain. This left the remaining two groups, one headed by Odinga, Muite, and Imanyara and the other by Matiba and Shikuku, more deeply divided than ever. In an attempt to resolve the leadership dispute, an election for delegates to the FORD national party congress was scheduled for August 1, with Odinga and Muite ultimately to run for chairman and vice chairman against Matiba and Shikuku. The results were indeterminate, and heated confrontations ensued between advocates of the two sets of candidates.[22] Adding to the turmoil, a cross-section of women met under the rubric of the National Committee for the Status of Women, urged FORD's Wangarí Maathai to run for parliament and perhaps for the presidency, and resolved to begin a fund-raising campaign on her behalf. Factionalism within FORD served only to benefit KANU. Given his years of protest against the Kenyatta and Moi regimes, Odinga was the sole opposition spokesman to have acquired a firm national reputation. Although Muite and Maathai were beginning to be considered rising stars, none of the remaining opposition leaders was readily distinguishable on any basis other than ethnic identity. Most important, KANU was the only party with a strong presence throughout the country.

Not content with its advantages, the KANU leadership persisted in its harassment of opposition hopefuls. Agriculture Minister Elijah Mwangale announced his support of Shikuku's bid for the FORD vice chairmanship, ostensibly because of their shared Abaluhya roots. In an effort to regain lost Kikuyu support, President Moi resurrected a former minister of state in the president's office, G. G. Kariuki, who had earlier been dismissed after he was linked to the deposed Charles Njonjo. Kariuki was easily elected KANU branch chairman for Laikipia and stood as a powerful candidate for the Laikipia West parliamentary seat. Opposition student organizations had formed at the University of Nairobi, the Student Organisation of Nairobi University (SONU) favoring FORD and Student Opinion (STOP) endorsing the DP. KANU hastened to sponsor its own student group, the Student Peace Initiative of Nairobi University (SPIN).[23]

The KANU government came under attack from another and more vital quarter. Public outrage followed a press revelation that the National Cereals and Produce Board (NCPB) had secretly extended credit to several hand-picked domestic companies so that they could import gunny sacks, at inflated prices, for the 1992 grain harvest. In July, serious shortages of maize meal and sugar were also reported. As shopkeepers took to price gouging, urban food riots erupted for the first time in Kenyan history. In Nairobi, angry poor people looted maize flour and burned a kiosk and a nearby store after the kiosk owner raised the retail price of flour from KShs.17 (50 cents) to KShs.50 ($1.50) per kilogram.

The Kenyan press blamed Supplies and Marketing Minister Musalia Mudavadi for the unexpected shortfall. Mudavadi had earlier assured the country that its food supplies were secured; now he timidly asked citizens to be patient with the shortage because supplementary imported maize would soon arrive at Mombasa. To make matters worse, the imported maize would be of the yellow variety, although Kenyans strongly prefer the white maize that is grown locally. The depth of public disgust with this situation was conveyed in a heated news commentary:

> What had happened to the more than enough food reserves in the NCPB stores in hardly a period of half a year? Somebody must have drained the food from the silos. That somebody must be known by the Minister and the person the Minister has put in charge of the NCPB. Kenyans are suffering shortages of maize and its by-products because of this person and the lack of foresight of the relevant government organisation. . . . This food . . . was sold either officially or unofficially within four months. Now Kenya has to use scarce foreign exchange to import the unpopular yellow maize for months to come.[24]

As 1992 approached its end, anger, foreboding, and mistrust spread across Kenya. In October the Moi-appointed electoral commission announced December 7 as the date for the national election. This left the opposition parties very little time to register candidates for parliamentary seats throughout the country. Facing the difficult task of organizing primary elections to identify candidates in such a large number of constituencies, FORD and other opposition parties insisted that the election date be moved forward.[25] Not surprisingly, KANU held out for December 7. FORD took the issue to the Kenyan high court, which ruled in its favor and set a new election date for December 29. The KANU leadership threatened to appeal but failed to do so. In the meantime, several new splinter parties had formed around individual personalities representing Kenya's major ethnic, regional, and ideological divisions.

The real threat to KANU, however, remained FORD, whose two competing leadership groups became consolidated according to their generational and philosophical differences. At the forefront of the old guard were the disillusioned former KANU politicians who had captured several FORD leadership positions on the party's formalization in December 1991. In addition to Matiba and Shikuku they included Philip Gathoka, George Nthenge, and Ahmed Salim Bamahriz. A year later it was widely believed that this clique in fact represented the political status quo and if elected would merely take up where the Moi regime had left off. The other faction enjoyed a much broader base of support and had triumphed at the September national convention following the August party election. It was led by Chairman Odinga, Vice Chairman Muite, and Secretary-General Imanyara. To underline its break with the past, FORD's new leadership embraced several young professionals who had been in the vanguard of Moi's opponents. These included Wangarí Maathai; Peter Nyong'o, a political scientist; Mukhisa Kituyi, an anthropologist; and Kiraitu Murungi, a human rights attorney. Odinga's son, Raila, also belonged to this group, which Nairobi commentators approvingly called the "young turks." FORD sympathizers among the press speculated that Muite would eventually be elected president of Kenya after Odinga had led the government through a transitional phase to fully representative democracy.

FORD's internal rifts had allowed Mwai Kibaki's DP to gain strength in Central Province, but it remained basically a regional, Kikuyu-sponsored party. As the election date approached, it seemed that KANU could be defeated only through a coalition uniting the DP and the FORD young turks. With December 29 nearly at hand, Moi's actions on behalf of KANU became increasingly irrational. He issued decrees banning truck transport and the sale of alcoholic beverages on the day before the election, explaining that opposition conspirators were planning to haul their voters to centers of strong KANU support and plotting to lace strong drink with hallucinogenic drugs so that KANU partisans would oversleep and miss the vote. In light of such actions and the widespread incidents of political violence in the preceding months, Western governments expressed considerable skepticism about how honestly the elections would be conducted. Germany, the United States, and several

Commonwealth countries offered to send a total of six hundred election observers, but the Moi government authorized fewer than a hundred—to cover more than one hundred thousand polling stations. The German delegation soon withdrew altogether, claiming that the government was obstructing its work. The American team released a report mildly critical of the KANU campaign and was answered in an angry rejoinder by the party's youth wing.[26]

The December 29 balloting produced an early lead for KANU and President Moi, but a heavy turnout required that vote counting be continued into the next two days. As expected, the first multiparty election in nearly three decades was accompanied by charges of illegal activities and a few violent confrontations in Kenya's urban centers, prompting some residents to stockpile food and several diplomatic missions to form evacuation plans. A crowd attacked an election officer suspected of vote tampering in Nairobi, and a Muslim demonstrator was killed in Mombasa, but the predicted mass violence did not materialize. In the end, Daniel arap Moi secured his otherwise uncontested Baringo Central parliamentary seat and captured more presidential votes than any of his opponents. For its part, KANU won a slim elective majority.[27] On January 4,

Swearing-in ceremony for President Moi, January 4, 1993 (courtesy the *Daily Nation*)

1993, Moi was sworn in for an unprecedented fourth term as president of the Republic of Kenya.

Despite their victories, the incumbent and his party could take little comfort in the 1992 electoral returns. When finally tallied, the results (Table 4.1) reflected a vote of no confidence in the richest and most heavily populated parts of Kenya. The president received strongest support in his Rift Valley homeland and in impoverished North-Eastern Province. Moreover, he obtained only 36 percent of the total vote, while the combined votes cast for opposition candidates Matiba, Kibaki, and Odinga exceeded 60 percent. In the parliamentary race, KANU gained a majority of seats (Table 4.2), but the party suffered major defeats in economically important and densely populated Nairobi, Central Province, and Nyanza Province. With the important exception of Vice President Saitoti, virtually all of Moi's senior ministers were defeated at the polls. In effect, the opposition lost the presidential election only because it was split three ways, and KANU retained its legislative preponderance only because of its strong base of support in heavily pastoral Rift Valley and North-Eastern Provinces and in the subsistence farming areas of Coast and Eastern Provinces.

The election demonstrated that KANU's domain had shrunk to the poorest parts of rural Kenya, that a new generation of young professionals (including an unprecedented six women) had now reached political maturity in the country's heartland, and that ethnicity was still a determining factor in Kenyan politics. Few parliamentary candidates won outside their own ethnic areas, Odinga dominated in his Luo stronghold of Nyanza Province, and the vital Central Province vote was neatly split between Kikuyu candidates Matiba and Kibaki. Most important, for the first time the Moi regime now faced an articulate and highly vocal opposition in government that would inevitably rally around its younger and more energetic leaders in demanding immediate policy reforms and greater executive accountability. How the president would respond to this new situation remained an open question.

THE POLITICAL STAKES IN MODERN KENYA

Looking beyond immediate events, the Moi era can be compared with Kenya's "dynastic" period under the paternalistic rule of Jomo Kenyatta. The main difference between the two leaders is that Kenyatta was a political monarch to himself and the nation and Moi is merely an astute political survivor. Kenyatta nurtured a broad form of nepotism through which any tie to his family, however remote, could be used in pursuing business contracts, land and other tangible assets, and favored treatment for oneself and one's own family. The medium of exchange in

TABLE 4.1 1992 Presidential Election: Reported Results

Province	Moi	Matiba	Kibaki	Odinga	Others	Voters	Turnout
Nairobi	2,410	165,553	69,715	5,888	1,944	674,564	375,465
Percentage	17	44	18	20	0.5	8	56
Coast	188,296	33,399	32,201	42,796	6,653	660,211	303,345
Percentage	62	11	11	14	2.2	8	46
North-Eastern	46,420	7,188	3,259	5,084	73	141,069	62,025
Percentage	75	11	5	8	0.1	1.8	44
Eastern	290,372	79,436	392,481	13,673	8,019	1,230,081	784,781
Percentage	37	10	50	1.7	1	15	64
Central	21,918	630,194	373,147	10,668	6,945	1,209,054	1,042,871
Percentage	2	60	36	1	0.7	15	86
Rift Valley	981,488	214,727	98,302	75,465	3,535	1,896,028	1,373,517
Percentage	71	16	7	5	0.2	24	72
Western	219,187	214,060	14,404	98,822	10,846	947,575	578,416
Percentage	38	37	2	17	1.9	12	61
Nyanza	117,554	10,299	51,998	581,490	9,807	1,197,772	773,562
Percentage	15	1	7	75	1	15	64
Total	1,927,645	1,354,856	1,035,507	903,886	47,822	7,956,354	5,293,982
Percentage	36	25	19	17	1	100	66

Source: Adapted from *Weekly Review* (Nairobi), January 1, 1993.

TABLE 4.2 1992 Parliamentary Seats by Province

Party	Nairobi	Coast	North-Eastern	Eastern	Central	Rift Valley	Western	Nyanza	Total
KANU	1	17	8	19	0	32	9	7	93
FORD[a]	1	2	1	1	1	2	3	20	31
FORD[b]	6	0	0	0	14	2	7	0	29
DP	0	1	0	9	10	2	0	1	23
Other	0	0	1	1	0	0	0	1	3
Total	8	20	10	30	25	38	19	29	179

Note: Returns from 9 constituencies not reported by January 1, 1993. KANU finally claimed 100 elected seats and 12 seats reserved for presidential appointment. The ruling party also gained an additional seat set aside for the attorney general and another provided for the speaker of the house, who sits as an ex officio member. This left 88 seats for the opposition in the 202-seat parliament.
[a]Young turks.
[b]Old guard.

Source: Adapted from *Weekly Review* (Nairobi), January 1, 1993.

all such transactions was support for Mzee Kenyatta and his regime. Daniel arap Moi began his presidency by reemphasizing constitutionality and the rule of law, sponsoring open elections and a relatively free press, and countering private and public corruption with heightened governmental regulation and internal self-policing. From the early 1980s onward, however, his approaches to politics and government came to resemble extreme versions of those employed by Kenyatta.

Defending the Status Quo

Concerned more with perpetuating itself than with accommodating public needs and demands, Kenya's second presidential regime oscillated between the suppression and the absorption of its real and imagined enemies. Economic policies continued to focus on growth and diversification at the expense of broad-based social equity, supposedly in the hope that an expanding economy would eventually benefit everyone. Economic recession, political corruption, and bureaucratic mismanagement soon changed all of this, and by the early 1990s governance in Kenya had become ossified as rule by the few with very little sharing of wealth and power. For this reason, the informal routines of the past were now constantly disrupted by increasingly open and structured confrontations between the political clan in power and several rival coteries, each bent on removing the president and his lieutenants from the entrenched positions of privilege that they had come to treat as sinecures. Police intimidation, ethnic clashes, and poverty-related mass outbursts added a violent dimension to this potentially explosive situation.

Like patronage politics, factionalism is nothing new in modern Kenya. Since before independence the public scene has been dominated by intense competition for influence among overlapping special interests. Chief among these are powerful civilian and military bureaucracies[28] and a small private-sector elite that commands senior offices in KANU, parliament, and the civil service. Ethnic cleavages cut across this establishment. While its members share goals, decisions on how to achieve them and in association with whom still tend to be framed in communal terms. Much of the country's business is conducted in Nairobi bars and clubs that also serve as ethnically discrete haunts for Luo, Kikuyu, Kamba, Abaluhya, Kalenjin, and other aspirants to wealth, power, and prestige.

Regardless of its deep internal divisions, the Kenyan establishment remains determined to preserve a status quo fashioned by Kenyatta and taken up again by Moi. Loyalty is rewarded, disloyalty is punished, and it is possible to be cast off only to be resurrected once issues, opportunities, and interpersonal alignments have changed. Politics means the pursuit of profit, the creation and maintenance of personal followings, and the garnering of favors from those above in order to enhance one's position. Formal status and rank continue to be heavily influenced by how rich one is and how good one's contacts are. The rules of the establishment can be reduced to three: "Honor the top," "Pay tribute," and "Use your *matatu* man."

"Honor the top" is a prescription to support the governing elite, to allay its insecurities, and to avoid political threats of any kind. Beyond the core formed by the president and his inner circle of cabinet ministers and business partners, "the top" includes other ministers and senior administrators, wealthy businessmen, and a handful of lawyers, academics, and church officials. In Kenyatta's time and in the early Moi period, most politically active Kenyans abided by the rule in exchange for a degree of mobility and opportunity within the system. As this type of participation was challenged by formal demands and outright opposition, the requirement of "honoring the top" was stressed to the point that foreign governments felt compelled to include it as part of their advice to tourists and investors: "Visitors to Kenya should show respect for the President and all he symbolizes. They should stop before a presidential motorcade, stand for the national anthem, and under no circumstances destroy or deface a portrait of the President."[29]

"Pay tribute" is an admonition to share profits with those in more powerful positions in return for career advancement and business protection. It underscores the intricate patronage network that connects the central core with the national elite, national with provincial elites, and provincial leaders with their district and village bases of support. The critical link in this chain is that of the district, where resident big men draw resources from above to distribute locally.[30] Kinsmen of urban influentials, traders and other entrepreneurs, local MPs and civil servants, chiefs and subchiefs are the brokers of political legitimacy and stability, and "the top" needs them as much as they need it.

"Use your *matatu* man" refers to the role of rural taxi operators, traders, and petty farmer-politicians as go-betweens in the patronage network. Mobile couriers circulating between Nairobi, the provincial and district capitals, and the outlying areas, *matatu* men mediate between the national and the local arena, between the formal and the informal economy, between haves and have-nots, between clients and their patrons.

These three rules have enhanced the status quo and promoted stability throughout Kenya. In the face of rising protest against what they have helped to create, their continuing applicability may now be seriously questioned.

The Politics of Change

Pressures for change currently emanate from several quarters. As might be expected, the KANU oligarchy's chief opponents are drawn

from the better-educated ranks of Kenya's first postindependence generation and make their presence known through a variety of modern secondary associations. The most orthodox of these are the denominational
churches, which also serve as powerful secular instruments of political
protest and demand for reform. Others include university students and
journalists and private voluntary organizations advocating environmental and other developmental causes, women's interests, and the protection of civil rights and liberties. These vehicles of dissent are strongly
representative of the country's larger ethnic clusters, but the issues they
raise are class-based rather than communal and the proposed solutions
legislative rather than patronage-related. Kenya's new political reformers embrace the concerns of the future, not of the past, and all have paid
the price of verbal harassment, arrest, and detention at the hands of the
Moi regime.

No group has been more vocal in its demands for political reform
or suffered more retribution for its efforts than the legal profession. After
the failed 1982 coup, President Moi and KANU hastened to extend their
control over countervailing centers of influence. In 1989 both the Maendeleo ya Wanawake and the Central Organization of Trade Unions
(COTU) were formally absorbed within the party. Led by the Law Society
of Kenya, concerned lawyers raised the alarm in an attempt to prevent
Kenya's justice system from suffering the same fate, and they had good
reason to be worried. In 1988 the position of attorney general, formerly
tenured, had become one of appointment at the president's pleasure.[31]
During the same year, an annual licensing of attorneys was mandated,
and, by constitutional amendment, judges' life tenure was abolished in
favor, again, of presidential appointment and dismissal. When the Law
Society protested these attacks on judicial independence, the president
accused it of being in league with foreign imperialists. The confrontation
came to a head in 1989, when Law Society activists protested the screening of ethnic Somalis to determine their citizenship. In his Independence
Day speech of December 12, Moi raged against the society and lawyers in
general, stating that "the identity of lawyers is not Kenyan."

Throughout this period, the Law Society leadership was subjected
to a continuous barrage of intimidation. Gibson Kamau Kuria was detained in 1987 for representing three earlier detainees in a suit against the
government claiming damages for torture while in custody. Paul Muite
traveled to the United States in 1989 to receive the Robert F. Kennedy
Human Rights Award for Kuria, and upon his return to Kenya his pass-
port was confiscated and his offices ransacked. Gitobu Imanyara was
arrested and remanded on at least two sedition charges stemming from
articles he had published in the *Nairobi Law Monthly*. Among other prominent attorneys, Kenneth Matiba and Charles Rubia were detained with-

out charge. Still others, including Rumba Kinuthia and Mirugi Kariuki, faced charges of treason. The former MP and political dissident Koigi wa Wamwere had been granted refuge in Norway and, on returning to eastern Africa, had apparently been abducted from Uganda to face charges in Kenya. His arrest caused Norway to suspend diplomatic relations with Kenya. In reaction to incidents such as these and to a growing number of other human-rights abuses and violent demonstrations against them, the International Bar Association switched the site for its 1990 biennial meeting from Nairobi to New York.

At home, the Law Society demanded that the government repeal its preventive detention act and that an investigation be launched into the conduct of Chief Justice Alan Hancox and Justice Norbury Dugdale. According to Muite, the society's chairman, and other members of his council, it was "quite clear that, in their efforts to suppress and even punish the advocates of fundamental rights, the authorities are readily assisted by a section of the judiciary."[32] Countering this accusation, Justice Dugdale granted an injunction requested by four lawyers opposed to Muite to prevent him from chairing the council and uttering "political" speech.[33] After some indecision, Muite, Imanyara, and the rest of the Law Society ignored the order and joined the effort of FORD and other opposition groups to reintroduce multiparty competition into Kenyan politics. The achievement of this goal in December 1991 paved the way for a more open albeit less predictable political process.[34] By the beginning of 1992, the battle lines between the KANU establishment and all of its challengers were at last firmly drawn. Unfortunately for those hoping to effect a smooth transition away from Moi and KANU, the opposition remained deeply divided among competing factions and shifting coalitions of antiestablishment politicians.

CONCLUSIONS: STABILITY AND REFORM

Stability is a perennial issue in modern Kenya. It was of fundamental concern in the transition from Kenyatta to Moi, became a central question again when the Kenyan economy began experiencing difficulty in 1979, and remained a major problem in the decade between the 1982 coup attempt and the 1992 election. Stability for Kenya ultimately requires that political change be moderated by sustainable economic growth. This means a favorable investment climate for Kenyans and foreigners made possible by the realistic expectation of continuity in public life.[35] The greatest fear for the business elite is loss of profitability, for the governing elite, loss of government, and for the new generation of political and economic reformers, loss of freedom and access to power.

Stability is usually determined by a government's response to crises and potential crises, but even the most adaptable regime may face structural forces beyond its apparent control. Kenya's freewheeling political economy may in fact carry the seeds of its own destruction. Already not well regulated, the entrepreneurial engine of growth operates on the fringes of legality. As resources become scarce, statutory boundaries are overstepped and administrative rules broken in a manner that undermines economic confidence, discourages foreign investors, and threatens the legitimacy of the leadership. External events often exacerbate these destabilizing tendencies. World recession and regional conflict in eastern Africa have stunted Kenya's economic expansion, led to a buildup of refugee populations and a problematic increase in police and military power, and entangled Kenya in the civil disturbances of neighboring states. Nairobi has served at various times as a base of operations for political exiles from Ethiopia, Rwanda, Somalia, Sudan, and Uganda. The presence of these groups has created justification for intensified attacks on the domestic opposition as exiles and local dissidents feed on each other's frustrations.

Another measure of a country's stability is the quality of its political leadership. Kenya has yet to evolve a firm set of enforceable rules for the exercise of power, and therefore personal factors play a decisive role in determining how leaders actually behave. Jomo Kenyatta's legitimacy was based on a Father of the Nation persona that he cultivated and built upon. To Daniel arap Moi fell the unenviable task of attempting to solve some very difficult national problems without the help of such an image and without Kenyatta's strong ethnic base of support, his well-placed political allies, and his wealth. It took him five years to acquire Kenyatta's level of control, and he has never achieved the prestige, let alone the adoration, that his predecessor enjoyed.

Beyond imagery, political relations in Kenya are inherently sectarian and sorely test the problem-solving capacities of individual leaders. Kenyatta managed schisms by manipulating them from above, Mboya by mediating among them, and Moi by continually balancing ethno-regional representation at the seat of influence and authority. Each approach has perpetuated the uncertainties of unfettered factional competition along ascriptive rather than instrumental lines. If the past is a preview of what is to come, future leaders will have to find their own formulas for accommodating communal and sectional instability, probably beginning with a resurgent struggle for power among the Kikuyu clans of Central Province.

Two other challenges to the next leadership generation should be emphasized. The first concerns the urban poor, including squatters recently arrived from the countryside, the perpetually unemployed, and the lower echelons of the working population. Sporadic rioting, looting, waves of petty crime, and other desperate protests against poverty have marred the urban scene since 1982 and speak to the existence of profound inequity that must be redressed if civil order is to be restored and social integration achieved. A second concerns the military. Among the many factors that can lead to direct military intervention in politics, some of the most dangerous arise from messages of distress and privation reaching soldiers from their families and kinsmen in Kenya's overcrowded and drought-prone hinterlands. If for no other reason than the military's increased size and strength, the safeguards installed by Kenyatta and Moi may no longer suffice to protect civilian rule.

Many of the means to political stability that worked for Kenyatta and Moi are now outmoded. Under the personalistic rule of these two presidents, regime security has depended "on a balance within the military system, on the centralization of power within the state structure, and on the neutralization of potential foci of organized opposition."[36] The Kenya of today is a much more complicated place of increasing inequality, rapid class formation, and highly vocal demands for political and economic reforms that extend far beyond established patronage relationships. This is not to say that the old alliances and animosities have disappeared. Ethnicity and sectionalism are still deeply embedded in the new political reality. As Kenya approaches the next century, the central question is whether its governing system will be capable of sharing opportunities for political participation and satisfying hitherto excluded elements of society without destroying itself in the process. In large part, the final answer to this question will turn on what is now happening in the Kenyan economy.

5

Modern Economic Realities

Kenya's economy reflects a peculiar blend of decentralized private enterprise and highly centralized state capitalism, both systems employed by those in power to foster politically enhancing patronage relationships. Aimed at encouraging but also controlling and manipulating large-scale foreign investment, this archetypical example of the "reorganizational"[1] approach to African development passed through its formative phases under the tutelage of Jomo Kenyatta. It reached maturity during the presidency of Daniel arap Moi, when many of the formula's inefficiencies and inequities became apparent and began to exert a decisive influence on society. In particular, Kenya now faces declining economic growth, widening trade deficits, mounting international debt, and deepening foreign-aid dependency. To some degree these problems originate in the international economic arena beyond the reach of domestic public policy. Beyond this, however, they are associated with inegalitarian industrial strategies emphasizing elite-oriented import substitution at the expense of mass consumables and with agricultural policies promoting exports more than food crops. No longer capable of coping with sweeping price increases for industrial inputs and fuels, fluctuating export prices, losses in local food production, rampant unemployment, and high-level corruption, the economy faces challenges demanding immediate attention. Politically as well as economically, the capacity for policy reform remains largely untested.

It is difficult to overestimate the urgency of the need for action in the current situation, due in no small measure to weakening activity in an underdiversified economy, a rapidly diminishing investment and resource base, and a concomitant rise in social discontent and disorder. For example, international tourism has replaced coffee as the country's richest source of foreign exchange. Tourist revenues depend in large part on the personal security of visitors and on the preservation of wildlife and wildlife habitats; yet tourists, wild species, and protected areas are placed at risk by gangs of unemployed marauders, well-armed and organized poachers seeking profit from ivory and rhinoceros horn, and land-hungry peasants. Mass expectations are rising in geometric proportion to flagging economic performance, resulting in sometimes violent confrontations and in a general rejection of authority that is intensified by the leadership's penchant for wealth accumulation while consigning much of the public interest to the vagaries of foreign aid.

This picture has a brighter and a darker side. The Kenyan GDP grew at an average annual rate of over 4 percent during the 1980s, as compared with average growth rates of 2.8 percent for Tanzania and Uganda. During the same period, however, percentage increases in non-emergency food aid exceeded population growth, and receipts of official development assistance swelled by 185 percent, from $351 million in 1979 to $1 billion by 1990. As Kenya entered the 1990s, it ranked behind only Egypt and Tanzania among African countries, as a consumer of concessional foreign aid.[2] More recently, this largess has been interrupted and its future placed in doubt. Donors have banded together in refusing to subsidize what they interpret as the Moi regime's flagrant abuses of human rights and its unwillingness to share power with a growing and increasingly vocal opposition. For their part, foreign investors have shrunk from the managerial and financial costs of doing business in a country where the acquisition of import licenses and government contracts turns on the delivery of corporate shares and outright payoffs to "the right people."

Kenya's economic universe is divided into two parts. Serviced by domestic investment and foreign capital, the formal economy consists of six key sectors: export agriculture, commercial energy, transportation and communication, industry and manufacturing, wholesale and retail trade, and tourism. A large informal economy surrounds this complex and, despite years of official neglect and even sabotage by government, helps cushion it by providing alternative means of livelihood for millions of rural and urban dwellers. The capabilities and mutual compatibilities of the two systems will be sorely tested in this decade, with the viability of the Kenyan society and state hanging in the balance. Only by stabilizing foreign economic contributions and investing much more heavily in the domestic economy—and especially in peasants and peasant agriculture—can planners and policy makers hope to avert a devastating national crisis.[3] Time is not on their side. Under present circumstances, the point will soon be reached at which the rural and urban areas can no longer absorb an inexorably expanding work force and the demands of frustrated retainers and needful dependents will finally overwhelm the resourcefulness of patronage politicians and job-holding relatives. The critical question is whether economic rationalization can proceed quickly and broadly enough to prevent sociopolitical disintegration and possible military intervention.

THE POLITICAL ECONOMY OF GROWTH AND RECESSION

Kenya's Economic Honeymoon

Since independence, the Kenyan approach to development has stressed economic growth above social equity within a mixed free-enterprise system managed by government. Until the end of the 1970s, the economy fared well under this strategy, especially in relation to the rest of Africa. Between 1964 and 1972, Kenya enjoyed an average growth rate of 6.8 percent, as compared with 4.5 percent for the continent as a whole. In the twilight of Kenyatta's rule, during the coffee-boom years of 1976 through 1978, economic growth peaked at 8.6 percent. Euphoria inspired by the coffee boom carried over into the Moi presidency in spite of declining export earnings prompted by a drop in world coffee prices. GDP growth fell to 4.3 percent in 1979 and averaged only 3.8 percent in the early 1980s.[4]

One reason optimism persisted in the face of a deteriorating international coffee market was that, over the previous decade, industry and manufacturing had replaced export agriculture as the economy's fastest-growing sector. During the 1970s, agricultural production increased at an average annual rate of 6.5 percent, while industrial output surged ahead at a rate of nearly 11 percent. This impressive showing contrasted sharply with activity in the stagnating industrial economies of Tanzania and Uganda. Worsened by the collapse of the East African Community in 1977, these countries' industrial growth rates averaged 2.7 percent and *minus* 6.4 percent respectively during the 1970s. By 1979, Kenyan industries accounted for 34 percent of GDP, the same percentage yielded by agriculture.[5] Confident of continuing economic growth and diversification, the government launched its fourth five-year development plan, the first "Moi" plan.

Spanning the period from 1979 through 1983, the fourth plan was ambitiously directed toward reducing poverty and providing for the basic needs of society while attaining a targeted economic growth rate of 6.3 percent.[6] Rather than through a significant extension of human services, the plan's social goals were to be reached through increases in formal employment. Over one million new jobs, many of them in the rural areas, were envisioned. This meant that export agriculture would have to be expanded and new industries encouraged. To help pay for these ad-

vances, additional revenues were to be extracted from foreign investments but under strict controls to preserve investor incentives.

As the 1980s approached, President Moi's closest advisors began to
worry that his development plan suffered from inconsistent objectives,
called for impossible growth performance, and failed to address the
country's mounting food and balance-of-payments deficits. Moi himself
was not entirely sanguine about the future. He instructed his vice president and minister of finance, Mwai Kibaki, to keep the public informed
of "hard options ahead" and to urge farmers toward largely self-financed
improvements in food production. Kibaki's ministry instituted import
controls and moved to stem the outflow of foreign exchange by restrict-
ing overseas travel and requiring advance deposits on imported goods.
These measures were not enough to prevent Kenya's slide into economic
recession.

End of the Honeymoon

Throughout Africa, the early 1980s were years of economic decline
and hardship. In Kenya, the number and magnitude of difficulties suddenly seemed overwhelming. Foreign-exchange reserves dwindled as
sagging earnings from coffee and tea were met by soaring oil prices and
rising costs for other imports. Industrial productivity fell victim to shortages of raw materials, equipment, and spare parts, as well as to power
outages caused by reduced generating capacity. In agriculture, dry
weather combined with tight credit, unfavorable producer prices (some
officially held down to allow urban food subsidies), and instances of governmental mismanagement to discourage farmers and lower their output. Domestic shortfalls were experienced in cereals, pulses, potatoes,
and milk. In some cases, as in coffee, sisal, and pineapples, production
actually increased, only to receive less return as world prices eroded.

In 1980 consumer prices rose by an average of 13.2 percent
and building activity slowed. As the realities of the new decade became
clearer, the government reduced its annual growth target to 5.4 percent
and initiated a program of belt-tightening. Import licenses were further
limited, greater emphasis was placed on agricultural growth, and novel
ways were sought to substitute Kenyan resources and products for foreign inputs and consumer goods. In fact, 1981 saw a slight upturn in the
economy. The maize crop came in well, although agricultural exports
were still plagued by depressed prices and high oil-import costs. At midyear Kibaki presented an annual budget applauded by parliament for its
austerity but criticized for not resolving the oil dilemma. In an urban-
izing society increasingly dependent on mechanized agriculture, industry, and transport, an oil problem meant a food and employment
problem. In 1981, Kenya's population stood at over 17 million, with a po-

tential work force of nearly 6 million.[7] During the year an estimated 250,000 Kenyans became available for work but only about 50,000 found wage employment. As school leavers and graduates flooded a saturated job market, instances of social unrest and petty crime became common-place.

The following year began with an inflation rate of almost 10 per-cent, a wave of industrial layoffs, and another set of restraints on import licensing. The government again reduced its planned rate of economic growth, this time to 4.3 percent. Perhaps most alarming, Kenya's interna-tional credit rating slipped from seventh to ninth in Africa.[8] A rapidly withering economy might well have led to an early downfall of the Moi regime. Food shortages, inadequate transportation services, unemploy-ment, corruption, economic mismanagement, and general social discon-tent were all implicated in the attempted air force coup of August 1982 and the subsequent urban disorders and financial losses. The episode was followed by a decline in tourism and tourist revenues, a flurry of official reassurances to international investors and donors, and a frantic search for scarce commercial credit to repair retail businesses devastated by looters.[9]

Shaken by these events, the Moi government took two important steps toward economic recovery. First, it commissioned a blue-ribbon panel, led by the economist and central bank director Philip Ndegwa to recommend a package of structural adjustments and policy reforms for the Kenyan economy. When completed, the Ndegwa Report unequivo-cally blamed a large share of Kenya's economic crisis on excessive official borrowing and spending, the private sector's addiction to external fi-nance and imports, and, most important, a "marked decline over the years in standards of management performance and financial control within the government."[10] The report further stated that efforts to stimu-late employment had ignored productivity considerations and that gov-ernment subsidization of commerce and industry consumed too much of the annual budget and often led to losses. In an indictment of the civil service, the panel charged that publicly supported development projects lacked effective planning, implementation, and evaluation. It urged greater economic self-reliance, austerity, and bureaucratic efficiency. These themes were incorporated into Kenya's fifth development plan, dedicated to the "mobilization of domestic resources for equitable development."[11]

A second and more immediate impetus for economic reform orig-inated in pressure from the International Monetary Fund for currency devaluation, enhanced export promotion, and a net reduction in govern-mental and parastatal employment. Not wishing to risk further depreci-ation of Kenya's eligibility for foreign credit, in 1982 the cabinet agreed to a 17 percent currency devaluation. Government hiring was curtailed and an inward-looking, export-oriented policy line promoted. Toward the end of 1983 these painful remedies seemed to have been accepted, at least in principle and to the extent that President Moi's reelection proceeded without serious disturbance.

SECTORAL PERFORMANCE IN THE 1980s AND EARLY 1990s

During the second and third terms of Moi's presidency, the Kenyan economy settled into the routines of a low-income country aspiring to middle-income status. The period produced a mixed record of advance and retreat for each of the country's six leading sectors, for its financial structures, and for the neglected informal economy upon which most citizens still depend.

Operating in both the domestic sphere of sectoral development and the international arena of foreign investment and aid, loose and ethnically shifting coteries of private entrepreneurs and public employees have carried on their quest for mastery over an erratic economy under the close scrutiny and ultimate control of President Moi and his coterie. Whether or not one accepts Freund's underlying premise about the motivating influences of African class formation, conspiracy, and conflict, he accurately captures some of what prompts these middle-level interactions—and the rising tide of protest against them—in modern Kenya:

> Whatever their specific relationship to foreign enterprise African accumulators in every bureaucracy have used their offices, connections and qualifications to further their personal advancement and feather their own nests. At the same time the state service contains a significant technocratic element, reproducing itself through education and envisioning itself as a permanent salariat. For this stratum anti-colonial nationalism has developed into an ideology of patriotism that sometimes supports and sometimes struggles with the private sector "national" bourgeoisie. The technocrats are not would-be capitalists, but nor are they simply selfless servants of the people. They have acceded to a standard of life enormously more affluent than that of the mass of the population, measured both in terms of private consumption and socialised benefits and entitlements. Within the general sea of African poverty lie considerable islands of welfareism, in which access to subsidised housing, free health care, schooling and other amenities is apportioned according to civil service rank. In defence of the island, technocrat and compradore, gatekeeper and national bourgeois unite.[12]

The largest expanses in Kenya's sea of poverty and some of its most impressive islands of privilege are still to be found in the rural areas.

Agriculture

The agricultural sector includes food and export crops, livestock, forestry, and fisheries. Taken together, farming, ranching, and herding employ over 80 percent of the population and yield the country's largest single share of domestic and foreign earnings. During the 1980s, nine crops (in descending order of economic importance: coffee, tea, cane sugar, maize, wheat, sisal, cashews, pyrethrum, and cotton) accounted for more than 70 percent of gross marketed production at constant 1982 prices. Livestock, poultry, and dairy products made up another 24 percent. Maize is raised on 40 percent of all cultivated land. Although the majority of farmers are no longer self-reliant in the crop, maize output is still sufficiently high and widely distributed to make this grain Kenya's main dietary staple. The bulk of the remaining major cash-crop inventory is exported. Also entering the local and international markets are forest and fish products, rice and barley, pineapples and coconuts, and assorted fresh fruits and vegetables.[13] About 42 percent of sales activity is organized under commodity-specific marketing boards,[14] but even their records underestimate total agricultural performance. Many small farmers bypass official buying agencies and sell informally on the open and clandestine market, where prices are usually higher and profits more quickly received. This practice applies especially to surplus maize, which serves as a vital source of supplemental income for large numbers of peasant cultivators. Maize is grown by more farmers than any other crop, and only about 25 percent of the annual yield is officially marketed.

Land shortages and inequality between commercial and subsistence enterprises have long been the most serious issues dividing rural society and constraining agricultural development. In a setting of epidemic landlessness, desperate attempts to bring arid and semiarid tracts under cultivation, and forced migration to already overcrowded towns and cities, those who are left behind have become increasingly polarized as economic haves and have-nots separated by an emerging agrarian middle class. During the 1980s, the proportion of total sectoral income derived from Kenya's multitude of unregistered small farms[15] fell from 54 percent to 47 percent. Among registered holdings, about 23 percent were less than 20 hectares (50 acres) and nearly 20 percent ranged from 500 to over 20,000 hectares (1,250 to 50,000 acres). Consisting of plantations, mixed farms, and ranches, about one third of these establishments employed fifty or more hired hands.[16] Regardless of the well-documented fact that, on a per hectare basis, smaller farms tend to be more productive than large ones in arable locations, the latter continue to receive preference in public and private economic support programs, which are also biased toward the ranching and dairy industries. In addition to pricing policies that benefit export producers at all levels, these advantages include privileged access to a variety of services, including agricultural research and extension, credit and marketing, hybrid seeds and chemical fertilizers, fuel and power, mechanization and transport, and veterinary assistance. Virtually the only exception to a total concentration of these technologies on exports is the successful dissemination of hybrid maize varieties in areas of moderate to high rainfall.

Biases in the delivery of modern agricultural services are encountered not only in the attention paid to large-scale holdings; their adverse effects are perhaps most pronounced in the generalized promotion of export commodities over food crops and livestock raised by peasant farmers and open-range herders. Part of Kenya's failure to regain food self-sufficiency relates to arable land shortages, part to an officially encouraged shift in registered small-farm production from subsistence to export crops. By the mid-1980s, smallholders accounted for 60 percent of coffee production (35 percent in 1964), 48 percent of tea output (5 percent in 1965), and 48 percent of sugar yields (11 percent in 1973).[17] These trends offer considerable hope for some degree of rural income equalization, but they do not include subsistence producers and have helped create a dangerous situation of structured food dependency. Between 1970 and 1985, Kenya recorded a 6.4 percent average annual growth rate in grain imports and a 43.1 percent growth rate in cereal food aid. By 1990, annual grain imports totaled about 250,000 metric tons. Nevertheless, food deficits continue to affect more than 80 percent of households in semiarid regions.[18]

Within this high-risk group, between 5 and 8 percent of society pursues pastoralism as a way of life. Fully committed pastoralists are still only tentatively involved in the national economy and have traditionally refused to sell their livestock except under adverse range conditions. They are typically seminomadic, moving their homesteads six to twelve times a year in search of grass and water. Cattle, sheep, and goats form the basis of most herds, although camels and other pack animals are also kept in the north. With over 80 percent of its area consisting of arid and semiarid rangelands, and notwithstanding large pockets of tsetse-infested bush, Kenya is physically able to support a substantial and environmentally sustainable livestock industry. Totaling about 25 percent of marketed agricultural production and only 2.5 percent of exports, however, the value of livestock products falls considerably short of its potential contribution to the national economy. In addition to drought and animal diseases, marketing and processing inefficiencies and a general failure to make economic use of pastoral livestock have figured prominently in this loss of domestic and foreign revenues. Export marketing is managed by the Kenya Meat Commission (KMC), a parastatal corporation that operates abattoirs near Nairobi and in other locations around the country. These facilities have experienced lapses in production for more than a decade because of desiccated ranges and competition from private slaughterhouses. The total number of harvested cattle and calves increased by 43 percent over the late 1980s, but KMC's intake declined by 76 percent.[19] Today, the KMC market share ranges between 3 and 4 percent of total output.

Reversing this trend requires that pastoralists be drawn more decisively into the formal economy. Most cattle arriving at KMC abattoirs are raised on ranches, but the supply of ranch-bred animals fell by nearly 30 percent during the 1980s. In an attempt since the 1960s to commercialize pastoral herds, the government has launched a series of livestock development projects designed to increase cattle sales through the creation of cooperative ranching schemes. Although liberally supplied with foreign technical and financial assistance, these efforts have proven largely unsuccessful in overcoming two fundamental problems: how to settle fiercely independent migratory communities, and how to convert pastoralists into ranchers without also destroying their ability to cope with the harsh and constantly changing conditions under which they live.

There is another side to the problem. For different reasons, central and provincial administrators, police and military authorities, missionaries, and community development workers agree that pastoral movements should be curtailed. Their position is that herders' highly mobile survival strategies usually place them beyond the reach of tax collectors, guardians of law and order, and providers of religious and social services. The military expresses further concern that, because of Kenya's insecure northern borders, wandering pastoralists may pose a security threat. It is often difficult to determine which of the cattle raids and killings that periodically disrupt the north are local affairs and which are the result of incursions from Somalia, Ethiopia, Uganda, and Sudan. The pastoral dilemma therefore has a political as well as a socioeconomic dimension.

Empowering Small Farmers? The District Focus for Rural Development. In March 1983, the office of the president announced a new policy aimed at stimulating social integration and economic development among smallholders, including previously neglected subsistence populations. Termed the District Focus for Rural Development, it was intended to "broaden the base of rural development and encourage local initiative in order to improve problem identification, resource mobilisation, and project design and implementation."[20] Its main provisions were subsequently incorporated into the 1984–1988 development plan, into another major policy statement emphasizing basic-needs satisfaction through renewed economic growth, and into the development plan for 1989–1993.[21]

In keeping with Moi's populist *Nyayo* ("Footsteps" of Kenyatta) philosophy, District Focus is the natural outgrowth of an earlier Special Rural Development Programme (SRDP), in which donor-supplied block grants were provided for small-scale integrated rural development projects administered by district development committees (DDCs) and district development officers (DDOs). Unpopular with central ministerial officials and suffering from a lack of donor coordination, the SRDP was terminated after seven years in 1974. Seeking to reinforce its grassroots patronage contacts and weaken the countervailing influences of ministers, provincial commissioners, and members of parliament, the Moi regime revived the DDCs and DDOs under District Focus.[22]

Partly financed under a nationwide Rural Development Fund (RDF), the policy shifts much of the responsibility for planning and implementing—but not for deciding on—rural development activities from ministerial headquarters in Nairobi to the districts. Therefore, and given that the RDF claims less than 1 percent of the total development budget, District Focus is more of a limited deconcentration of administration than a real devolution of decision-making and budgetary authority. DDCs are supposed to gather ideas from committees of local residents at the divisional, locational, and sublocational levels, but such groups are still largely absent in poorer, sparsely settled regions, and there is no provision for direct popular representation on the DDCs themselves.[23] Ministerial staffs and development budgets are disaggregated on a district-by-district basis, and some funds now flow directly from the Treasury instead of having to pass through individual ministries and provincial offices, but ultimate control over projects and project finance remains centralized at the national level. RDF monies are disbursed according to the size of the district population, which means that more is spent in cash-crop locations where population densities are high than in less crowded arid and semiarid zones.[24]

In short, sensitivity to local conditions and developmental requirements may have been heightened under District Focus, but the program has not had the effect of dramatically improving the productivity of the disadvantaged rural communities whose need and potential for economic development may be the greatest. Rather, the District Focus for Rural Development has once again demonstrated that in the political economy of contemporary Kenya, "decentralisation to the district level and the empowerment of the rural population are not the same."[25]

Empowering Pastoralists? ASAL Development. Half of Kenya's predominantly rural districts contain large expanses of arid and semiarid lands. These areas continue to absorb a relentless flow of immigrants from densely populated wetter areas given over to commercial agriculture, producing a steady increase in environmentally risky dryland farming and an equally dangerous loss of pastoral rangelands. Although ASAL regions vary widely in potential for economic development, the official tendency has been to treat all of them as "low-potential areas." ASAL development has thus taken a back seat to investment in "high-potential areas," most recently according to a rationale presented in the strategy statement upon which the 1989–1993 development plan was based:

> Forward budgets will be further guided by a programme of *budget rationalization* that will identify high-productivity projects for additional funds and speeded implementation; identify low-potential projects to be postponed or cancelled; ensure that recurrent resources are available in the future to operate and maintain completed priority projects and generally to improve the utilization of completed facilities; and fund new projects only if they pass stringent tests of high productivity and cost-effectiveness. Aid donors are being asked to adjust their assistance to conform with this approach.[26]

As in the failed Special Rural Development Programme, donors are called upon to supply the bulk of support for ASAL development projects approved under the District Focus for Rural Development. According to another official pronouncement, "the achievement of sustainable and accelerated development [in ASAL] is truly a long-run, and often expensive, enterprise. Thus the [government] continues to look to the donors both to identify more cost-effective production strategies for these areas in the future and to stimulate the rate of progress there now."[27]

Heavy foreign involvement is employed to compensate for a lack of commitment within the domestic leadership. This abdication of responsibility brings all of the problems of official development assistance directly to bear on the inhabitants of the ASAL, including weak project coordination among donor agencies, delays and interruptions in funding and staffing, an absence of local involvement in and responsibility for development activities, shifting donor priorities and faddism in project selection and administration, and an uneven geographical and topical application of problem-solving efforts. The sheer magnitude of the role assigned to foreign technical specialists inflates the costs of attempts at economic diversification and commercialization, often beyond whatever improvements ASAL dwellers may hope to derive from them. Responsive as they must be to their own public constituencies, aid officials soon lose enthusiasm for projects with such obviously unfavorable cost-benefit ratios.

Kenya's drylands offer considerable hope for economic productivity increases, but only if concerted action is taken to resolve a number of problems. First among these is migration-induced population growth, ranging from two to ten times the country's rate of natural increase, in the semiarid hinterlands of arable locations. In addition to rapid environmental degradation, this overcrowding results in increasingly frequent and violent land conflicts among ethnic groups, between new arrivals and established residents, and between pastoralists and farmers. Also constraining agricultural and rural development are national policies that continue to draw rigid distinctions among ministerial responsibilities, between export-crop and food production, between livestock promotion and wildlife protection, and between "progressive" farmers and subsistence peasants.

Overcoming these obstacles will expand Kenya's capacity for economic development by allowing fuller use of assets already present in the ASAL. Over 50 percent of the national livestock herd is located there. As low-input agriculture proves incapable of supporting the growing number of ASAL farmers and herders, out-migration for employment returns income to those remaining behind and makes them more willing to risk innovation.[28] Under the coordinating influences of the District Focus program, existing user-managed irrigation systems can be expanded at relatively low cost to stimulate other changes that will enhance income generated locally. These include cattle dips to control livestock disease, soil and water conservation, afforestation and tree nurseries, grazing regulation, fuel and fodder production, and supporting human services. The ASAL can also be viewed as gateways to export marketing. An all-weather road now links Nairobi, Isiolo, and Marsabit with the Ethiopian capital of Addis Ababa. Southern Sudan is more easily reached from the northwestern town of Lodwar than from Khartoum. Mombasa already receives more exports from northern Tanzania than Dar es Salaam. The airport at Wajir could become a transit point servicing air freight bound for the Arabian Gulf and beyond and might also anchor a free-trade and reexport manufacturing zone.[29] Feeder roads to arterial highways and marketing facilities could assist in the commercialization of cottage industries and help to create healthier, more productive cattle herds.

In summary, the ASAL may contribute much to Kenyan economic development through greater attention to small-scale irrigated and dryland farming, livestock and wood products enterprises, trade, transport, and wildlife tourism, and conceivably mineral exploitation. Capitalizing on many if not most of these opportunities will require an official determination, independent of foreign-aid considerations, to share wealth and power with disadvantaged local communities and with the many nongovernmental organizations concerned with rural development, natural resource conservation, and basic needs satisfaction.[30] At present, however, a redefinition of the leadership's own enlightened self-interest seems remote. Economic conditions in the rural areas have not advanced from the early 1980s, when subsistence farmers received less than 3 percent of the income gained by commercial producers. In rural Kenya the question is, "How much longer can the . . . elite ignore the disastrous scenario that combines limited land availability, lack of employment, rapid population growth, and scattered food shortages?"[31] The relationship among these inexorably worsening problems is both synergistic and antithetical to economic growth and development.

Energy

Kenya must also contend with what may be evolving into a permanent energy crisis. Wood fuels account for nearly 80 percent of domestic energy consumption, and this high level of demand is steadily depleting already limited supplies. In spite of attempts at agroforestry, afforestation, reforestation, and the development of more efficient cookstoves,[32] population growth combined with inefficiencies in charcoal manufacture and wood fuel usage have imposed hardships throughout the country—especially for poor women in the drylands, who are compelled to forage farther from home in search of firewood for cooking and heating. Commercial charcoal production and small-scale wood scavenging also result in progressive loss of ground cover and topsoil. Deforestation is proceeding at an average annual rate approaching 2 percent, and Kenya has already lost more than 70 percent of its original forest canopy.[33]

Kenya's main sources of commercial energy are hydroelectricity and fuels derived from imported petroleum, and here too the country faces a dire situation. Hydroelectric stations have provided some degree of energy independence, and their installed capacity was increased from 353.5 megawatts in 1985 to 497.5 megawatts by 1989.[34] Yet river silting, equipment breakdowns, and inefficient management continue to cause frequent power shortages. More than that of any other eastern African country, the Kenyan economy is dependent on Middle Eastern oil. In 1988, for example, Kenya imported 14.3 billion gallons as opposed to Tanzania's 3.9 billion gallons.[35] Some is refined at Mombasa for reexport, but rising costs, lowered export earnings, and a weak currency have dictated that increasing quantities be retained for domestic use.[36] Even before the Arabian Gulf crisis of 1990–1991, these factors resulted in higher and higher import bills, mushrooming fuel prices, and depressed consumption. Oil costs swelled by 21 percent between 1988 and 1989 alone, from K£250.1 million ($268.9 million) to K£303.4 million ($326.2 million), while the volume of purchases declined from 2.187 to 2.169 million metric tons. During the same period, the per liter price of regular gasoline and diesel fuel rose from KShs.8.63 (46 cents) and KShs.5.72 (31 cents) to KShs.10.18 (55 cents) and KShs.6.76 (36 cents) respectively.

Kenya's energy consumption grew at an average annual rate of 4.5 percent between 1965 and 1980; between 1980 and 1990 average growth fell to 1.1 percent.[37]

The economy had suffered under two previous oil crises, in 1973–1974 and in 1979–1981. Growth in GDP deteriorated from 6.8 percent in 1972 to 3.1 percent in 1974; it recovered to 8.2 percent in 1977 only to reach a 1984 low of 0.8 percent in the world recession that followed the second price surge in crude petroleum. By the beginning of 1990, gasoline and diesel fuel prices had reached KShs.10.7 (57 cents) and KShs.7.65 (41 cents) per liter. Iraq's invasion of Kuwait on August 2, 1990, and the ensuing Gulf war served to accelerate these downward economic trends. In response to the most recent oil shock, the government raised the official price of gasoline by 32 percent and the price of diesel fuel by 42 percent. This inevitably led to soaring industrial and transportation costs, higher bus fares, and—not least disturbing—a 41 percent increase in the price of kerosene, from KShs.5.7 (31 cents) to KShs.8.02 (43 cents) per liter. This fuel has come into widespread domestic use for cooking and lighting not only in cities and suburbs, where wood fuels are scarce, but also in the rural areas. The price controls on kerosene that previously subsidized politically restless urban consumers led to shortages as marketing companies became reluctant to meet a growing demand at what they viewed as unprofitable official prices. The oil companies benefited from a lifting of the controls, but popular discontent over these and other price increases doubtless contributed to the urban riots of July 1990 and thereafter.

Like its pastoral dilemma, Kenya's energy problem is both political and economic. As in so many other spheres of national life, there are also environmental dangers: "The results of the price increases are yet to be seen, but if the upsurge in kerosene usage over the past few years has also resulted in a decrease in the use of firewood and charcoal, then there may well be a return to the latter two as sources of domestic fuel. The resulting impact on the environment could be disastrous."[38] Equally ominous are the implications of future energy shortfalls for every other sector of the Kenyan economy and for the country's sociopolitical stabilization and integration.

Transportation

By most African standards, Kenya enjoys a well-developed transportation system, including fairly extensive road and rail networks, a modern deep-water port and international airport at Mombasa, eastern Africa's major air hub at Nairobi, and a high-capacity oil pipeline linking the two cities. Steady growth occurred during the 1970s in such categories as road vehicles registered, rail and air freight shipments, and num-

bers of passengers arriving at airports. By contrast, the early 1980s witnessed a serious loss of transport revenues induced by high fuel costs,
world economic recession, and tight foreign-exchange controls aimed at
reducing the international debt. Optimism returned to the transportation
sector later in the decade, but new economic uncertainties have brought
questions and doubts to the 1990s. Like its overall approach to development, Kenya's approach to transportation policy is characterized more
by short-term economic pragmatism, political opportunism, and occasional good fortune than by a careful weighing of long-term ends and
means.

To a greater extent than its general economic health might warrant,
Kenya is rapidly becoming a society on the move. More than twenty
thousand vehicles were registered in 1989 (48 percent more than in 1985),
and 60 percent of these were passenger cars and other personal convey-
ances. Approximately 75 percent of newly registered vehicles were assembled in Kenya. Passenger journeys on trains increased by 69 percent
between 1985 and 1989. Kenya Airways, the country's national airline,
carried 375,736 domestic passengers and 384,725 international passengers in 1989. More than 2 million travelers passed through Nairobi's
Jomo Kenyatta International Airport in that year, and another 574,500
were accommodated at Mombasa's Moi International Airport.[39]

This growth occurred without a significant extension of rail lines
and roads and was not matched by rail freight haulage. In 1978, 2,601
kilometers (1,561 miles) of rail were in use; by 1988 only 172 kilometers
(103 miles) had been added. In its scant attention to the road system, the
1989–1993 development plan aimed merely at upgrading 13,500 kilometers (8,100 miles) of dirt roadways to gravel and, to a lesser extent, bitu-
men. This would reduce the length of unimproved roads from 117,400
kilometers (70,440 miles) to 103,900 kilometers (62,340 miles) but would
not add to the 150,600-kilometer (90,360-mile) national total. Perhaps influenced by this conservative approach to infrastructural development,
rail freight tonnage increased by less than 2 percent in the last half of
the 1980s, and freight handled at Mombasa harbor increased by only 14
percent.[40]

Nevertheless, between 1985 and 1989 the value of road, rail, water,
air, and pipeline transport expanded by 56 percent—from K£482.6 million ($592.7 million) to K£754.1 million ($810.9 million). The historic
main railway line connects Mombasa with Nairobi and continues on to
Uganda. Spur lines extend to Lake Magadi, Nanyuki, Kitale, and Kisumu
and to northern Tanzania through Voi and Taveta. Also concentrated in
the south on an axis from Mombasa to Nairobi and Uganda, a web
of arterial highways and rural roads links high-population areas. The
north is virtually bereft of all-weather roads, the primary exceptions

being feeder roads to Lodwar, Garissa, and Wajir and an international highway linking southern Kenya with Ethiopia through Moyale. Inadequate ground transport has long been recognized as contributing to the underdevelopment of the north, but little real thought has yet been given to ways of overcoming this obstacle. The north also lacks the airstrips and radio relay stations that could assist in promoting economic growth and diversification.

Beyond its neglect of the north, Kenya's transportation system displays the negative effects of unplanned and unbalanced growth. During its first year of operation, Kenya Airways had gross revenues of K£23.58 million (about $62.3 million). In subsequent years it extended its routes outside eastern Africa and began receiving government subsidies and loans. Ten years later, as a result of unexpectedly high costs for fuel and maintenance, a softening Kenya shilling, and a series of management and labor difficulties, it grossed K£128.6 million but only $7.8 million in hard currency. The acquisition of much-needed new aircraft and the most recent oil price increases further weakened the corporation and robbed Kenya of development funds.

At ground level, although heavy commercial traffic between Mombasa, Nairobi, and Kisumu overburdens the road surface and causes urban congestion, the rail line paralleling the Mombasa road remains underused. This is partly because the railroad is a state-run affair and trucking is highly profitable. An equally heavy and sometimes illegal traffic in transport licenses has led to a proliferation of both freight and passenger carriers. Kenyans may choose among a variety of bus lines, including Kenya Bus Services, East African Road Services, Akamba, Coast Bus, Malindi Taxis, Mawingo, Gold Line Bus Services, and Nyayo Bus Service and a seemingly limitless number of *matatu* (rural-urban taxi) companies. This road-based commercialism is the product of Kenyan ingenuity in keeping old vehicles running, finding cargoes and passengers, opening new routes, and avoiding police checks. Typically overlooked are the concomitant problems of extensive road damage, high fuel consumption, localized air pollution, truck and bus overloading, and lethal high-speed accidents. Perhaps nowhere is the frenetic quality of Kenya's modern economy more apparent than on its roads.

Industry and Manufacturing

During the first decade and a half of independence, the industry and manufacturing sector was the fastest-growing sector of the Kenyan economy. Until 1980, the annual industrial growth rate averaged over 10 percent, twice that of agriculture and nearly twice that of social services. During the 1980s, industrial growth slowed to slightly more than 4 percent, but the sector still managed to hold its own at about 20 percent of GDP, employing nearly a quarter of a million workers in some five thousand firms with an average annual output of about $5 billion. Today, leading growth industries include processed foods, refined petroleum products, beverages and tobacco, textiles and clothing, paper and paper products, printing and publishing, chemicals and cement, rubber and plastics, clay and glass products, building and construction, vehicle assembly, and industrial machinery.

In keeping with its "reorganizational" approach to development, the Moi regime has encouraged private domestic and foreign investment but maintained firm ultimate control over the industrial sector. By 1982, government's industrial holdings included 47 wholly owned companies and majority or minority interests in 129 other firms. Statutory boards managed the activities of 147 private concerns.[41] At mid-decade, parastatal corporations accounted for 8 percent of GDP, 55 percent of public-sector capital formation, 31 percent of public employment, and 15 percent of formal-sector employment.[42] Responding to the economic declines of the 1980s and the demands of foreign donors and lenders, Kenya has since joined other African countries in lowering its profile of public corporate ownership. Exclusive state ownership in industry is today mainly confined to utilities and infrastructural services. In addition to Kenya Airways, these include the postal and telecommunications systems, ports, and railways. Government continues to participate in industry by acquiring equity shares through parastatal development finance institutions such as the Industrial and Commercial Development Corporation, the Industrial Development Bank, the Development Finance Company of Kenya, and the Tourist Development Corporation.[43] At present, the Kenya Fluorspar Company is the only fully state-owned firm engaged in manufacturing and mining.

Aside from reducing the managerial burden on government, privatization may well improve industrial efficiency and ensure a favorable environment for foreign and local investment. It will not be a panacea for the more serious difficulties affecting Kenyan industry. In 1986, a conference organized by the Kenya Association of Manufacturers and the University of Nairobi produced eight basic critiques of Kenyan industrial development:

- underused industrial capacity and skills;
- existence of major gaps in the industrial structure while redundant investment still flows into sectors with excess capacity;
- failure to move on to the second stage of import substitution, the production of intermediate inputs;
- the planners' lack of a long-range vision and systematic policies for industrialization and development of technological capacity in the [eastern African] region;
- the need to negotiate better with foreign investors and donors;

- importance of giving good incentives to farmers so as to earn the foreign exchange still needed, on net, by industry;
- the untapped ability of many economically strategic governmental organs . . . to promote local industry; and,
- adverse implications for industry from the alliance of local monopolists and traders with some politicians.[44]

These problems are symptomatic of a heavily politicized bias toward unbalanced economic growth, and their effects are now being felt not only by industry but throughout the economy.

While paying lip service to export promotion (utilizing local resources to enhance foreign-exchange earnings), Kenyan industrial policy remains committed to first-stage import substitution (creating finished products for domestic consumption by employing technologies and contents produced elsewhere). Kenyan industry is therefore increasingly dependent both on foreign investment and ties with multinational corporations and on imported raw materials, components, and spare parts. Moreover, industrial decisions depend more on the perceived interests of international capitalism and its local representatives than on the developmental needs of Kenya and the eastern African region as a whole. When national, regional, and multinational priorities coincide, it is usually more by chance than by design.

Kenya's postindependence orientation toward industrial import substitution has reduced the country's need for imported machinery, equipment, and other manufactures (Table 5.1). At the same time, international food and fuel dependency has grown, and although the percentage share of manufactured exports has increased slightly, export revenues are still largely derived from unprocessed primary commodities and reexported petroleum products, to which comparatively little value has been added. On the domestic scene, the structure of manufacturing has remained virtually unaltered since 1970, when food, beverages, and tobacco accounted for 33 percent of industrial value added, textiles and clothing for 9 percent, machinery and transport equipment for 16 percent, and chemicals for 9 percent. By 1990 these proportions had risen only marginally for food, beverages, and tobacco (to 41 percent) and for textiles and clothing (to 10 percent) and had fallen or remained unchanged for machinery and transport equipment (11 percent) and for chemicals (9 percent). Growth of manufacturing earnings per employee recovered from an average of minus 3.4 percent between 1970 and 1980 to 0.1 percent between 1980 and 1989, but the cost of imports from major industrial countries rose from $16 million in 1970 to $111 million by 1990, representing a twenty-year increase of 594 percent.[45]

Underlying this performance is a pattern of politically endorsed

TABLE 5.1 Structure of Kenyan Imports and Exports, 1965 and 1990

| | Percentage Share | |
Type	1965	1990
Imports		
Machinery and transport equipment	34	25
Other manufactures	46	30
Food	6	10
Fuels	10	32
Other primary commodities	4	4
Exports		
Machinery and transport equipment	0	0
Other manufactures	10	12
Fuels, minerals, and metals	13	19
Other primary commodities	77	70

Source: Adapted from World Bank, *World Development Report 1992* (New York: Oxford University Press, 1992), pp. 246 and 248.

multinational involvement in the Kenyan economy, giving rise to a significant loss of national self-determination in the formulation, adoption, and execution of industrial policy. Localization or Kenyanization of many top managerial positions has been achieved, often through the appointment of senior politicians and civil servants as directors of the subsidiaries of multinational corporations or distributors of their products. As Nyong'o has pointed out, however, parent firms typically retain control over the most critical policy areas, among them decisions on investment planning, capital expenditure, equipment replacement, budgeting, personnel management, profit targeting, and production for export versus local consumption.[46] By the early 1990s, moreover, about 70 percent of manufacturing value added was still in foreign hands.

Linking the economic success of multinational corporations with that of senior government officials seriously compromises the agenda-setting and regulatory functions of government. Approvals of import licenses and the coveted Certificate of Approved Enterprise are purposely granted and withheld on an ad hoc basis. This informality benefits the elites who control the process and the companies afforded bargaining advantages because of their size and wealth, but it disrupts relations between the private sector and government and leads to conflicts of interest, bribery, and tax evasion. The system is presided over by President Moi and his circle of retainers, who amass large private holdings by obtaining shares and outright ownership of foreign subsidiaries. Asian intermediaries are sometimes employed to mask these transactions, intensifying the public's negative perceptions of both the African leadership and the Asian business community.

Political interference in the guise of Kenyanization has also helped to distort the structure and operation of Kenyan industry. Under the protection of elite self-interest, multinational corporations undermine local firms, create oligopolies and monopolies that manipulate prices and product lines, dominate choices pitting capital investment and technology selection against job creation, and deepen the economy's addiction to imported inputs while weakening Kenya's competitiveness in African regional markets. At the domestic level, import-consuming firms and state control over trade in raw materials weaken cottage industries and prevent local firms from becoming more efficient. All these misdirections retard the growth and diversification of Kenyan industry and not only lessen its contributions to agriculture but actually discriminate against the economy's leading export sector.

Comparatively efficient local establishments and potentially efficient infant industries are placed at a disadvantage in competition with foreign subsidiaries and importers while inefficient local enterprises are protected. Favored by exemption from duties on inputs and low tariffs for finished products, the multinational Bata Shoe Company and Taiwanese shoe exporters have stunted the growth of a domestic footwear industry. In 1987, a cabinet minister began importing refined sugar under license, and this forced two Kenyan sugar refineries, one of which had just been built at a cost of KShs.100 million (about $5.5 million), to close. In 1989, the East African Bag and Cortage Company was placed in receivership as foreign-made paper bags flooded the market. Plastic baskets were manufactured and sold at the expense of Kenyan women who had converted the weaving of baskets from sisal into a profitable domestic and export venture. By the late 1980s, locally produced cotton cost 25 to 30 percent more than cotton sold at world market prices because of price fixing and inefficiencies in processing and distribution at the hands of the Cotton and Lint Seed Marketing Board, Kenya's only cotton purchaser and supplier to textile mills. This, in turn, has "hampered the textile factories' ability to export cotton fabrics and has greatly encouraged the shift in the domestic market toward synthetic fibres whose raw materials must be imported."[47] In general, while importers are favored with tax exemptions and protection from competition, export agriculture and related enterprises are taxed rather than encouraged. At times even the purposes of import substitution are ignored; agricultural equipment enters Kenya duty-free while the parts to assemble it are subject to import duties.[48]

Domestically and internationally, the Moi regime's preoccupation with short-term profit taking has had a number of adverse economic effects. Capital-intensive technologies directed toward elite consumption have led to poor job creation in an exploding industrial labor market, inhibited both unprocessed and processed agricultural exports, and promoted a redundant and expensive proliferation of imported and locally fabricated luxury consumables. A brisk trade is conducted in import licenses for computers and other electronic devices. Kenya assembles more than ninety models of trucks and buses. Automobile production began in 1985, and by 1987 fourteen separate models were being locally assembled. Today, more than sixty makes of automobile in more than two hundred models ply the Kenyan roads. Import controls have been placed on luxury vehicles and other expensive items to protect domestic assemblers and save foreign exchange. A single visit to central Nairobi will confirm that these restrictions are commonly honored in the breach. Heavily protected Kenyan monopolies charge high prices for unreliable supplies of often inferior goods, leading to an insufficient use of industrial capacity as discriminating buyers choose imports instead. A bias toward luxury consumer goods leaves large gaps in industrial output, especially in the production of pesticides, fertilizers, and other agricultural inputs that could help reduce Kenya's import dependency and boost export earnings.

Kenya has long served as eastern Africa's economic powerhouse, and this dominance precipitated the demise of the regional East African Community (EAC) in 1977. An outgrowth of the colonial East African Common Services Organization, the EAC and its East African Common Market were intended to further trade and the equitable distribution of economic and infrastructural services among Kenya, Tanzania, and Uganda. The EAC's enabling Treaty for East African Co-operation also established an East African Development Bank with instructions to make 80 percent of its investments in less prosperous Tanzania and Uganda. These arrangements failed to slow Kenya's economic ascendancy over its partners, and the EAC finally collapsed amid charges and countercharges of unfair advantage and default on obligations.[49] In 1983 Kenya joined a larger and perhaps more promising regional alliance, the Preferential Trade Area (PTA). The PTA agreement provides for the liberalization of trade among countries in eastern and southern Africa and eventual economic integration within and between these regions. The 1988–1993 development plan reinforced the Kenyan commitment by calling for increased economic activity within the framework of the PTA, including an expansion of manufacturing-under-bond enterprises and the development of major export-processing zones beginning with sites near Nairobi and Mombasa.[50]

Since 1983, Kenya has maintained a highly favorable trade balance with other African countries. In recent years, manufacturing-under-bond agreements have been reached with a variety of multinational corporations, including Cadbury-Schweppes, Boots, Cussons, Aspro Nicholas, ICI, Warner-Lambert, Johnson & Johnson, and Buitoni. Nonprimary exports have not, however, risen appreciably (Table 5.1), and this suggests little change in such exports within the PTA because Kenya's manufactured exports would likely enter regional instead of world trade. The problem is not import substitution versus export promotion but rather the *type* of import substitution practiced in Kenya's politically influenced version of state-managed capitalism. At present, little effort is made to link industrialization, intersectoral integration, domestic needs satisfaction, and export promotion. Official tender boards still favor multinationals and importers. Foreign-assistance projects continue to include unnecessary tied-aid components with foreign suppliers. Price controls—some justifiably aimed at combatting inflation—persist in inhibiting investment and agricultural production.[51] Industries still rely on costly imported materials to assemble redundant consumer durables at below capacity instead of using less-costly indigenous and imported resources in the production of intermediate and finished products to stimulate employment and mass consumption, reduce foreign economic dependency, and encourage exports. At root, Kenya's industrial development problem results more from political choice than from economic constraint. In an effort to preserve their hegemony by resisting an extension of economic participation and the growth of class politics and compromise, the political, bureaucratic, and entrepreneurial powers that be retard future industrial growth and diminish support for and from a now-faltering agricultural economy. In the words of a resident economist at University of Nairobi, "only after more Africans own and manage manufacturing enterprises and ensure that their economic interests are well represented politically will policy become better harmonized with the needs of industry."[52]

Trade

Since independence, Kenya's external trade has expanded more in volume than in variety. Excluding profits gained from the transportation of goods to nearby landlocked countries, the country's main foreign-exchange earners remain tourism, tea, and coffee. Because of this lack of diversification and because of sagging export prices and soaring petro- leum costs, the Kenyan foreign trade deficit has hovered at slightly over $1 billion since 1980.[53] In the challenging world economy of the 1980s, export growth declined to 26 percent of that attained in previous years and import growth to 67 percent. Not including foreign aid transfers, a balance-of-payments deficit approaching $700 million was recorded for 1990. This left the country with $236 million, or less than one month of import coverage, in international cash reserves.[54]

For many years, the government has ostensibly sought to improve trade balances. The 1979–1983 development plan proposed a "vigorous campaign of export promotion rather than import substitution," and this theme was repeated in successive plans with little effect. Imports have indeed been curtailed but as a consequence of cash-flow difficulties rather than long-range planning decisions (Table 5.2).

Kenya is constrained not only by a paucity of export products but also by a dearth of equal trading partners (Table 5.3). The economy suf- fers from negative trade balances with every world region except Africa and is locked into lopsided relationships with Europe, North America, the Middle East, and Asia. Favorable trade ledgers are maintained on neighboring and other PTA countries, but the books are awash in red ink regarding the country's most critical suppliers: Britain, Germany, the United Arab Emirates, and Japan (Table 5.4).

A large part of the trade problem lies in the fact that Kenyan indus- trialization is taking place behind a wall of tariff quotas, bureaucratic prohibitions, and other forms of restriction on commerce. In recent years, the International Monetary Fund and the World Bank have achieved some success in moving Kenya toward export promotion through low- ered trade barriers. Nevertheless, a policy bias persists that makes assembly of foreign components for home consumption usually more profitable than adding value to primary and intermediate inputs, both domestic and imported, for local markets and export. Trade restrictions are justified in terms of foreign-exchange conservation, but at issue are the specific *types* of commodities restricted and for *whom*. In this context,

TABLE 5.2 Kenyan Trade Growth, 1965-1990 (average annual growth rate in percentages)

	1965-1980	1980-1990
Exports	3.9	1.0
Imports	2.4	1.6

Source: World Bank, *World Development Report 1992* (New York: Oxford University Press, 1992), p. 244.

TABLE 5.3   Destination and Origin of Kenyan Exports and Imports, 1989 (1986 US$ millions)

Region	Exports	Percentage	Imports	Percentage
EEC	559.3	47.0	1,266.1	45.2
Other West Europe	52.5	4.4	151.3	5.4
East Europe	25.1	2.1	32.0	1.1
North America	73.9	6.1	212.3	7.5
Africa	284.0	23.8	91.5	3.3
Middle East	36.6	3.1	437.1	15.6
Far East	158.3	13.3	597.3	21.5
Other	0.8	0.2	11.2	0.4
Total	1,190.5	100.0	2,798.8	100.0

Source: Republic of Kenya, Economic Survey 1990 (Nairobi: Central Bureau of Statistics, Ministry of Planning and National Development, 1990), pp. 96 and 97.

an economic analyst's complaint of more than a decade ago remains valid today:

> With one hand, the Finance Minister calls on local industries to become more competitive against foreign ones. On the other hand, the same Finance Minister imposes high rates of duty on raw materials with which competing industries are not burdened. . . . Import duty on raw materials entering Kenya defeats the whole purpose of import substitution. It puts at risk Kenya's large import-substitution industries set up at a vast cost, much of it in foreign exchange for items such as machinery.[55]

In short, the national leadership has made the Kenyan economy a landing place for foreign investment and products instead of a takeoff point for income-earning local manufactures and exports.[56]

Tourism

International tourism has until recently been one of Kenya's biggest economic success stories. Between 1972 and 1982, Kenya received some 350,000 visitors annually. Although the number of vacationers and other guests remained fairly constant during the 1970s, earnings from tourism increased fourfold. This period followed a massive postindependence expansion of the industry, in which 40,000 jobs were created for Kenyans as compared with 95,000 jobs in manufacturing. By 1982 more than twenty-four thousand beds had been made available in Kenyan hotels, up from fewer than six thousand in 1963. During this time, tourist earnings grew from K£7.9 million ($22.6 million) to K£118 million ($185

TABLE 5.4 Kenya's Major Trading Partners, 1989 (1986 US$ millions)

Partner	Exports	Imports
U.K.	248.4	438.8
PTA (excluding Tanzania, Uganda, and Zambia)	163.6	62.45
West Germany	110.9	248.4
Netherlands	62.2	90.0
Tanzania	34.3	16.6
Uganda	82.4	1.3
U.A.E.	3.4	316.7
Japan	15.9	307.0

Source: Republic of Kenya, *Economic Survey 1990* (Nairobi: Central Bureau of Statistics, Ministry of Planning and National Development, 1990), pp. 96 and 97.

million).[57] Confident of continued growth, the government projected a doubling of international arrivals over the life of the 1984–1988 development plan, a 10 percent annual increase in tourist revenues, and the addition of 3,264 jobs for Kenyan service personnel.[58]

A large share of the sector's total income is earned from visitors to Kenya's spectacular national parks and game reserves (Table 5.5). Although their numbers generally increased during the 1980s, declines were recorded in 1983 and again in 1986. Nineteen eighty-three was the year after the aborted coup against Moi's government, and in 1985 and 1986 Kenya was recovering from the physical effects and negative publicity of a disastrous drought. As the country entered the 1990s, the impact of these perturbations was reduced by others, notably marked increases in crimes against tourists and other foreigners, violent urban demonstrations against the Moi regime, attacks by heavily armed poachers on wildlife and occasionally on game-watching visitors, and politically motivated ethnic conflict in Rift Valley and western locations containing several popular national parks and reserves.

Other developments have helped to depress both wildlife tourism and the lucrative trade in package tours to Kenyan beach resorts. Kenya has become less attractive to many travelers because of their own reduced means, inflated prices for airplane tickets, and correspondingly higher costs for local amenities such as food and drink, transportation, and lodging. Persistent urban unrest associated with demands for political and economic reform has caused foreign embassies to issue travel advisories to their nationals. The Iraq-Kuwait crisis and the Gulf war of 1990–1991 resulted in a 60 percent loss of tourist revenues. The war's end

TABLE 5.5 Visitors to National Parks and Reserves, 1981-1989

Year	Number	Percentage Change
1981	804,430	
1982	968,110	+16.9
1983	957,663	-1.1
1984	1,011,199	+5.3
1985	986,676	-2.5
1986	924,139	-6.8
1987	976,595	+5.4
1988	1,063,254	+8.1
1989 (est.)	1,200,800	+11.4

Sources: Republic of Kenya, Statistical Abstract 1989 (Nairobi: Central Bureau of Statistics, Ministry of Planning and National Development, 1989), p. 31, and Republic of Kenya, Economic Survey 1990 (Nairobi: Central Bureau of Statistics, Ministry of Planning and National Development, 1990), p. 160.

brought more reductions as port calls to Mombasa by U.S. Navy ships became less frequent. More recently, civil strife and famine in Somalia have resulted in a burgeoning refugee problem for Nairobi and further altered travelers' perceptions of Kenya as a desirable place in which to spend time and money.

Even under more favorable conditions, the profitability of tourism has been limited by the fact that most trips are booked from abroad and by the depletion of wild animals and the shortage of funds to maintain and appropriately extend facilities in the national parks and game reserves. More than ten years ago the government attempted to redress the first imbalance by imposing restrictions on visas and charter carriers, which led to a 15 percent drop in tourism and to the bankruptcy of several beach hotels.[59] Between 1977 and 1987, the Kenyan elephant population declined by 57 percent in preserved areas and by 73 percent in unprotected forests and savannas because of drought, peasant encroachment on elephant habitats, and commercialized ivory poaching.[60] Until President Moi took a personal interest in the crisis, the Department of Wildlife Conservation and Management was too underfunded to maintain its own vehicles, regulate tour bus operators, and offer anything but token opposition to poaching, let alone undertake much-needed improvements in the parks and reserves.

Alarmed by the rapid depreciation of Kenya's valuable wildlife resource, conservationists finally managed to convince the president that wildlife tourism is often an economically more promising use of

Tourist attractions: two of Kenya's many wildlife species (photo of elephants by David Keith Jones/Images of Africa Photobank; female lion by Alain Gille/UNESCO)

marginal lands than farming and pastoralism. In 1987 Moi removed the head of the wildlife department (who was also operating a private tour company) and replaced him with Perez Olindo, a professional wildlife manager. Olindo promptly fired seven senior parks officers and placed twelve others under investigation for corruption. He halted economically questionable lodge construction projects influenced by public officials with high stakes in the safari business and ordered a reexamination of all previously approved projects and future priorities for park development. These actions brought him into direct confrontation with powerful vested interests in the African elite community, and in April 1989 Moi replaced him with a Kenyan of European extraction, the prehistorian and director of national museums Richard Leakey. Leakey immediately launched a vigorous campaign to eradicate poaching—some of it involving government officials—and to raise money for the wildlife department.[61] He was moderately successful in these efforts, but not even President Moi's ostentatious public burning of contraband ivory enabled him to achieve his most urgent goals.

The social costs of international tourism are part of the reason the wildlife department has been unable to counter short-term avarice with the promise of long-term economic reward. Rich foreigners engaging in conspicuous consumption and other types of objectionable behavior disturb many Kenyans, especially when the profits from tourism seem so narrowly distributed. Forecasting a growth in sectoral earnings from K£735 million ($790 million) to K£1.2 billion (about $946 million), the 1989–1993 development plan committed government to "educating the public on the continuing importance of protection and conservation of wildlife for aesthetic value, and as a natural heritage, and for their role in maintenance of proper ecological balance and sustaining the tourist industry."[62] Under the circumstances, and given increasing land shortages, Kenyans have shown little enthusiasm for this kind of education. As if in anticipation of such indifference, the government earlier began a program to encourage domestic tourism, but after nearly a decade this initiative has yet to produce measurable social, ecological, and economic benefits.[63]

MACROECONOMIC PERSPECTIVES
ON MULTINATIONALISM

In each of its six main sectors, the Kenyan economy has exhibited the strengths and weaknesses of politically manipulated, state-managed capitalism. Although serious economic distortions and social inequities are apparent in each area, significant and imaginative advances have been made. In agriculture, research and crop breeding have improved production. In energy, the domestic refining of crude oil has increased local stocks and earned precious foreign exchange. In transportation, small and large businesses compete so aggressively that at times they create a public nuisance on the country's streets and roads. In trade, Kenya has become a leading seller to eastern and southern Africa. In tourism, Kenya has far surpassed Tanzania even though Tanzania is more richly endowed with natural treasures. And in industry, multinational investment and domestic entrepreneurship have placed the Kenyan economy ahead of its counterparts in eastern Africa and in most other parts of the continent. A mixed legacy of success and failure is closely related to Kenya's long-standing economic integration with the West and has important implications for the last part of this century and thereafter.

The Roots of Kenyan Multinationalism

The modern Kenyan economy is largely the product of a long tradition of foreign involvement. During the 1950s the country emerged as eastern Africa's undisputed leader in commerce, industry, and banking. Kenyatta took additional steps to encourage foreign capital by assuring new investors that their interests would be well served. A postindependence Foreign Investment Protection Act generously provided for the recovery of investment costs and repatriation of corporate profits. These guarantees reinforced the attractiveness of Nairobi's advanced communications facilities and temperate climate to release a flood of multinational investment and to stimulate the growth of a rapidly expanding expatriate population. By the late 1970s, the value of foreign corporate investment totaled nearly $1 billion. A large portion of the industrial sector had come under foreign ownership, with the remainder controlled by Kenyan parastatal bodies, the resident Asian community, and the African and European business elite. Approximately 350 multinational corporations had established large-scale operations in Kenya, and another 250 maintained some degree of sales presence.[64]

Three important trends appeared during the early years of the Moi presidency. First, private foreign investment leveled off as a result of international recession, local shortages of foreign exchange, a shrinking export market following the demise of the East African Community, a proliferation of competing if struggling domestic firms, high corporate taxation, and worsening political interference, bureaucratic inefficiency, and corruption. The 1982 coup attempt discouraged investment and even precipitated the withdrawal of a few multinational corporations, including Coca Cola, Pepsi Cola, and Union Carbide. At the same time, a countervailing trend emerged as public agencies such as the World Bank, the German Development Bank, and the Commonwealth Development Fund became major sources of industrial finance and began exerting in-

fluence over sectoral, particularly industrial, policy. To counter this progressive internationalization of the national economy, the government
initiated a third trend by evolving from a passive partner in a few enterprises into an active participant in many. Joint ventures typically incorporated local private and public capital, multinational investment, and
funding from multilateral and bilateral lending institutions. By the early
1980s, many of the ninety-three companies in which government maintained an interest followed this pattern.[65] The formula was applied
throughout the decade and was paralleled by a steady extension of parastatal control over those sectors of the formal economy that attracted
only secondary international interest. Although some parties to these
arrangements still view them as sound or susceptible to reform, significant and widening cracks have opened in the foundations of Kenyan
capitalism.

Macroeconomic Challenges in the 1990s

Employment. Although the national economy continues to grow
at over 4 percent per annum, fewer than 90,000 private-sector jobs are
created each year. New employment accommodates only one-fifth of en-
trants into the work force, who will arrive at an annual rate of about
400,000 for at least the next fifteen years. Current growth is clearly too
slow to reduce unemployment through accelerated economic diversification and improved productivity, and here one of the chief culprits is a
parastatal sector whose inefficiency may be reducing the growth rate by
an estimated two percentage points.[66] More responsive to political pressures than to economic need and capacity, a relentlessly expanding civil
service merely adds to the problem. Excluding teachers, central government employment rose by 70 percent between 1979 and 1990,
from 158,977 to 270,005.[67] Despite these inverted relationships between
productive potential and employment, the government has yet to develop and implement effective action plans for parastatal and civil
service reform. Kenya's job situation offers one of the clearest examples
in modern Africa of how widely political necessity can diverge from
economic rationality.

Consumption and Investment. In comparative economic terms, Kenya's plight might seem somewhat less menacing, but this appearance is
largely illusory. Across the Third World, growth in public consumption
fell by nearly 100 percent between 1965–1980 and 1980–1990 and growth
in private consumption by over 70 percent. During the same period,
public-consumption growth in Kenya declined by more than 300 percent
but increases in private consumption by less than 2 percent. Kenyans'
private consumption of wealth is growing at a rate more than double
the Third World average while growth in public consumption averages
nearly 1 percent less.

The real difficulty, however, involves not consumption but investment. Average Third World growth in investment plummeted from a
high of 8.8 percent during the relative boom years of the 1960s and 1970s
to 1.3 percent during the recessionary 1980s. In Kenya, investment
growth remained behind these averages for both periods, lagging at rates
of 7.2 percent and 0.6 percent respectively.[68] The country's government
and its private citizens are simply consuming more than they produce
and reinvest. As is invariably the case under such circumstances, the outcomes are mounting debt and deepening dependency on others.

Debt and Dependency. Kenya began the 1990s with a swelling budget
deficit and an increasingly structured reliance on external assistance to
cope with it (Table 5.6). Cash balances improved between 1985/86 and
1989/90 (Table 5.7) but only because external loans virtually replaced
borrowing from the faltering domestic economy (Table 5.8). As the 1980s
ended, external grants and loans and total government expenditure
occupied dubious positions on the positive side of the fiscal ledger. All
other indicators were negative. Normally optimistic in its projections, the
1989–1993 five-year plan predicted a continuation of deficit financing
through external loans (Table 5.9).

From a broader historical perspective, Kenya's long-term public
debt mushroomed from $319 million in 1970 to $4.8 billion by 1990, while
the long-term private debt rose from a mere $88 million to $578 million.
In 1970, the country's outstanding domestic and foreign obligations
totaled less than $1 billion; twenty years later they neared $7 billion.[69]
The severity of external debt is always closely linked to gross national
product and export earnings. In 1980, the Kenyan external debt stood at

TABLE 5.6 Kenya's Growing Budget Deficit (current US$ millions)

Category	1985/86	1989/90*	Percentage Change
Current revenue	1,506.9	2,173.7	+44.2
Current expenditure	1,563.5	2,368.1	+51.5
Current surplus	-56.6	-194.4	-243.5
Capital revenue	4.7	4.4	-5.7
Capital expenditure	221.2	650.9	+194.2
Net lending	63.1	74.8	+18.5
External grants	68.5	448.8	+555.2
Overall deficit	-267.7	-466.9	+74.4

*Provisional.

Source: Republic of Kenya, *Economic Survey 1990* (Nairobi: Central Bureau of Statistics,
Ministry of Planning and National Development, 1990), p. 72.

TABLE 5.7 Trends in Kenyan Deficit Finance (current US$ millions)

Category	1985/86	1989/90ᵃ	Percentage Change
External loans	118.0	339.6	+387.8
Domestic borrowing	255.2	72.2	-71.7
Changes in cash balances	-131.3	-55.07	+58.05

ᵃProvisional.

Source: Republic of Kenya, *Economic Survey 1990* (Nairobi: Central Bureau of Statistics, Ministry of Planning and National Development, 1990), p. 72.

48.3 percent of GNP and 165.1 percent of international sales. By 1990, foreign arrears had grown to 81.2 percent of GNP and 306.3 percent of export earnings. In that year, total debt service claimed 33.8 percent of income earned from the export of goods and services, and interest payments alone consumed 14.8 percent.[70]

TABLE 5.8 Key Fiscal Trends, 1985/86, 1989/90

Trend	1985/86	1989/90ᵃ
Current deficit as a percentage of current revenue	-3.7	-8.9
Overall deficit as a percentage of current revenue	-17.8	-21.5
Overall deficit as a percentage of total expenditure	-13.0	-13.3
External grants and loans as a percentage of capital expenditure plus net lending	-17.7	108.6
Total government expenditure as a percentage of GDP at current prices	37.3	47.8
Overall deficit as a percentage of GDP at current prices	-4.8	-6.4

ᵃProvisional.

Source: Republic of Kenya, *Economic Survey 1990* (Nairobi: Central Bureau of Statistics, Ministry of Planning and National Development, 1990), p. 73.

TABLE 5.9 Targeted Deficit Financing Through External Loans (current K£ millions)

	1988/89	1989/90	1990/91	1991/92	1992/93
Deficit	362.9	357.8	354.4	357.5	378.2
Loans	200.0	223.6	255.0	249.4	256.2
Percentage	55.1	62.4	71.9	69.8	67.7

Source: Republic of Kenya, *Development Plan for the Period 1989 to 1993* (Nairobi: Government Printer, 1988), p. 62.

A twenty-year history of high consumption without commensurate increases in investment and productivity has brought the economy dangerously close to permanent indebtedness, if not insolvency.[71] It has also raised Kenya's political susceptibility to the demands of official donors and lenders, each with an agenda that may or may not correspond with Kenyan priorities.

CONCLUSIONS: THE CONSEQUENCES OF KENYAN CAPITALISM

Kenya's economy remains a dual economy in two senses. Still distinguishable as "modern" or "traditional," economic relations can also be differentiated in terms of goals and performance. Kenyan planners continue to identify objectives that few in today's Africa could quarrel with:

1. Rationalization of import-substituting and export-promoting industries by reforming trade controls, exchange rates, and prices to favor exports and reduce the import intensity of domestic production "while at the same time exploring possibilities for further efficient import substitution."
2. Decentralization of policy planning, decision making, and management, together with greater interministerial and intersectoral integration and coordination.
3. A public-investment emphasis on income-producing activities of all types and a better balancing of investment between arable and semiarid-to-arid rural areas, between rural and urban areas, and between cities and towns.
4. Increased private-sector responsibilities matched by closely controlled growth in public employment, especially a "gradual decrease of the Government's interest in parastatals which it has long held on behalf of the citizens. The citizens themselves will hence become the owners of these companies."

5. "Diffusion of ownership to avoid over-concentration of economic power" and "an equitable distribution of wealth and income" through more progressive taxation.[72]
6. A "vibrant capital market" for domestic and foreign investment, further stimulated by measures to increase the absorption of external resources and a new emphasis on effective policy implementation, monitoring, and regulation at all levels.
7. Protection and further development of tourist attractions and their key infrastructure.[73]

Proposals of this sort are not new; most were prescribed over ten years ago by the World Bank and also by the Moi-appointed Working Party on Government Expenditure chaired by Philip Ndegwa.[74] As one observer was soon to point out, however, "the acquisitiveness of Kenya's elites was not fully addressed by the Ndegwa committee for understandable reasons, [and] the Bank has similarly failed to identify it as an obstacle to the implementation of the reforms it recommends."[75] In predicting that "the structural adjustments undertaken by the Moi government in 1982 and 1983 should be a basis for renewed growth,"[76] the first edition of this book was likewise overoptimistic for esssentially the same reason.

Several factors do, however, suggest real possibilities for economic recovery and growth, fuller diversification of production and consumption, and wider distribution of employment and income. First and foremost, Kenya is a country of economic survivors—resilient, enterprising, and ultimately pragmatic. Society is provided a short-term economic cushion in that a majority of the population still pursues a rural life-style offering subsistence, meager but important cash surpluses, and social support through an "economy of affection"[77] based on kinship and friendship. Similar patterns of self-help, mutual assistance, and reciprocity extend even to urban slums.

Itself undiminished by economic hard times, Kenya's entrepreneurial spirit is also infectious. It has spread throughout the country, leading land-hungry peasants into off-farm employment and enticing previously excluded minorities such as the Maasai and other pastoralists into mixed enterprises in herding, farming, and small business. Not least, women are now entering the market economy in greater numbers, and new educational and occupational opportunities are being opened for young people, particularly through the efforts of churches and nongovernmental development agencies. All of this dynamism confirms that Kenya's greatest assets are its human resources, which stand ready to be mobilized if given the chance.

During the 1980s, the informal economy grew by about 25 percent, as much as formal economic growth measured at constant 1982 rates. Although worth only 5 percent of the formal economy, informally generated wealth succeeded in preventing Kenya's per capita GDP from falling even lower than its minus 0.1 percent annual average.[78] This long-neglected sector and its millions of occupants must be brought into the mainstream of economic life, where they will nourish and be nourished by an emerging working middle class in business and agriculture.

In 1987, 13,237 wage-paying establishments were operating in Kenya. Of these, 51 percent employed one to nine workers, 31 percent had ten to forty-nine employees, and 18 percent retained more than fifty on the payroll. Only 15.3 percent of all wage labor was engaged by foreign-owned businesses.[79] A World Bank study considered these figures to demonstrate "a layer of modern African entrepreneurs lying between the informal sector on the one hand and large foreign-owned or state-owned enterprises on the other."[80] The bank also found that, during the 1980s, between 880 and 1,695 locally owned companies were registered each year in Kenya, whereas the annual rate of newly registered foreign companies varied from 10 to 58.[81]

The study concluded that, in spite of inadequate access to bank credit and little assistance from central government and aid donors,[82] African-owned and registered small businesses are economically far more efficient than informal enterprises and should receive commensurate support. Conversely,

> an alternative strategy that would rely mainly on the informal sector as the engine for growth looks less promising. An increase in the share of this sector in total employment has been associated in the past with poor overall performance on both the job and income fronts. Good economic performance has been linked with rapid expansion of the modern private sector and a decline in the contribution of the informal sector to the economy, initially in relative terms and eventually in absolute terms.[83]

The World Bank investigation determined that foreign investment does not block African entrepreneurship, but it failed to consider the impact on small African enterprises of high-level political collusion with foreign companies and their local subsidiaries and partners. Had this topic been examined, the full potential of Kenya's small businesses might have been better estimated.[84]

Reporting on a forthcoming study, Lewis offers similar hope for the future contributions of peasant farmers and pastoralists, including those deriving their livelihoods from supposedly "low-potential" arid and semiarid lands. In their consideration of district-level economic linkages,

Lewis and a research colleague discovered an intrasectoral relationship somewhat different from the conventional wisdom:

> the *general* superiority of agricultural sectors in generating regional income growth in Kenya. Regardless of assumptions pertaining to the extent of supply constraints in agriculture, the livestock, coffee, and foodcrops sectors predominate in terms of multiplying value added. Moreover, all three subsectors perform comparably well, suggesting that traditional production activities (livestock and foodcrops production) need to be considered along with cash crop production (coffee) in the formulation of income generation strategies.[85]

If it is to proceed with its quest for economic prosperity and for social integration and political stabilization, Kenya must evolve into a haven of opportunity for all of its people and not just for a favored few. The time has passed when the regime could rely on a quiescent majority and on the automatic backing of foreign capital and a Western coalition of industrial states pursuing Cold War objectives. Kenya and its economic fortunes remain of great interest to private and public actors in the world arena but in ways and for reasons significantly different from those of the past. No longer is the country simply being hailed (and by some condemned) as a paragon of African capitalism through the successful adaptation of Western economic values. In the post–Cold War era, linkages between domestic and international processes have become much more complicated and their outcomes much less predictable.

6

The International Dimension

Kenyan foreign policy is pragmatic, traditionally pro-Western, and consistently driven by economic self-interest. In recent years, the Moi regime's record on human-rights abuses and official corruption has tarnished a once cordial relationship with trading partners and aid donors. Manifested in mounting verbal criticism and in two suspensions of military and economic assistance, international pressure has played an important part in stimulating the country's halting movement toward political and economic reform. Foreign doubts about Moi's sincerity are further evident in subsequent donor reviews of the Kenyan aid package and in the dispatch of foreign observers to monitor the 1992 election.

Historically, Kenya has been aggressive in its search for overseas markets, foreign investors, and economic assistance—with the result that, despite the excesses of the Moi presidency, cooperative links are still maintained with a wide range of states including Britain, the United States, Canada, Germany, France, the Netherlands, Japan, the Scandinavian countries, China, India, Saudi Arabia, and now even South Africa. Kenya has also competed for international tourist revenues, afforded preferential treatment to multinational corporations, and promoted its capital as a regional and world center of affairs. In addition to serving as headquarters for the UN Environment Programme and the UN Center for Human Settlements, Nairobi is host to thirteen other multilateral organizations, a full range of bilateral foreign-aid missions, and hundreds of international private organizations. Beyond the expected exchange in terms of diplomatic representation, many Kenyan students vie each year for opportunities to study abroad, continuing a tradition initiated by Tom Mboya in the early 1960s.

Conditions seem less settled concerning international security relations. Britain remains Kenya's closest military ally and has maintained a discrete but important "training" mission in the country ever since

161

British commandos assisted in putting down the army mutiny of 1964. U.S. military links grew stronger during the Reagan and early Bush administrations and once represented a pragmatic quid pro quo, U.S. arms funding, training, and equipment being traded for access to Mombasa's deep-water port and air bases. Partly because of this aid, augmented by assistance from Britain, Canada, and other countries, Kenya's military expenditures increased by 312 percent between 1973 and 1982, and the size of the armed forces grew by 137 percent.[1] In more recent years, U.S. military support has dwindled as a result of Cold War–ending changes in eastern Europe and the former Soviet Union, an enhanced American military presence in the Arabian Gulf region, and U.S. displeasure with Kenya's economic, political, and human-rights performance. The impact of these cuts on the Kenyan armed services and on the future stability of the country has yet to be assessed.

Overall, the Kenyan orientation to foreign policy is best described as undefined and open-ended. Although more of an internationalist than Kenyatta, Moi has established few theoretical or ideological principles for relations with other states either in Africa or elsewhere. His central and somewhat fanciful precept has been that Kenya's regional and global policies should reflect a dedication to "love, peace, and unity": "This should be the guiding light to all as we face the turbulence of the decade. More than ever before, love for humanity, international peace, and unity among nations is needed to provide the perspective for our actions."[2] Both at home and abroad, cynicism about such rhetoric has steadily mounted in the early 1990s, pointing to the need for a new and more realistic rationale for Kenyan foreign policy.

AFRICAN RELATIONS

Kenya's relations with other African states, particularly its closest neighbors, have ranged from benign to hostile. Between 1977 and 1985 the country was locked in disputes along all of its borders except the Ethiopian. Although relations with Tanzania have since been normalized, confrontations, sometimes violent, continue to erupt intermittently with Uganda and Somalia. Civil war in southern Sudan has destabilized the northwestern border area including the Elemi Triangle, a contested territory possibly containing petroleum deposits. For Kenya as for most of postcolonial Africa, regional reciprocity among states seems to improve with distance.

Tanzania

Relative cordiality has returned to the Kenyan relationship with Tanzania after more than a decade of acrimonious ideological haranguing and border closings, mainly at Tanzania's initiative. Economic near-collapse and a change in presidential leadership have induced Tanzania virtually to abandon its experiment in self-reliant socialism and to reactivate some of the linkages with Kenya that were terminated in 1977 with the demise of the East African Community. Tanzania's willingness to open its northern border to Kenya-based tourists, reintroduce trade between the two countries, and curb its criticism of Kenyan capitalism have made this normalization of relations possible.

Curiously, it was Uganda that brought the Kenyan-Tanzanian conflict to a head. In 1971, when Idi Amin seized power in Uganda, Tanzanian President Julius Nyerere granted sanctuary to his friend and deposed colleague Milton Obote. He also broke all ties with Uganda, thus driving a fatal wedge into the tripartite EAC. These events had an important economic and diplomatic impact on Kenya, and in spite of Kenyatta's attempts to mediate the quarrel[3] the EAC's fate was sealed. Tanzania had already expressed resentment over Kenya's dominant economic position in eastern Africa; Kenyatta's decision to curry favor with the Amin government by authorizing the transshipment of arms to landlocked Uganda merely hastened the breakup. In early 1977, following a series of charges and countercharges about EAC debts and service obligations, Tanzania severed economic relations and closed its border with Kenya. Aside from the Uganda situation, Nyerere justified this action on ideological grounds, arguing that the separation would encourage Tanzania to build socialism on its own and avoid becoming a permanent vassal to capitalist Kenya.

From the Tanzanian perspective, economic and political realities eventually intervened to foster an accommodation with Kenya. Moi and Nyerere met three times between 1979 and 1982, but it was not until late 1983 that the Tanzania-Kenya frontier was opened to modest commercial traffic. A period of uneasiness and bureaucratic border delays finally ended in 1986, after Tanzania had accepted the export-oriented conditions of the World Bank and the International Monetary Fund and Nyerere had stepped down. As one of his first official acts, Tanzanian President Ali Hassan Mwinyi made a state visit to Kenya, and President Moi returned the visit in 1988. Subsequent relations have stiffened somewhat, particularly since Kenya's expulsion of a number of Tanzanians identified as illegal aliens, but Mwinyi has seemed determined to resurrect some semblance of the regional cooperation abandoned in 1977. For Kenya and Uganda, more so than for Kenya and Tanzania, this may prove a daunting task.

Uganda

Uganda's lifeline to the sea runs through Kenya, which has usually abided by international conventions pertaining to the interests of landlocked countries. In return, Kenya enjoys access to the Uganda market and to electric power generated at Owen Falls Dam on the Nile. At the same time, verbal hostilities between Presidents Moi and Yoweri Museveni have often been accompanied by violent border incidents and threats of war. Relations between the two countries began to deteriorate in the late 1960s, just before Milton Obote's abortive proposal that Uganda "move to the left." When Obote was overthrown, the Kenyatta government adopted a wait-and-see attitude despite Idi Amin's threat to "reclaim" large parts of western Kenya for Uganda. The Kenyan stance angered both Ugandans opposed to Amin and the Tanzanian government, which was receiving similar threats. Nairobi's rationale was that, as unpalatable as he was, Amin at least prevented Kenya from being all but surrounded by socialist regimes. Kenyan neutrality continued into the Tanzania-Uganda war of 1978–1979,[4] and as successive Ugandan governments later came to power and fell, political exiles from every camp streamed eastward.

After the disputed Ugandan national election of December 1980 returned control to Obote and his Uganda People's Congress, Obote made it clear that he now favored a mixed economy instead of the socialist program he had advocated before the coup. A month later, Presidents Moi, Obote, and Kenneth Kaunda of Zambia met to discuss better communications, trade, and joint antismuggling activities. Unfortunately for this new beginning, the Obote regime soon descended into a period of corruption and violence. It was replaced by a military junta headed by Lieutenant-General Tito Okello, which fell in early 1986 to the National Resistance Army of Yoweri Museveni.

Tensions mounted again in 1987 because of several border incidents including the apparent killing of a Ugandan teacher by Kenyan police and the smuggling of food and weapons to Museveni's political enemies. Kenyan troops were ordered to the border and there killed twenty Ugandan soldiers in isolated skirmishes. Amid the confusion, some two thousand Ugandan refugees crossed into Kenya, prompting a border closing. Charging that Museveni had sent two hundred Kenyan boys to Libya for insurgency training against his regime, Moi also closed the port of Mombasa to Ugandan trade. In 1988, the Organization of African Unity (OAU) stepped in to mediate the dispute. OAU Chairman Kaunda managed to extract pledges from both sides to pursue peaceful negotiations. Later that year, however, when the Kenyan courts sentenced a Ugandan to ten years in prison for spying, Museveni accused Moi of delivering arms and ammunition to antigovernment guerrillas holding out in northern Uganda, and on March 7, 1989, an unidentified MiG aircraft dropped two bombs on Lokichoggio, in northwestern Turkana District. The bombs landed within 200 meters (660 feet) of the army's local GSU headquarters, and five persons were killed. Despite strong evidence that the plane was Libyan and based in Sudan and that the raid had been conducted in retaliation for Kenyan support of southern Sudanese rebels, President Moi insisted that Uganda was responsible. The incident followed several weeks of clashes over cattle rustling along the Uganda border.[5]

In more recent years, strains between the two countries have mainly had their source in Uganda's alleged support of a Tutsi insurgency against the Rwandese government of Moi's personal friend, Juvenal Habyarimana, and allegations that Museveni was encouraging Kenyan dissidents and even planning to invade western Kenya. Uganda, for its part, has consistently protested the discriminatory treatment of Rwandese refugees and its own nationals living in Kenya. In 1990, Moi and Museveni met in the Ugandan border town of Tororo to find ways of resolving their problems, and although the discussions went well, little has since happened to reduce conflict and increase cooperation between these historically linked states.[6]

Sudan

Kenya and Sudan maintained a basically convivial relationship during the Kenyatta and early Moi presidencies, when President Gaafar Nimeiri ruled in Khartoum.[7] Although their common frontier traverses an arid 320-kilometer (200-mile) sector of the isolated Lotikip Plain, a new road carries some trade between the two states. In the 1980s, other ties included a five-year agreement on the sharing of agricultural and arid-lands water technology, a joint committee on telecommunications, and an exchange of press coverage. These initiatives were directed at bringing Sudan and Kenya closer together, an appealing notion for both Nimeiri and Moi in view of their shared antipathy for several neighboring regimes.

Since the early 1980s, however, Khartoum's problems with its non-Muslim south have spilled over into Kenya. Refugee border crossings, cholera, and cattle thefts have become common in the Elemi Triangle region. Until the Nimeiri regime was toppled in April 1985, both governments played down these problems in deference to their mutual interests. Most important, a vital trade route extends from the southern Sudanese capital of Juba through Nairobi to Mombasa; it is more efficient for imports to be shipped to the southernmost reaches of Sudan from Mombasa than from Port Sudan on the Red Sea.

Since Nimeiri's fall, stability has eluded Sudanese politics, civil war and famine have ravaged the south, and cordiality has faded from Nairobi's relations with three consecutive governments in Khartoum. Kenya has sent famine relief to Sudanese populations in the south, and much of it has been diverted to the rebellious Sudanese People's Liberation Army (SPLA). Khartoum has suggested that the Kenyans have allowed arms and other military equipment to accompany these shipments. A dispute has been revived over ownership of the Elemi Triangle, which both countries claim as a result of separate preindependence agreements with the British. Most recently, Sudan threatened to offer sanctuary to Kenyan political dissidents unless Kenya stopped providing assistance to the SPLA, and in 1992 the current head of the Sudanese government, General Omar Hassan Ahmed al-Bashir, announced that Kenya had submitted to this ultimatum.[8]

Ethiopia

Until the 1991 departure of Mengistu Haile Mariam, head of state and chairman of the Provisional Military Administrative Council, Marxist-Leninist Ethiopia was distinguished as the ideologically most radical country in eastern Africa. Even when Mengistu was in power, relations between Kenya and Ethiopia remained remarkably friendly. In the early years of Kenyan independence, Jomo Kenyatta developed a personal friendship with Emperor Haile Selassie on the basis of their similar ages, Christian religious identifications, and common mistrust of Islamic Somalia, which laid claim to portions of both countries. Kenya and Ethiopia signed a mutual defense treaty in the early 1960s and attempted to form closer economic ties. A highway was completed linking Nairobi with Addis Ababa, only to fall into disuse for want of trade.

A brief hiatus followed the overthrow of Selassie in 1974. Kenya expressed official disapproval over the palace coup and the deaths of the emperor and his family, but, true to his inclination toward realpolitik, Kenyatta quickly normalized relations with the new military government. Mengistu proceeded to convert Ethiopia into an Afro-Marxist state,[9] and with the Ethiopian-Somali war of 1977–1978 and the arrival of Soviet and Cuban troops in Ethiopia, Kenya could have been expected to recoil from its northern neighbor. The Mengistu junta privately assured Kenya of its intention to coexist peacefully, adding that the Soviet and Cuban presence was simply a short-term necessity. Also finding comfort in Ethiopia's Coptic Christianity and denunciation of their common adversary, Somalia, the Moi government maintained the status quo. Kenya's main interest lay in strict adherence to existing boundaries, to which Ethiopia agreed.

The ultimate collapse of Mengistu's regime and Ethiopia's ensuing period of internal political turbulence has led to an influx of refugees into Kenya. By March 1992, the Nairobi-based UN High Commissioner for Refugees estimated that, in one month, at least ten thousand southern Ethiopians had entered Kenya to escape interethnic violence, drought, and famine.

Somalia

Somalia has long been Kenya's northeastern nemesis. It is the only country with which Kenya has fought a war and the only one to have laid serious claim to Kenyan territory. Kenya is the main recipient of the direct and indirect consequences of the collapse of civil order in this monoethnic republic. From the Kenyan point of view, Somalia is a focal point of hostility in eastern Africa.

Tensions with Somalia extend back at least eighty years and can be partly attributed to the British Colonial Office. At the turn of the century, Somali peoples of the Darod and Hawiye clans were expanding southward and westward out of their central homeland in the horn of Africa. Somali pastoralists staked claims to territory southwest of the Juba River in what is now northeastern Kenya. In 1916 the area was divided by the British and the Italians as part of an agreement to ensure Italy's support of Britain in World War I. This decision absorbed up to 150,000 ethnic Somalis into the East Africa Protectorate and Kenya Colony, and their descendants remain ethnically, religiously, and linguistically Somali.

Prior to Kenyan independence, local Somali leaders petitioned for a boundary adjustment to include their kinsmen in the recently independent Somali Republic. A British commission appointed to survey the wishes of these people reported a near-unanimous desire to become part of Somalia instead of Kenya. Britain failed to act on these findings and allowed independence to proceed with Kenya Colony's existing frontiers intact. As we have seen, the colonial flag had hardly been lowered when the Kenyatta government was plunged into an undeclared border war with Somalia. Although the Somali government denied supporting the insurgent *shifta*, these guerrillas were in fact encouraged and supplied from Mogadishu. In 1968, an uneasy peace settled over the region.

Despite continued animosity and violence, informal communications proceeded unabated. Large-scale smuggling was carried out throughout the 1970s and 1980s, particularly in *miraa*, a mildly intoxicating, grasslike weed grown near Mt. Kenya and chewed in Somalia. Foodstuffs, petroleum fuels, small manufactures, and gold also traveled overland and by coastal vessel in what had become a firmly established, aggressive, and often ingenious illegal trade.[10] Improved formal relations followed the 1981 OAU meetings, where talks between governments led to a reconciliation made possible by a Somali renunciation of any further claims to Kenyan territory. Moi visited Mogadishu during 1984, and a joint communiqué was issued in 1987 outlining provisions for monitoring and regulating border crossings. When friction developed two years later over evidence that Somali poachers were decimating northern Kenyan elephant populations and murdering helpless villagers, it precipitated screening to determine the citizenship status of all ethnic Somalis living in Kenya. The roundups ended in 1990, but by this time more than fifteen hundred Somalis, fearing that they would be deported to a Somalia now on the verge of civil collapse, had fled to Uganda. Thousands of other local Somalis were ordered to evacuate pastoral lands surrounding the northern game reserves.

The government of Siad Barre was overthrown in January 1991, and the anarchic clan warfare and famine that immediately engulfed southern Somalia created an enormous refugee problem for Kenya. Starving Somalis began arriving in North-Eastern Province at midyear and by December numbered more than seventy-five thousand. In the closing weeks of 1992, an estimated three hundred thousand severly undernourished refugees were camped on Kenyan soil. At the Liboi border camp alone, an estimated fifty thousand were dying at the rate of up to three hundred a day from starvation, lack of water, and disease.[11] Refugee issues preoccupied Kenya into 1993 as airports became hastily arranged points of departure for relief shipments, border towns were converted into immigrant reception centers, Nairobi and other cities began to receive an influx of impoverished and sometimes armed aliens, and southern Somalia succumbed to gang violence, civil breakdown, and foreign military intervention.

Other African States

According to one recent assessment from Nairobi, Kenya faces difficult times in its effort to secure a viable place in the unsettled political arena of eastern Africa:

> For some time to come ... Kenya will have to live with its troublesome neighbors, unless some kind of regional security arrangement can be worked out with the consent of all the nations involved. Given the rivalries of the past, the formation of any such regional security arrangement within the forseeable future appears to be a very tall order indeed.[12]

Elsewhere in Africa, relations have been more predictable and have been driven by a less complicated agenda centering on business and trade. Nowhere are the wider regional advantages of Kenya's relative economic strength more visible than in its emergence as a leading member of the Preferential Trade Area. Because of distance and poor communications, West Africa figures less prominently in commercial terms, but this situation may soon change. In addition to established trade links with Ghana and Algeria, a pan-African highway has been discussed that would eventually extend from Mombasa to Lagos, Nigeria. Road expansion is seen as a key factor in increasing trade through Tanzania to Zambia, Zimbabwe, Botswana, and other PTA countries.

Periodically, President Moi has offered to mediate the internal disputes of other African states. He tried to help resolve the Obote-Okello-Museveni leadership struggle in Uganda in 1985, and in 1989 he endeavored to bring together the contending sides in the Eritrean war of secession against Ethiopia. He has made similar overtures with a view to ending a protracted guerrilla war in Mozambique between the Front for the Liberation of Mozambique (FRELIMO) government and the South Africa–backed Mozambique National Resistance Movement (RENAMO).[13] Such apparent altruism has not entered into Kenyan relations with the Libyan government of Muammar Qaddafi. Moi severed diplomatic relations with Libya in 1987, accusing Tripoli of interfering in Kenyan affairs through its military adventures in Sudan and Uganda. Insulting as this action may have been to the radical wing of the Arab world, it succeeded in reinforcing the close alliance Kenya has traditionally maintained with pro-Western Egypt.

RELATIONS OUTSIDE AFRICA

Key relationships in Kenya's broader international universe include those with Britain and other members of the European Community and with the United States, several Middle Eastern states, and Japan. The former Soviet Union and the People's Republic of China once figured more significantly in Kenyan foreign policy than they do today. Soon after the transition from Kenyatta to Moi, the U.S.S.R. invaded Afghanistan, and Shi'ite followers of the Ayatollah Khomeini captured the U.S. embassy in Tehran. To the West, these crises gave Kenya a new strategic importance in the Indian Ocean region and the Middle East that inexorably drew the country into an equally new and potentially fluid set of international opportunities, obligations, and dangers. Even before this turning point, conditions had already changed considerably from the early independence period, when Kenya's chief opening to the non-African world was through Britain.

Britain

Britain remains Kenya's leading trade partner, long-term source of economic aid and investment, and supplier of foreign military assistance. The Moi government has nurtured the special relationship that Jomo Kenyatta forged with Britain at independence, but a number of minor disruptions that arose during the Kenyatta presidency have carried over into the 1980s and 1990s. Kenya expressed official outrage at Britain's failure to reverse white Southern Rhodesia's unilateral declaration of independence in 1965,[14] but stopped short of recalling its ambassador. Until recently, British arms sales to South Africa formed another bone of

contention between the two states, and taxes, levies, and other restrictions on resident British firms are perennial issues. Since Britian is still
Kenya's principal source of overseas investment, often-heated negotiations are constantly in progress over the rights and responsibilities of
British enterprises operating in the country. In the past decade, economic
tensions have revolved around fluctuations in the prices paid for Kenyan
exports to Britain, annually valued at over $200 million, the local pricing
policies of British oil companies, and the distribution of revenues from
the British portion of Kenya's tourist industry.

Relations are more harmonious on the political front. In spite of
United States–led foreign criticism of the Moi regime's human-rights
practices and tolerance of economic inefficiency and corruption, Britain
has remained largely silent on these issues. Correspondingly, Kenya
supports British positions at the United Nations, offers residence to more
than twenty thousand British citizens, and avoids situations that might
induce the thirty to forty thousand Asians and other Kenyans holding
British-protected status to seek refuge in England. In fact, the Kenyan
government has relied on the British to supply much-needed international legitimacy to President Moi and his beleaguered circle. Prime
Minister Margaret Thatcher visited Kenya in early 1988 and hailed
the president's "strong and decisive leadership within a constitutional
framework." She went on to praise the country's "peace and stability,
policies which recognize the worth of individual effort and personal
endeavor . . . and an economy in which private ownership and private
industry have been encouraged."[15] While this flowery tribute was somewhat self-serving from the perspective of British investors, it was well
received. In 1991, while other donors were reducing their aid, Kenya
received about £44 million (approximately $78 million) from Britain,
which made it the second-largest recipient of British assistance for that
year. In 1992, a confidential memorandum from Her Majesty's High
Commission in Nairobi, apparently leaked to the Kenyan press, conveyed the suggestion that, from a diplomatic point of view, Daniel arap
Moi was the best possible presidential candidate in the forthcoming
national election.[16]

United States

North America made its first definitive contact with eastern Africa
after 1833, when the United States established a consulate on Zanzibar to
oversee the coastal trade. After World War I, American missionaries com-
menced work in Kenya, and in the 1950s U.S. labor organizations began
discreetly to support the independence movement. As chairman of the
Kenya Federation of Labour, Tom Mboya became a conduit for this assistance. During the same period the American Pathfinder Fund initiated

family planning programs in Kenya, and shortly thereafter American private contributions facilitated an airlift of Kenyan students to the United States. By 1965, thirteen hundred students had taken advantage of this opportunity.

Official relations were less convivial in the immediate postindependence period. Diplomatic stresses first surfaced over U.S. intervention in the Congo (now Zaire), an episode that led to a large anti-American demonstration in Nairobi. As occurred throughout Africa, criticism was later voiced about the U.S. role in Vietnam, U.S. policy toward South Africa, and the building of an American military base on the Indian Ocean island of Diego Garcia.

Conditions improved in the 1970s as U.S. development assistance and corporate investment increased; teachers, missionaries, and Peace Corps volunteers arrived in greater numbers; and the flow of American tourists swelled to nearly forty thousand per year. In 1979 President Moi led a ministerial delegation to Washington, where he and President Jimmy Carter settled upon an aid package to help offset Kenya's first major food shortage. Further agreements, concluded in 1980, traded U.S. military access to Mombasa harbor and Nanyuki air base for Kenyan access to U.S. military equipment and training. Under these terms, the two countries drew closer during the eight-year presidency of Ronald Reagan as Kenya became the United States's best friend in eastern Africa.

From 1987 until the beginning of the Clinton administration in 1993, U.S.-Kenyan exchanges became increasingly quarrelsome. In effect, the problem represented a clash between the self-serving economic policies of an increasingly authoritarian and capricious Kenyan elite and a rigid and demanding U.S. policy agenda expressing President George Bush's vision of a post-Soviet "new world order" in Africa. Economically, the Bush protocol could be reduced to five basic "structural adjustments," also advocated by the World Bank and the International Monetary Fund:

- Establish realistic exchange rates.
- Reduce or eliminate government price controls.
- Reduce government budget deficits.
- Reform parastatal organizations.
- Achieve realistic interest rates.[17]

Regarding civil rights and liberties, the Bush mandate reflected American priorities for African and Third World "democratization": "The US supports ... efforts toward democracy in the belief that human rights cannot be secured in Africa without political pluralism. The US encourages economic and political pluralism in Africa through funding projects that promote the administration of justice and rule of law."[18]

With these policy lines serving as a backdrop, President Moi and Ambassador Smith Hempstone entered into a highly personalized dialogue of mutual admonition and recrimination.[19] In the midst of this spectacle, three U.S. senators visited Kenya and recommended that further economic assistance be withheld until political prisoners were either charged or released, until they were guaranteed against physical abuse while in detention, and until the autonomy of the courts and the press was restored.[20] The executive branch persuaded all major donors to curtail their aid until the fall of 1992, the approximate time of the next parliamentary and presidential elections. With foreign aid then underwriting almost 30 percent of the Kenyan national budget, the effect of this cutback was immediate if not catastrophic. Although the country continued to receive $865 million in international economic assistance, most of this was in the form of already-committed project support. About $360 million in quick-disbursement program aid was lost, and, as one U.S. government agency pointed out, "Because this is cash and directly affects foreign exchange availability, the suspension has had a negative effect on imports, economic growth, and new investment."[21]

In November 1992, what was interpreted as the employment of excessive police force to end a prodemocracy rally in Nairobi brought official protests from Washington, London, Stockholm, Copenhagen, Bonn, and other capitals. In response, Kenya accused the U.S. embassy of masterminding an opposition attempt to take over the government. The situation remained in limbo as the Kenyan election returned Moi to power, the U.S. presidency shifted from the Republican incumbent to his Democratic challenger, and the flamboyantly provocative American ambassador prepared to leave Nairobi.[22]

The Former Communist States and China

Whereas Kenyatta, Mboya, and other KANU nationalists courted Britain and the United States during and after the transition to independence, Odinga and a small group of supporters looked instead to the Soviet Union and, later, the People's Republic of China. Odinga, pushed toward the Marxist-Leninist camp by ideological inclination and deep-seated political rivalry with his Luo kinsman Mboya, by 1963 had become Kenya's leading advocate of closer cooperation with Moscow and Beijing. In 1964, the new vice president led a mission to both capitals and, without cabinet authorization, signed agreements for interest-free loans, technical assistance, and weapons transfers. These pacts quickly became a cause célèbre in Nairobi and backfired when the Soviet arms that finally arrived seemed to be of World War I vintage. This insult and the fact that the Soviets were also supplying weaponry to hostile Somalia provided Kenyatta with all the justification he needed to cool relations with the East and to fetter Odinga. Nevertheless, Kenya continued to receive assistance from both Marxist-Leninist states, including a large Soviet-built hospital at Kisumu, in Odinga's home area. This is not to say that Kenya's central problems with the Soviets, involving Kenyatta's avowedly pro-Western sentiments and the U.S.S.R.'s persistent support of Somalia, simply disappeared. By the time the latter alliance was terminated in 1977, Soviet and Chinese influence in Kenya had stabilized at a very low level.

From its inception in 1978, moreover, the Moi government made anticommunism an important policy theme. Speaking on behalf of the recently installed president, Vice President Mwai Kibaki stated flatly, "There is no room for communists in Kenya." Shortly thereafter, President Moi himself informed a graduating class at the University of Nairobi that, in his opinion, idealistic and easily misled students should not be exposed to theories of scientific socialism. Alleged campus implication in the 1982 coup attempt included a charge that some lecturers and student agitators had been secretly funded from external communist sources. At the same time, a partial exception to this anticommunist stance was initiated as early as 1980, when Chinese Vice Premier Ji Penfei paid a state visit to Nairobi. A month later President Moi went to Beijing and concluded agreements for economic, technical, and cultural cooperation. The relationship was solidified in January 1983, when Premier Zhao Ziang made a reciprocal trip to the Kenyan capital. Since then, the China linkage has been maintained on the basis not of any ideological affinity but of shared Third World identity. Kenya's future relations with the former Soviet Union remain open to speculation but cannot be expected to become any more significant than they were during the pre-Yeltsin period of communist rule.

The Middle East

By contrast, Kenya's dealings with the Middle East and the greater Arab world figure very importantly in the country's foreign policy. In 1973, the Kenyatta government made a difficult choice in the Arab-Israeli conflict. Since independence the country had pursued a pro-Israel policy line in pursuit of trade preferences and development assistance and also, in the light of Arab support of Somalia's irredentist claims to the Ogaden region of Ethiopia and to its own northeastern territory, out of fear of Islamic expansionism in eastern Africa. Coming at a time of relative quiet in Kenya-Somalia relations, the 1973 global oil crisis changed this equation. To protect its precarious access to oil imports, the government gave way to growing economic pressure from Arab members of the Organization of Petroleum Exporting Countries (OPEC) and broke diplomatic relations with Israel. To most Kenyans this move represented an unfortunate but necessary quid pro quo, with Kenya receiving oil products at concessionary prices in exchange for taking sides against Israel.

Under Moi and successive foreign ministers, the connection with Jerusalem has been partially reopened through Israeli participation in large construction projects and other development activities. At the same time, the Kenyan side has taken great pains to preserve Arab goodwill. During his first three years in office, Moi traveled to Saudi Arabia, Abu Dhabi, and Iraq in search of oil concessions, financial aid, and trade. An arrangement worked out in Baghdad for enough crude oil to satisfy one-third of Kenya's requirements collapsed in the 1980s Iraq-Iran war. Since then, the country's main suppliers have been the Arabian Gulf states.

Kenyan export revenues from the Middle East today include proceeds from fruits and vegetables, tinned meats, wood and dairy products, and international tourism. Because of oil, the region receives about 16 percent of Kenya's import expenditures, the third-largest share behind the European Economic Community (EEC) and the Far East. The dollar value of imports from the United Arab Emirates alone is second only to the value of imports from Britain.[23]

RELATIONS WITH INTERNATIONAL ORGANIZATIONS

Besides the Preferential Trade Area, Kenya participates in four regional and global associations of states—the Organization of African Unity, the British-originated Commonwealth of Nations, the European Economic Community, and the United Nations. In terms of foreign-policy priorities, the OAU and the UN have taken a back seat to the Commonwealth and the EEC, which are treated as mechanisms for fostering trade and to channeling foreign aid into the country.

In the case of the Commonwealth, Britain and Canada figure prominently as preferred sources of economic and military assistance. Monies for coffee and tea development and for land-use and human-settlement projects are among several important contributions to Kenya from the Commonwealth Development Fund. Relations with Commonwealth partners are not always smooth, however. In November 1989, while Canada was investing $8.8 million to help Kenya develop a comprehensive energy policy, a diplomatic crisis arose over the treatment of the country's ethnic Somali community. This incident paralleled an interruption of assistance from Norway and Sweden resulting from these countries' objections to the suppression of anti-KANU political dissidents.

Multilateral links to the EEC are typically less politicized. Since 1969 Kenya has been party to two Yaoundé conventions and four Lomé conventions that have extended preferential trade status and enabled

Kenyan ministries to obtain long-term loans from the European Development Fund.[24] In recent years, EEC-sponsored projects have included $26 million for integrated arid-lands development in Machakos District and funding for transport and road improvements to facilitate communications with neighboring countries. Commonwealth and EEC assistance programs are important components of Kenya's development portfolio but not nearly so important as help from the World Bank, the International Monetary Fund, and bilateral sources.

THE POLITICS OF FOREIGN AID

Kenya's relatively open society and essentially laissez-faire economy have made it a favorite target for purveyors of official development assistance and private support and opened it to the vagaries and political liabilities inevitably associated with foreign aid. By the beginning of the 1990s, foreign assistance had become a vital part of the Kenyan national economy. The importance of political, as well as purely humanitarian and economic, motives for this support is suggested by the fact that Kenyan receipts per capita and as a percentage of gross national product fell below the African averages (Table 6.1).

In the year that Daniel Moi assumed the presidency, total aid disbursements amounted to $350 million in addition to an accumulated $1.45 billion in previously contributed grants and loans.[25] By 1982, annual aid had risen to $428 million, or $26 per capita, and in the following year to $450 million for 517 projects sponsored by thirty-five donors and lenders.[26] Between 1974 and 1984, Kenya's largest bilateral aid partners were Britain, West Germany, the United States, the Netherlands, and Sweden. Responsible for 9.5 percent of total assistance and 19.4 percent of all resource transfers, the World Bank was already well established as the country's biggest multilateral financier and coordinator of bilateral assistance.[27]

TABLE 6.1 Official Development Assistance to Kenya, 1990 (current US$ millions)

	Receipts	Per Capita ($)	Percent GNP
Kenya	1,000	41.4	11.4
Africa (av.)*	417	53.7	15.3

*Excluding Algeria, Egypt, Libya, Morocco, and Tunisia, and also Cape Verde, Comoros, Djibouti, Equatorial Guinea, Gambia, Guinea Bissau, São Tomé and Principe, Seychelles, and Swaziland.

Source: World Bank, World Development Report 1992 (New York: Oxford University Press, 1992), pp. 256-257.

As Kenyan economic performance declined in the 1980s, international influence over domestic policy progressively increased. In 1986, a consultative group of donors led by the World Bank pledged $900 million over two years to help implement the 1984–1988 national development plan. The International Monetary Fund encouraged modifications to the plan by allowing the purchase of standard drawing rights, worth up to $85.2 million, in support of what it considered essential economic and financial adjustments. During the same year, fourteen bilateral and nine multilateral representatives met in Paris and estimated that Kenya would need grants and loans in the amount of $600 million per year to meet its economic growth and investment objectives.

By 1987, Kenya's main donors had become Britain, West Germany, the United States, the Netherlands, and Japan. The proportion of American aid had fallen substantially because of a reduction in military assistance from $111 million in 1984 to $57 million in 1987. U.S. political influence intensified in 1988 with a $17.2-million grant to effect structural adjustments in the Kenyan economy and again in 1989 with an offer to cancel Kenya's debt if plans for the Kenya Times Media Trust building project were abandoned. The World Bank's International Development Association (IDA) pressed for further policy changes with a $5-million credit for the training of staff to implement reforms in the Kenyan banking system and an additional $45-million credit for adjustments in the industrial sector. The IDA reinforced its presence in 1990 with a credit of $6 million to restructure the Kenyan Industrial Development Bank and the Industrial and Commercial Development Corporation. Japan had become Kenya's largest official donor in an atmosphere of Western disenchantment with the Moi regime, and a year later the country's committed and temporarily deferred aid package exceeded $1 billion, $400 million of which targeted toward parastatal and other reforms urged by an increasingly united donor community to reduce governmental involvement in the economy.

Following a high-level meeting organized in 1992 by the International Monetary Fund, the World Bank released approximately $300 million in balance-of-payments support to allow fiscal reforms, reductions in public employment, and privatization of parastatal corporations. The government created a new agency, the Department of Government Investment and Public Enterprise (DGIPE), to administer these divestitures and sales. Led by George Mitine, former director of government investment in the Treasury, the DGIPE began to address problems of mismanagement and corruption that over the years had plagued the parastatal sector. Many public companies had never paid taxes, and some had failed even to remit all of the revenues they collected for government. Most were headed by politically appointed chairmen and directors, and a number of firms perennially defaulted on their foreign debts.

Mitine and his colleagues faced the difficult and potentially dangerous task of reducing pervasive inefficiency and corruption in these organizations as a condition for Kenya's receiving future resource transfers.

Until the donor community's outright suspension of foreign aid to force political and economic reforms, the Moi government had successfully managed the aid process by setting its own terms and playing donors off against each other. The 1989–1993 development plan strictly delimited the discretionary power of foreign lending and granting institutions over national policy:

> External resources in the form of grants and loans will only be received where the anticipated local cost component is not very high and conditionalities are not too stringent. The grant element of such assistance will be expected to be at least 25 percent. Government will establish priority areas and determine where specific donor funds and activities will be channelled. Donor flexibility will be required in rescheduling undisbursed funds and in taking on programme as opposed to project funding. Donors will be expected to allow for competitive bidding, without insisting that goods and services must come from their own country.[28]

Donor influence and coordination were further constrained by the restriction of expatriate advisors mainly to staff instead of line functions and by the aid agencies' own failure to suppress rivalries and exercise their relative advantages in providing assistance.[29]

The balance of power has now shifted in Kenya toward what David Abernethy has termed "the informal governance of Africa by aid agencies." This situation creates both a problem and an opportunity for the Moi regime in its latest incarnation. In Abernethy's formulation:

> To the extent that the macro-level policy changes insisted upon by the major aid agencies benefit large numbers of food producers while reducing living standards for many urban dwellers, rulers of authoritarian no-party or one-party African regimes face a serious political dilemma. On the one hand, the rural beneficiaries of reform have virtually no voice in government and hence no way effectively to support the regime. On the other hand, urbanites who lose out from reform are able to exert real political leverage against the regime by engaging in demonstrations, riots, and coup attempts. Authoritarian rulers can respond to this dilemma by undermining structural adjustment reforms that threaten to harm previously favored urban populations. . . . Alternatively, rulers could conclude that it is in their own interest to broaden political participation to include the rural food-producing beneficiaries of reform as a significant (supportive) constituency. In this case . . . economic crisis, coupled with structural adjustment policies, could be the precursor of government-sponsored moves toward genuine electoral democracy.[30]

If Kenya is to reclaim its earlier high ground of international policy independence and turn foreign conditionalities to the purposes of politically and economically sustainable development, its governing system must now eschew the former course of action and embrace the latter.

CONCLUSIONS: KENYA AND THE WORLD

From the 1970s to the early 1990s, tensions in the eastern African, Indian Ocean, and Arabian Gulf regions were of primary concern to the Moi government and its foreign policy. Because of the centrality and strategic importance of its location, Kenya was repeatedly drawn into conflicts with neighboring states and larger struggles disrupting northeastern Africa and the Middle East. In addition to ongoing problems with Uganda and Sudan, the Soviet invasion of Afghanistan, the U.S.-Iran hostage crisis, the Iraq-Iran war, the Gulf war, and the United States–led military intervention in Somalia have all occurred during the Moi presidency. The last two of these crises have required Kenya to become more or less directly involved. Relations with Tanzania have improved with time, but until the collapse of the Soviet Union and the fall of Afro-Marxist regimes in Ethiopia and Somalia, Kenya perceived this former superpower and its successive surrogates as genuine threats to its security. The human effects of anarchy and violence in southern Somalia continue to spill over into Kenya and preoccupy the country's policy makers and law-enforcement agencies. And as if these regional predicaments were not enough, three wider challenges to Kenya's international autonomy[31] have grown into major issues for the 1990s and probably beyond.

The first is heavy international pressure on the government to stop depriving its opposition of civil liberties and rights as a means of retaining control. Past official practice has been to reject the criticism of foreign governments as meddling in Kenyan internal affairs and to suppress churches, human-rights groups, and other internationally connected nongovernmental organizations when they have voiced their own objections. A recurrent theme has been that Kenya's overwhelming need for national unity is not really understood in the West and that, well-intentioned or not, short-term diplomats and aid workers, visiting academics, and expatriate NGO representatives aid and abet ethnic dissension and communal strife when they complain about how the country's citizens are subjected to authority. This argument may have carried some weight when Cold War expediencies induced Western governments to turn a blind eye to authoritarianism under otherwise friendly regimes and before democratization was transformed from a tiny rivulet of hope into a rushing torrent of demand across Kenya and the rest of Africa,[32] and across other developing areas and the former communist world. The Kenyan government has already bent under the weight of this movement, and unless some accommodation is made with the forces of political diversification and participation, whatever their bases of loyalty and support, it may break.

A second problem area is the relationship between local corruption and foreign business investment. The modern Kenyan leadership has always viewed a certain amount of nepotism, bribery, and favoritism as simply good business practice. So long as profits could still be made, moreover, foreign investors tended to write off such inconveniences as a necessary cost of doing business. The central assumption on both sides was that Kenya's pragmatic economic policies and its anticommunist foreign-policy positions were good for private enterprise—that its open markets, promotion of tourism, and welcoming of multinational corporations were sufficient to guarantee a steady influx of financial and technological backing from abroad. This supposition even extended to multilateral trade forums and United Nations institutions, which Kenya influenced to help stabilize world prices for its exports and to claim its share of development monies and international prestige. With the ending of the Cold War and the opening of new and vibrant markets in Asia, eastern Europe, and elsewhere in Africa, Kenya's easy access to international capital is fast disappearing. Led by a 50 percent reduction in U.S. operations, multinational companies and private foreign investors have already fled the domestic marketplace, initiating a trend that is almost certain to continue unless decisive and politically very risky steps are taken to restore the country's tarnished image as an attractive center for international profit taking. Because many members of an elite that is responsible for these measures will also suffer under them, prospects for a meaningful reform of the economy remain uncertain.

International constraints on domestic choice are not limited to issues of personal freedoms and economic affairs. They affect the very manner in which governance is structured and operates. For the first time since independence, formerly close allies are granting asylum to Kenyan political dissidents and to refugees from other African countries. For the first time, ambassadors and visiting official delegations are lecturing Kenyan leaders on the need for unrestricted party competition, free and fair elections, and a wider and deeper sharing of power. Multilateral financial institutions have turned from offering free economic advice and assistance to imposing conditions for political and policy reform. National elections are being closely monitored from without and their results pointedly questioned. The international community is imposing itself on Kenya as never before, and the circumstances and potential consequences of these pressures are more complicated and unpredictable than those extolled in standard development theory, criticized in statist approaches, and lamented in underdevelopment, dependency, and world-system constructs.[33] At this critical juncture in Kenyan history, it remains to be seen whether the country will be able to prosper in a changing international environment by renewing its quest for prosperity at home.

7

Kenya at the Crossroads of Development

What is Kenya after thirty years of independence, and what is it likely to become? Political science, economics, and other social sciences offer seemingly contradictory answers to these questions. According to the orthodoxies of modernization theory, economic growth and diversification have made Kenya one of Africa's leaders in per capita income, international investment and technology transfer, industrial and commercial development, and trade. Although a small elite may have benefited most from these achievements, about 60 percent of the population has attained relative security in terms of basic-needs satisfaction and improved life chances. The infant mortality rate declined from 112 per thousand live births in 1965 to 67 per thousand by 1990, a better result than recorded for all but five of the world's forty-three low-income countries and the best for low-income countries in Africa. By 1989, 94 percent of school-age children and 92 percent of young girls were enrolled in primary education. Between 1965 and 1989, the ratio of females to males attending secondary schools had risen from 38 percent to 70 percent. In spite of severe drought and an annual population growth rate of 3.8 percent, the average index of per capita food production increased by 6 percent from 1979–1981 to 1988–1990.[1] By all of these measures, Kenya has emerged from a period of expansive economic modernization with at least a modicum of social equity.

As other observers have pointed out, however, the costs of these advances have been high. Rigid class distinctions based on wealth and power are rapidly emerging. A small elite dominates much of society and has created severe inequality not only in economic and political rewards but also in education, employment, health, and social welfare. Rural women and remote pastoral minorities are routinely subjected to socioeconomic and political discrimination. Corrupt practices have proliferated in both business and government, and those who have protested

181

these illegalities have been stripped of their rights and freedoms. An incessant wooing of foreign investment and aid has outpaced Kenya's ability to absorb new assistance and made it at least to some extent dependent on an increasingly demanding and fickle coalition of investors, lenders, and donors. Abject poverty continues to be the lot of possibly 20 percent of the population, whose predicament is more desperate than that of the poorest of the poor in other African countries with much lower levels of overall economic performance.[2]

Underdevelopment and dependency theorists blame this situation on global capitalism and its links to a class of local exploiters.[3] Scholars working within the statist framework hold, in contrast, that it has been created by mismanagement and abuses of power on the part of an essentially autonomous national leadership.[4] More than international servility, domestic realpolitik has been determinant in independent Kenya. The entrepreneurial elite can still trace its roots to the structures of colonialism. It controls much of Kenya's agricultural economy and is the leading partner with international capital in controlling the industrial and commercial sectors. It has retained its ability to curtail dissent through the manipulation of parliament and local government, the shaping of public opinion, pressure on the press and on protest groups, and a perennial "harvesting" of material resources to sustain its life-giving patronage system.

Until quite recently, and with notable exceptions in 1975 and 1982, the ruling system has not been seriously challenged. This relative calm is due in part to the fact that the powerful constitute a semi-isolated urban clan in a largely rural country and in part to a popular perception of them as worthy of emulation. Much of their wealth, status, and power is the product of a single generation, and only now is hope fading that the process of accumulation can be broadened as well as deepened as they pass from the scene. Many of the wealthy have used their riches to support relatives, friends, and political followers back home. Absentee-owned estates and businesses have been worked by retainers considering themselves subordinates but not victims of feudalism and capitalism. Emerging class distinctions have produced occasional outbursts but not yet the deep cleavages that, left unattended, might lead to revolutionary violence or—perhaps more likely—coups d'état. This has been the reality of Kenya, but events are rapidly undermining the country's apparent stability.

In the final analysis, the most serious problems facing Kenya are matters of choice. Central to these is the systemic problem of broadening political and economic participation. At the policy level, crucial questions revolve around Kenya's capacity to feed itself and to slow population growth through expanded education, employment, and incomes.

Also at issue are appropriate ways to conserve and, where possible, regenerate precious natural resources, to promote social equity without sacrificing economic growth, and to reverse the present slide toward political instability and international intervention in domestic affairs.[5]

In order to increase capacity in each of these areas, the formula employed in the past to maintain legitimacy and stability will have to be fundamentally overhauled. The politics of patronage and interethnic bargaining will have to be supplemented and then replaced by the politics of class compromise and the rule of law. Corruption will have to give way to more rational and legally regulated mechanisms of problem solving and goal attainment. Responsibility for establishing societal obligations and incentives will have to devolve from corporatist centers of power to formally representative decision-making structures at all levels of both the public and private sectors.

Set against these awesome tasks are the enduring and stabilizing features of the Kenyan entrepreneurial culture. The system is still valued by its participants because it has worked for them in the past. Even the largely excluded have extracted some reward. For them and for the better-off as well, Kenya has not yet lost its rural cushion. In the countryside and in the burgeoning towns and cities, small-scale entrepreneurs—ordinary farmers, traders, and artisans—operate from communities in which family and communal values still provide the social cement that keeps things from falling apart.[6] Most citizens want the system to survive, although they also want their stake in it to increase.

The alternatives to orderly and equitable change are not pleasant. The game of patronage politics, played with diminishing resources and returns on the basis of primordial ethnic loyalties and antipathies, could very well degenerate into unbridled factional conflict and thence into military takeover and dictatorship. In place of all-out military rule, a self-appointed coalition of the armed forces and the civilian bureaucracy could take over to reform (i.e., to "depoliticize") the faltering old order. As the status quo comes under attack by a new generation of more liberal and politically conscious reformers, the only real possibility for avoiding either of these authoritarian outcomes may be through pragmatic changes that lead to a greater sharing of social, economic, and political opportunity throughout Kenya. Reason for hope is found in the fact that, for this country and its peoples, pragmatism has always gone hand in hand with the quest for prosperity.

Notes

INTRODUCTION

1. World Bank, *World Development Report 1992* (New York: Oxford University Press, 1992), p. 278.

2. For detailed geographical and human-ecological descriptions of Kenya, see Francis F. Ojany and Reuben B. Ogendo, *Kenya: A Study in Physical and Human Geography* (Nairobi: Longman, 1973); Simeon H. Ominde, *Land and Population Movements in Kenya* (London: Heinemann, 1968); Alan Best and Harm J. de Blij, *African Survey* (New York: Wiley, 1979), Chapter 25; and G. M. Hickman and W.H.G. Dickens, *The Land and Peoples of East Africa* (London: Longman, 1960).

3. See Rodger Yeager and Norman N. Miller, *Wildlife, Wild Death: Land Use and Survival in Eastern Africa* (Albany: State University of New York Press, 1986), pp. 82–83.

CHAPTER 1

1. Our evolutionary origins in eastern Africa are discussed in Sonia Cole, *The Prehistory of East Africa* (New York: Mentor Books, 1963); Richard E. Leakey and Roger Lewin, *People of the Lake: Mankind and Its Beginnings* (New York: Avon Books, 1979); David Pilbeam, "The Descent of Hominoids and Hominids," *Scientific American* 250 (March 1984), pp. 84–96; and Laurel Phillipson and David Phillipson, *East Africa's Prehistoric Past* (Nairobi: Longman, 1978).

2. See Roland Oliver, "The East African Interior," in Roland Oliver, ed., *The Cambridge History of Africa*, Volume 3 (Cambridge: Cambridge University Press, 1977), pp. 621–669.

3. For an analysis of early trade between the Kikuyu and the Maasai, see Peter Marris and Anthony Somerset, *African Businessmen: A Study of Entrepreneurship and Development in Kenya* (London: Routledge and Kegan Paul, 1971), pp. 34–42.

4. Eastern Africa's Arab, Shirazi, and Swahili cultures are portrayed in

A.H.J. Prins's classic study *The Swahili-speaking Peoples of Zanzibar and the East African Coast* (London: International African Institute, 1961).

5. The Portuguese may also have brought millets and cereal grains—crops that had originally come to Africa with Indo-Polynesian migrations across the Indian Ocean—to Kenya from their southern African enclaves. See George P. Murdock, *Africa: Its Peoples and Their Culture History* (New York: McGraw-Hill, 1959), pp. 21–24.

6. Western interest in the domain of Sayyid and his successors was not confined to eliminating slavery. The United States concluded a free-trade agreement with Zanzibar in 1833 and opened a consulate on the island in 1837. Similar arrangements were made by Britain, France, and the Hanseatic German Republics in 1839, 1844, and 1859. For further discussion of this period, see Richard D. Wolff, *The Economics of Colonialism: Britain and Kenya 1870–1930* (New Haven: Yale University Press, 1974), p. 32, nn. 155, 156; Kenneth Ingham, *A History of East Africa* (New York: Praeger, 1962), Chapters 1–3; and Thomas Spear, *Kenya's Past: An Introduction to Historical Method in Africa* (London: Longman, 1981), Chapter 5.

7. Wolff, *Economics of Colonialism*, p. 36. Other factors promoted the early development of commercialism in Kenya. Markets were often located on the borders of different ecological zones, for example, between the coastal belt and the dry interior, between open grasslands and forests, and at the foot of hills and mountains. They were also situated along ethnic borders (such as those shared by the Kikuyu and the Maasai) and on interregional trade routes to provide travelers with food and shelter. Even in the absence of Omani, Swahili, and European influences, Kenya's varied ecology, diverse ethnic makeup, and crisscrossing trade networks made the region highly conducive to commercial growth. Cf. P. L. Wickens, *An Economic History of Africa from the Earliest Times to Partition* (London: Oxford University Press, 1981), p. 118.

8. Antislavery and other missionary interests, the strategic port of Mombasa, and the German presence to the south also figured prominently in the decision to establish the East Africa Protectorate. When the fertile lands and commercial potential of southern Kenya became known, they provided the final justifications for declaring the territory a formal British possession.

9. The Uganda Railway has generated an extensive literature. See Charles Miller, *The Lunatic Express* (New York: Macmillan, 1971), for a highly readable overview and excellent bibliography.

10. By the 1880s, a significant number of Asian merchants and traders were already living on Zanzibar and in Mombasa. See Wolff, *Economics of Colonialism*, pp. 31–32, for further information on the early economic impact of Asians in eastern Africa. For a later view, see Dharam P. Ghai, ed., *Portrait of a Minority: Asians in East Africa* (Nairobi: Oxford University Press, 1965), Chapter 4.

11. A few years earlier and slightly to the north, a child was born who would later call himself Jomo Kenyatta and become the father of independent Kenya. In *Kenyatta* (London: George Allen and Unwin, 1972), pp. 21–32, Jeremy Murray-Brown offers a background sketch of this seminal period.

12. Following his retirement in 1919 from the governor-generalship of Nigeria, Sir Frederick (later Lord) Lugard set forth the details of his African

policy in *The Dual Mandate in British Tropical Africa*, 5th ed. (London: Frank Cass, 1965).

13. Officially termed "indirect administration," the concept of indirect rule was developed by Lord Lugard in northern Nigeria and later transferred to Tanganyika Territory by one of his lieutenants, Sir Donald Cameron. See Margery Perham's introduction in Lugard, *The Dual Mandate*, pp. xxxviii–xlviii, and Rodger Yeager, *Tanzania: An African Experiment*, 2d ed. (Boulder: Westview Press, 1989), pp. 14–15. Pacification came more easily in central Kenya than farther west, where it took a series of paramilitary and military expeditions to suppress the Nandi and other peoples living beyond the eastern Rift Valley. Sporadic resistance continued until 1912. Some of these campaigns are recorded firsthand in Richard Meinertzhagen, *Kenya Diary (1902–1906)* (Edinburgh: Oliver and Boyd, 1957).

14. Alan Best and Harm J. de Blij, *African Survey* (New York: Wiley, 1979), pp. 434–451.

15. See V. I. Lenin, *Imperialism, the Highest Stage of Capitalism* (Moscow: Foreign Languages Publishing House, n.d.). Lenin originally published this pamphlet in 1917.

16. Today as then, 83 percent of Kenya's land area is arid or semiarid, and only 12 percent has high potential for rain-fed agriculture. This environmental constraint is the basis for many of the political, human-ecological, and economic problems discussed in subsequent chapters.

17. Paul von Lettow-Vorbeck, *My Reminiscences of East Africa* (Nashville: Battery Press, n.d.), p. 44. This edition is reprinted from the original English-language edition (London: Hurst and Blackett, 1920).

18. The African combatants and porters were a mixture of a dozen or more indigenous ethnic groups. Represented in larger numbers than the rest were the Nandi and the Kamba. The British had found it difficult to pacify these peoples and therefore respected them as spirited fighters. The Germans favored certain groups, notably the Hehe of south-central German East Africa, for the same reason.

19. Robert B. Asprey, *War in the Shadows: The Guerrilla in History*, Volume 1 (Garden City: Doubleday, 1975), pp. 273–274. For other estimates, see Vincent Harlow, E. M. Chilver, and Allison Smith, *History of East Africa*, Volume 2 (Oxford: Clarendon Press, 1965), p. 156, and Leonard Mosley, *Duel for Kilimanjaro: An Account of the East African Campaign, 1914–1918* (London: Weidenfeld and Nicolson, 1963), pp. 234–235. An informative popular account of World War I in eastern Africa is presented in Charles Miller, *Battle for the Bundu* (New York: Macmillan, 1974).

20. Zoe Marsh and G. W. Kingsnorth, *An Introduction to the History of East Africa* (Cambridge: Cambridge University Press, 1961), p. 186. Those who continued to farm for the war effort faced serious labor shortages, and even when food crops could be collected, considerable postharvest losses resulted from a general lack of transport. Most of the protectorate's motor vehicles and railway wagons were committed to the conflict in the south.

21. Ibid., p. 187.

22. Wolff, *Economics of Colonialism*, pp. 119–120.

23. Ibid., p. 126. Wolff reports that between 1921 and 1931 the squatter population increased by 6.2 percent, as compared with a total Kikuyu increase of 1.5 percent. He estimates that by the early 1930s as many as a hundred thousand squatters resided on European farms. For an excellent oral history of the socio-economic, political, and everyday personal aspects of Kikuyu squatterism, see Tabitha Kanogo, *Squatters and the Roots of Mau Mau: 1905–63* (London, Nairobi, and Athens, OH: James Currey, Heinemann Kenya, and Ohio University Press, 1987).

24. Lord Hailey, *An African Survey*, rev. ed. (London: Oxford University Press, 1956), p. 750.

25. Although European farmers experienced economic reversals between 1919 and 1922 and again during the 1930s depression, 1923 through 1929 was a growth period for agriculture and for Kenya's infant industrial sector as well. Until the late 1920s, corporate growth was weak. Most of the thirty-three firms registered during this time failed in their first nine years of operation. Many early companies were organized as interlocking directorates of the same families, for example those of Evert Grogan and Lord Delamere. Although Africans were excluded from this process, Asians were not. As a result, substantial capital for new enterprises flowed into Kenya from India. As corporate expansion accelerated, however, British capital superseded investment from other sources.

26. Wolff, *Economics of Colonialism*, p. 145.

27. Ibid., pp. 132–133 and 144–146. See also C. C. Wrigley, "Kenya," in Harlow, Chilver, and Smith, *History of East Africa*, pp. 204–264.

28. In 1925, for example, Kenya imported 24 million square yards of cotton goods, despite repeated Asian attempts (all rejected by the Colonial Office) to capitalize on eastern Africa's comparative advantage in raw cotton by establishing domestic textile mills in Kenya. Swainson argues that had settler capital been involved in the attempt to create a textile industry, a protective Kenyan administration would have resisted the metropole. During the 1920s and 1930s the Colonial Office undermined existing colonial industries only in Uganda and Tanganyika (former German East Africa), both with minute settler populations. A Japanese-financed match factory collapsed after the Colonial Office instructed the local administration to tax it to the point that its import-substituting pricing edge was removed. A sisal twine company established by a British firm suffered a similar fate when it tried to export twine to Britain. Nicola Swainson, *The Development of Corporate Capitalism in Kenya, 1918–1977* (London: Heinemann, 1980), pp. 27–28, and E. A. Brett, *Colonialism and Underdevelopment in East Africa: The Politics of Economic Change, 1919–1939* (New York: NOK, 1973), Chapter 9.

29. See Ingham, *History of East Africa*, p. 281.

30. Johnstone Kenyatta, *Facing Mount Kenya: The Tribal Life of the Crikuyu* (London: Secker and Warburg, 1938). For additional details on this period in Kenyatta's life, see Murray-Brown, *Kenyatta*, Chapters 9 and 10.

31. Best and de Blij, *African Survey*, p. 439.

32. Brett, *Colonialism and Underdevelopment*, p. 276.

33. George Bennett, "Settlers and Politics in Kenya," in Harlow, Chilver, and Smith, *History of East Africa*, p. 330. This trend is further discussed in George

Bennett, *Kenya, a Political History: The Colonial Period* (London: Oxford University Press, 1963).

34. Carl G. Rosberg, Jr., and John Nottingham, *The Myth of "Mau Mau": Nationalism in Kenya* (New York: Praeger, 1966), p. 303.

35. Colonial Office, *Historical Survey of the Origins and Growth of Mau-Mau*, Corfield Report, Cmnd. 1030 (London: Her Majesty's Stationery Office, 1960).

36. For further analysis of settler politics during the 1950s, see Rosberg and Nottingham, *The Myth of "Mau Mau,"* pp. 308–319; M.P.K. Sorrenson, *Land Reform in the Kikuyu Country: A Study of Government Policy* (Nairobi: Oxford University Press, 1967), pp. 236–252; Elspeth Huxley, *The New Earth: An Experiment in Colonialism* (London: Chatto and Windus, 1960); Elspeth Huxley and Margery Perham, *Race and Politics in Kenya*, rev. ed. (London: Faber and Faber, 1955); and Gavin N. Kitching, *Class and Economic Change in Kenya: The Making of an African Petite Bourgeoisie, 1905–1970* (New Haven: Yale University Press, 1980), pp. 159–324.

37. The Swynnerton Plan and its impact are more fully discussed in Chapter 5.

38. Marris and Somerset, *African Businessmen*, p. 46.

39. Ibid., p. 12, and Arthur Hazlewood, *The Economy of Kenya: The Kenyatta Era* (London: Oxford University Press, 1979), p. 7. Hazlewood reports that in 1960, with only 61,000 Europeans and 169,000 Asians resident in Kenya, "eighty percent of the value of the marketed produce of agriculture came from the European-owned farms and estates [and] fifty-five percent of the total wage bill accrued to non-Africans, though they amounted to only ten percent of the labour force. Profits from manufacturing and trade were received almost entirely by non-African individuals or companies. . . . Africans received money income from wages and from the sale of agricultural produce, and it is this sale of produce which constituted virtually the whole of the monetary output of the African-owned economy . . . no more than three to four percent of the gross domestic product in 1960."

40. Swainson, *Development of Corporate Capitalism*, pp. 180–182.

41. Marris and Somerset, *African Businessmen*, p. 48.

42. Of forty-eight African states in existence today, thirty-two (or more than 65 percent) became independent during the 1960s. This rush to create new states began when fourteen French and Anglo-French territories were granted independence in 1960, followed by the British release of another twelve, including Kenya, between 1961 and 1968.

43. The best-known of these efforts was the Million Acre Scheme, begun in 1962 to resettle impoverished African farmers on former white estates. By the early 1970s, about 34,000 families had been located on approximately 430,190 hectares (1.1 million acres). In fact, only 15,000 of these were landless squatter families, settled on about 67,200 hectares (168,000 acres). Uma Lele, *The Design of Rural Development: Lessons from Kenya* (Washington, DC, and Baltimore: World Bank and Johns Hopkins University Press, 1975), p. 214.

44. Actually, these thirty-three seats were to be contested in nonracial "open" elections, while ten seats were reserved for Europeans, eight for Asians, two for Arabs, and twelve for "national members" selected by an electoral col-

lege. As Bennett and Rosberg have pointed out, however, an African majority was guaranteed because "the franchise would be so wide as to ensure that the electorate would be overwhelmingly African" (George Bennett and Carl Rosberg, *The Kenyatta Election: Kenya 1960–1961* [London: Oxford University Press, 1961], pp. 21–22).

45. Ibid., p. 141.

46. Although subsidized by the British, settler land transactions placed a financial burden on the domestic economy and aroused dismay and anger among former Mau Mau fighters and other landless Kikuyu. In her oral history of the period, Kanogo emphasizes that these groups "had come to equate Kenyatta's release and person with the inception of a millennium that would be epitomized by the recapturing and redistribution of the stolen lands" (Kanogo, *Squatters and the Roots of Mau Mau*, p. 171). The resulting perception of betrayal would later return to trouble Kenyatta and his successor, Daniel arap Moi. Lonsdale captures the poignant dilemma confronting the young Mau Mau veterans: "On emerging from forest or detention they were landless still, indeed more so than before in a rural world now realigned by land consolidation and freehold title. They remained debarred from the creation of order, outside its boundary fence. And on his release back to political life in 1961 Kenyatta took up his old refrain. His government would not be hooligan rule; Mau Mau had no moral claim on power" (John Lonsdale, "Mau Maus of the Mind: Making Mau Mau and Remaking Kenya," *Journal of African History* 31 [1990], p. 420).

47. Rosberg and Nottingham, *The Myth of "Mau Mau,"* p. 319.

48. Ibid.

49. Republic of Kenya, *The Constitution of Kenya (Amendment) Act,* No. 28 of 1964 (Nairobi: Government Printer, 1964), and Republic of Kenya, *The Constitution of Kenya (Amendment) (No. 2) Act,* No. 38 of 1964 (Nairobi: Government Printer, 1964). Other early amendments imposed controls on members of parliament, increased presidential authority over the civil service, relaxed restrictions on the president's use of emergency powers, and established parliamentary participation in the presidential selection process. In 1968 the constitution was changed again to provide for direct popular participation in presidential selection and at the same time to link parliamentary and presidential elections under the leadership of the leading party (of course, KANU). Under these provisions, each party is required to name a presidential candidate to run for a parliamentary seat. The candidate who wins more presidential votes than any other while winning a seat is declared president. Republic of Kenya, *The Constitution of Kenya (Amendment) (No. 2) Act,* No. 45 of 1968 (Nairobi: Government Printer, 1968).

50. Republic of Kenya, *The Constitution of Kenya (Amendment) (No. 4) Act,* No. 40 of 1966 (Nairobi: Government Printer, 1966), and Republic of Kenya, *The Constitution of Kenya (Amendment) Act,* No. 16 of 1968 (Nairobi: Government Printer, 1968).

51. For an example of this view (later modified by the author), see Colin Leys, *Underdevelopment in Kenya: The Political Economy of Neo-Colonialism, 1964–1971* (Berkeley: University of California Press, 1974, and London: Heinemann, 1975).

52. Wolff, *Economics of Colonialism,* p. 143.

53. Kenya white settlers are both praised and vilified in the literature on British colonialism in Africa, but they were neither saints nor demons. Most were ordinary people caught up in a socioeconomic and political context that dictated even as it was created by the terms of their presence. As one of our close friends and colleagues once observed about the settler situation, "If they were going to survive as agricultural producers, they had to *take* the land, *coerce* labor, *prevent* peasant production, *bias* the administrative infrastructure and tax system, and *keep* a monopoly on power" (Frank Holmquist, personal communication, March 15, 1983.) The system shaped settler behavior, and systemic changes eventually rendered this behavior obsolete. For an excellent interpretation of the transition period, see Gary Wasserman, *The Politics of Decolonization: Kenya Europeans and the Land Issue, 1960–1965* (Cambridge: Cambridge University Press, 1976).

CHAPTER 2

1. Although the ten constitutional amendments enacted between 1964 and 1968 were focused on consolidating power in the central government and specifically in the office of the president, that these changes were formally incorporated into Kenya's basic law seems to imply a degree of elite respect for the concept of constitutional limitations on political expediency. In any event, constitutional limits on power were not among Kenyans' highest priorities at independence. As Christopher Leo has noted in his review of this book's first edition, "liberal political ideals were certainly not the main things for which African nationalists were fighting. Most of all, the nascent bourgeoisie wanted access to the opportunities which members of their class among the white population took for granted but which had been denied to Africans: land, capital, franchises, and directorships. Peasants wanted the right to own their own land and to engage in the husbandry of their choice. They wanted marketing facilities and good roads to markets. For all classes, education for their children was a priority second to none" (*Canadian Journal of African Studies* 20 [1986], p. 302). For a more detailed analysis of the strengths and limitations of constitutionalism in Kenya, see J. B. Ojwang, *Constitutional Development in Kenya: Institutional Adaptation and Social Change* (Nairobi: African Centre for Technology Studies Press, 1990).

2. Republic of Kenya, *African Socialism and Its Application to Planning in Kenya* (Nairobi: Government Printer, 1965), really a blueprint for state-managed capitalist development.

3. See Rodger Yeager, *Tanzania: An African Experiment*, 2d ed. (Boulder: Westview Press, 1989), pp. 31–35, and Cranford Pratt, *The Critical Phase in Tanzania, 1945–1968: Nyerere and the Emergence of a Socialist Strategy* (Cambridge: Cambridge University Press, 1976), especially Chapters 4–8.

4. Henry Bienen, *Kenya: The Politics of Participation and Control* (Princeton: Princeton University Press, 1974), p. 74.

5. M. Tamarkin, "The Roots of Political Stability in Kenya," *African Affairs* 77 (1978), p. 308.

6. A later constitutional amendment established regulations governing periods of detention in criminal matters. Republic of Kenya, *The Constitution of Kenya (Amendment) Act*, No. 4 of 1988 (Nairobi: Government Printer, 1988).

7. For example, preventive detention was used in 1975 against two members of parliament who had taken controversial positions in legislative debate. Ojwang, *Constitutional Development in Kenya*, p. 150.

8. These were Oginga Odinga (1963–1966), who resigned to form and lead the KPU; Joseph Murumbi (1966–1967), who soon retired for health reasons; and Daniel arap Moi (1967–1978), who served Kenyatta faithfully and succeeded to the presidency after Kenyatta's death. Under the constitution, the death of a president calls for an interim period in which the vice president serves as acting president. An election must be held within three months, the new president taking office the day after voting is completed.

9. Government service remains a career much sought after by secondary, postsecondary, and university graduates. Since government is still the predominant wage employer in Kenya, civil service entry is very competitive and is generally stratified according to level of educational attainment. Senior positions are divided into "administrative" and "executive" classes; the former, generalist category carrying greater status and the latter reserved for professionals and technicians. Pay scales may be higher for executive than for administrative personnel, however, and transfers rarely occur from executive to administrative roles for this reason and because many executive officers are physicians, engineers, and other specialists. In 1969, about 77,000 people were employed by the central government. By 1980, the number had risen to 214,800 in central administration with another 257,000 retained mostly as teachers, employees of parastatal corporations, and local government workers. Public employment totaled 680,600 in 1989 (representing an increase of 31 percent since 1980), 280,800 being central civil servants. Republic of Kenya, *Economic Survey 1981* (Nairobi: Central Bureau of Statistics, Ministry of Finance and Economic Planning, May 1981), p. 55, and Republic of Kenya, *Economic Survey 1990* (Nairobi: Central Bureau of Statistics, Ministry of Planning and National Development, May 1990), p. 48.

10. Kenyan provinces are headed by commissioners who are responsible for between three and seven districts. Each district administration is led by a district commissioner (DC), the highest-ranking central government official in direct daily contact with local residents. DCs are assisted by headquarters staffs and by district officers, who preside over smaller geographic areas termed divisions. Below the divisions are locations and sublocations, managed by chiefs and subchiefs. Abandoned elsewhere in eastern Africa, chiefly titles are a carryover from colonial times, when the British appointed local influentials to serve as petty administrators and magistrates. Today most chiefs and subchiefs are formally educated civil servants.

11. Cf. Nicola Swainson, *The Development of Corporate Capitalism in Kenya, 1918–1977* (London: Heinemann, 1980), p. 183, in reference to G. Lamb, *Peasant Politics, Conflict and Development in Murang'a* (Lawes, Sussex: Julian Friedman, 1974), p. 25.

12. See Frank Holmquist, "Defending Peasant Political Space in Independent Africa," *Canadian Journal of African Studies* 14 (1980), pp. 157–167, and "Class Structure, Peasant Participation, and Rural Self-Help," in Joel Barkan and John D. Okumu, eds., *Politics and Public Policy in Kenya and Tanzania,* (New York: Praeger,

1979), pp. 130–153. See also P. Mbithi and B. Rasmussen, *Self-Reliance in Kenya: The Case of Harambee* (Uppsala: Scandinavian Institute of African Studies, 1977).

13. Cf. Njuguna Ng'ethe, *"Harambee* and Development Participation in Kenya" (Ph.D. thesis, Carleton University, Ottawa, Canada, 1979), Chapter 4.

14. The future political importance of religious groups was enhanced by the appointment of African bishops and other high officials to the Kenyan branches of the Anglican and Roman Catholic churches. These denominations enjoyed substantial international influence and extensive missionary networks that could be mobilized on behalf of causes taken up by the local clergy.

15. Tamarkin, "Roots of Political Stability," pp. 303–305.

16. No press representatives or other outside observers were permitted to witness the execution. See David Goldsworthy, *Tom Mboya: The Man Kenya Wanted to Forget* (Nairobi: Heinemann, 1982), pp. 279–289, and Norman N. Miller, *Assassination and Political Unity: Kenya*, American Universities Field Staff Reports 1969/8 (Hanover, NH: American Universities Field Staff, 1969).

17. Emmet B. Evans, Jr., "Sources of Socio-Political Instability in an African State: The Case of Kenya's Educated Unemployed," *African Studies Review* 20 (1977), p. 39. See also Stanley Meisler, "Tribal Politics Harass Kenya," *Foreign Affairs* 49 (1970), pp. 111–121.

18. John R. Nellis, *The Ethnic Composition of Leading Kenyan Government Positions* (Uppsala: Scandinavian Institute of African Studies, 1974), pp. 14–15. In addition to the presidency, the offices Nellis surveyed included cabinet ministers, assistant ministers, permanent secretaries, deputy permanent secretaries, provincial commissioners, and district commissioners.

19. See Victor A. Olorunsola, ed., *The Politics of Cultural Sub-Nationalism in Africa* (Garden City: Anchor Books, Doubleday, 1972), especially Donald Rothchild, "Ethnic Inequalities in Kenya," pp. 289–321. The regime responded to this situation in a largely symbolic manner. Secretaries at the University of Nairobi were instructed not to answer telephones in the Kikuyu language, variations on the president's "unified nation" speech were delivered more often, and token appointments of non-Kikuyu were made to higher government posts. Kenyatta proudly pointed to his multiethnic cabinet, although in fact an informal Kikuyu subcabinet continued to make important decisions.

20. The Kenyan constitution guarantees citizenship to anyone born in the country since independence, anyone born in Kenya before independence if one parent was Kenya-born, and any registrant for citizenship married to a Kenya national. A final category of citizenship includes adults who have resided in Kenya for five years and who satisfy tests of language, personal character, and intention of permanent residence. For further details, see Ojwang, *Constitutional Development in Kenya*, pp. 203–208.

21. Mainly small units ostensibly on training rotation from Britian, these troops were usually kept inconspicuously away from the capital but were widely believed to be available if called upon by the civil government.

22. Alan Best and Harm J. de Blij, *African Survey* (New York: Wiley, 1979), pp. 442–444. See also Gary Wasserman, *The Politics of Decolonization: Kenya Europeans and the Land Issue, 1960–1965* (Cambridge: Cambridge University Press,

1976), Chapters 2 and 3, and John W. Harbeson, *Nation-Building in Kenya: The Role of Land Reform* (Evanston: Northwestern University Press, 1973), especially Part 2.

23. Colin Leys, "Development Strategy in Kenya since 1971," *Canadian Journal of African Studies* 13 (1979), p. 299.

24. A term originally employed during the colonial period to distinguish ordinary subsistence farmers from subordinate African participants in the European agricultural economy.

25. International Labour Office (ILO), *Employment, Incomes, and Equality: A Strategy for Increasing Productive Employment in Kenya* (Geneva: ILO, 1972).

26. Irving Kaplan, ed., *Area Handbook for Kenya* (Washington, DC: American University, 1976), pp. 304–307, and Gavin N. Kitching, *Class and Economic Change in Kenya: The Making of an African Petite Bourgeoisie, 1905–1970* (New Haven: Yale University Press, 1980), p. 325. As proof of the relative efficiency of smallholders, Livingstone estimated that in 1967–1968 an average of K£31.75 ($90.70) per acre was earned on settlement-scheme farms with an average size of 7.3 acres. This compares with average earnings of K£5.55 per acre ($15.80) from farms averaging 124.8 acres and K£3.25 ($9.28) from farms averaging 2,979 acres. I. Livingstone, *Rural Development, Employment, and Incomes in Kenya* (Aldershot, Hants., U.K.: Gower, 1986), pp. 230–231. For further analysis of policy changes promoting this differentiation of growth, see Hans Ruthenberg, *African Agricultural Production Development Policy in Kenya, 1952–1965* (Berlin: Springer-Verlag, 1966).

27. This discrepancy in patronage awards was not suffered entirely by other ethnic communities. During his rule, for example, Kenyatta appointed one cabinet minister each from Kikuyu strongholds in Embu, Kitui, Machakos, Meru, Murang'a, and Nyeri while distributing six key cabinet posts among his Kiambu Kikuyu supporters.

28. Mwithaga was singled out for special punishment because he had aroused backbench Kikuyu protest against an attempt by Kenyatta's attorney general, Charles Njonjo, to circumvent parliament by submitting the Kariuki case to a judicial board of inquiry. Following Mwithaga's conviction, riot police were required to disperse a crowd of supporters assembled at the courthouse.

29. "Kenya on the Brink," *Sunday Times* (London), August 10, 17, and 24, 1975.

30. Arthur Hazlewood, *The Economy of Kenya: The Kenyatta Era* (London: Oxford University Press, 1979), pp. 24–28. For statistical evidence of strong economic growth in the late 1970s, see Chapter 5 and also Republic of Kenya, *Economic Survey 1979* (Nairobi: Government Printer, 1979).

31. The ILO recommendations urged government to spend more in the rural areas, to generate more labor-intensive employment, to facilitate both food and export-crop production, to extend land allocations, extension services, and favorable prices to small farmers, and to assist the informal sector of small industrial enterprises instead of concentrating exclusively on large capital-intensive firms. ILO, *Employment, Incomes, and Equality,* "Summary of Recommendations," pp. 9–30. See also Leys, "Development Strategy in Kenya," pp. 305–306.

32. Republic of Kenya, *Employment—The Government Response,* Sessional Paper No. 10 of 1973 (Nairobi: Government Printer, 1973). See also Swainson, *Development of Corporate Capitalism,* p. 184, and Dharam Ghai, Martin Godfrey,

and Franklin List, *Planning of Basic Needs in Kenya* (Geneva: International Labour Office, 1979), pp. 155–161. The World Bank sponsored a group of experts to examine the results of the ILO recommendations. See Hollis Chenery et al., *Redistribution with Growth* (London: Oxford University Press, 1974).

33. Njuguna Ng'ethe, "Income Distribution in Kenya: The Politics of Mystification," in J.F.R. Rweyemamu, ed., *Industrialization and Income Distribution in Africa* (London: Zed Press, 1980), pp. 1–5.

34. E. Crawford and E. Thorbecke, *Employment, Income Distribution, Poverty Alleviation, and Basic Needs in Kenya: Report of an ILO Consulting Mission* (Ithaca: Cornell University, 1978).

35. For early but still useful conceptualizations of interest articulation and aggregation in the comparative study of political development, see Gabriel A. Almond and G. Bingham Powell, Jr., *Comparative Politics: A Developmental Approach* (Boston: Little, Brown, 1966), Chapters 4 and 5.

36. Quoted in Hazlewood, *Economy of Kenya*, p. 13.

37. For assessments of these firms from the standpoint of international dependency theory, see Steven W. Langdon, *Multinational Corporations in the Political Economy of Kenya* (London: Macmillan, 1981), and Raphael Kaplinsky, ed., *Readings on the Multinational Corporation in Kenya* (Nairobi: Oxford University Press, 1978). Case studies of Kenyan multinationals are provided in Swainson, *Development of Corporate Capitalism*, pp. 250–284, and Hazlewood, *Economy of Kenya*, pp. 59–65. For broader views on the role of multinationals in developing countries, see Joseph LaPalombara, *Multinational Corporations and Developing Countries* (New York: Conference Board, 1979), and V. N. Balasubramanyam, *Multinational Enterprises and the Third World* (London: Ditchlong, 1980).

38. Langdon, *Multinational Corporations*, pp. 34 and 194. Prior to 1972, international firms earned 60 percent of Kenya's value added in manufacturing and local enterprises, 40 percent. More recently, outright foreign ownership has steeply declined as government and private parties have increased their participation in these enterprises.

39. Swainson, *Development of Corporate Capitalism*, p. 235.

40. Guy Arnold, *Modern Kenya* (London: Longman, 1981), p. 235, and World Bank, *World Development Report 1986* (New York: Oxford University Press, 1986), p. 220. U.S. assistance totaled $30 million in 1978 and rose to $50 million in 1979. After Britain, the United States became Kenya's second-largest source of private capital in 1978, with $110 million invested in the country.

41. For background on these arrangements, see Norman N. Miller, "The United Nations Environment Programme," and Norman N. Miller and James F. Hornig, *Habitat: The New UN Initiative in Human Settlements*, American Universities Field Staff Reports (Hanover, NH: American Universities Field Staff, 1979 and 1981).

42. In addition to the 1975 London *Sunday Times* series, instances of corruption in Kenyatta's Kenya are reported in Tamarkin, "Roots of Political Stability," pp. 303–307; Goran Hyden, Robert Jackson, and John Okumu, *Development Administration: The Kenyan Experience* (Nairobi: Oxford University Press, 1970), pp. 31–37 and p. 60; Arnold, *Modern Kenya*, pp. 84–85; and Norman N. Miller, *The Indian Ocean: Traditional Trade on a Smuggler's Sea*, American Universities Field

Staff Reports 1980/7 (Hanover, NH: American Universities Field Staff, 1980). For contemporaneous general discussions of corruption in Third World settings, see R. Wraith and E. Simpkins, *Corruption in Developing Countries* (New York: Norton, 1963); Joseph Nye, "Corruption and Political Development: A Cost-Benefit Analysis," *American Political Science Review* 61 (1967), pp. 417–427; James C. Scott, "Corruption, Machine Politics, and Political Change," *American Political Science Review* 63 (1969), pp. 1142–1158, and *Comparative Political Corruption* (Englewood Cliffs: Prentice-Hall 1972).

43. See Kenneth King, *The African Artisan: Education and the Informal Sector in Kenya* (London: Heinemann, 1979), pp. 48–65. For a recent comparative assessment of local entrepreneurs in Botswana, Côte d'Ivoire, Ghana, Kenya, Malawi, and Tanzania, see Keith Marsden, *African Entrepreneurs: Pioneers of Development*, International Finance Corporation Discussion Paper No. 9 (Washington, DC: World Bank, 1990). With regard to the illegal aspects of small-scale entrepreneurship in Kenya, not all crimes are viewed as equally criminal. Petty smuggling, street hawking, and beer brewing are considered normal activities, and poaching is treated only slightly more seriously. In contrast, outright theft by civil servants, stealing from primary cooperative societies, and shoplifting in retail markets are abhorred. The more overt the offense and the more damaging to the interests of the poor it is perceived to be, the greater the public outrage. Mob beatings of thieves caught in the act are not uncommon in rural and urban Kenya.

44. See, for example, Raphael Kaplinsky, "Capitalist Accumulation in the Periphery: Kenya," in Martin Fransman, ed., *Industry and Accumulation in Africa* (London: Heinemann, 1982), pp. 193–221, and Steven W. Langdon, "The State and Capitalism in Kenya," *Review of African Political Economy* 8 (1977), pp. 90–98. André Gunder Frank originally proposed international dependency as a root cause of Latin American developmental problems in *Capitalism and Underdevelopment in Latin America: Historical Studies of Chile and Brazil* (New York: Monthly Review Press, 1967).

45. Public complaints were occasionally lodged against MPs who were too busy with their business ventures even to attend legislative sessions. See, for example, *Sunday Nation* (Nairobi), September 10, 1977.

46. See Yeager, *Tanzania*, especially Chapters 2 and 4, and Martin R. Doornbos, "Changing Perspectives on Conflict and Integration in Uganda," in G. N. Uzoigwe, ed., *Uganda: The Dilemma of Nationhood* (New York: NOK, 1982), pp. 313–332, especially pp. 322–329. In the Arusha Declaration of 1967, Tanzanian president Julius Nyerere defined *ujamaa* in terms of the country's domestic and foreign-policy commitment to democratic socialism and self-reliance. Three years later, President Milton Obote proposed a similar doctrine in his Common Man's Charter for Uganda. The Tanzanian version of this ideology was later blamed for much of Tanzania's economic decline in the 1970s and 1980s, and Obote's attempted move to the left was so unpopular in Uganda that it became the proximate cause of his downfall in January 1971.

CHAPTER 3

1. See W. H. Whitely, ed., *Language in Kenya* (Nairobi: Oxford University Press, 1974). Kiswahili and English, serving as effective lingua francas, have largely eliminated these barriers to cross-cultural communication.

2. The number of children a woman would bear if she were to reproduce at the average rate for each age-group through which she passes from puberty to menopause.

3. Allen C. Kelley and Charles E. Nobbe, *Kenya at the Demographic Turning Point? Hypotheses and a Research Agenda*, World Bank Discussion Paper 107 (Washington, DC: World Bank, 1990), p. 6; World Bank, *World Development Report 1992* (New York: Oxford University Press, 1992), pp. 268 and 270; and U.S. Census Bureau estimates.

4. Between 1979 and 1988, for example, USAID transferred more family planning assistance to Kenya than to any other African country except Egypt. This aid totaled $32.5 million in mission-level support (i.e., not including centrally or regionally allocated funds). U.S. General Accounting Office, *Foreign Assistance: AID's Population Program*, GAO/NSIAD-90-112 (Washington: U.S. General Accounting Office, May 1990), p. 22. After years of mainly rhetorical expressions of concern for family planning through child spacing, moreover, the Kenya government responded to a sudden presidential change of heart on the matter. Beginning in 1984, a series of policy guidelines, strategy statements, and surveys was prepared that led to the incorporation of family planning activities into the 1989–1993 national development plan. See, for example, Republic of Kenya, *Population Policy Guidelines*, Sessional Paper No. 4 of 1984 (Nairobi: National Council for Population and Development, Office of the Vice-President and Ministry of Home Affairs, 1984). For largely political reasons in this strongly pronatalist society, the plan's comparatively high level of commitment to fertility control is still couched in cautious terms: "While a rapidly growing population has been regarded as a constraint to development and to the provision of health, education and other social services, it should be realised that the greatest resource this country has is its people. Furthermore, it has been established that higher levels of education and incomes lead to a decline in population growth. Therefore, whereas family planning programmes will continue to be expanded and intensified, greater emphasis will be laid on the generation of increased wealth" (Republic of Kenya, *Development Plan for the Period 1989 to 1993* [Nairobi: Government Printer, 1988], p. 35).

5. For further analysis of the relative significance of these factors, see Kelley and Nobbe, *Kenya at the Demographic Turning Point?* pp. 7–71.

6. U.S. Census Bureau estimates. Average life expectancy is also expected to increase from 57.6 years in 1980 to 68.7 years by 2000. For older studies of Kenya's exploding population, see Simeon H. Ominde, *Land and Population Movements in Kenya* (London: Heinemann, 1968); Norman N. Miller, *Population Review 1970: Kenya*, and *Politics of Population*, American Universities Field Staff Reports 1970/1 and 2 (Hanover, NH: American Universities Field Staff, 1970); J. C. Likimani, *Country Profiles: Kenya* (New York: Population Council, May 1971); Republic of Kenya, *Kenya Fertility Survey, 1978*, Volumes 1 and 2 (Nairobi: Central Bureau of Statistics, 1980); Frank L. Mott and Susan H. Mott, *Kenya's Record Population Growth: A Dilemma of Development*, Population Bulletin (Washington, DC: Population Reference Bureau, October 1980); United Nations International Children's Emergency Fund (UNICEF), *Country Profile: Kenya 1981* (Nairobi: UNICEF East Africa Regional Office, 1981); and Rashid Faruguee, "Fertility and Its Trends in Kenya," *Rural Africana* 13 (1982), pp. 25–48.

7. U.S. Census Bureau estimate.

8. World Bank, *World Development Report 1981* (New York: Oxford University Press, 1981), p. 172; and World Bank, *World Development Report 1992*, p. 278.

9. In 1990, 49.9 percent of the Kenyan population occupied the 0–14-year age-group, and another 2.8 percent was 65 years or older. World Bank, *World Development Report 1992*, p. 268.

10. UNICEF, *Country Profile: Kenya 1981*, pp. 3–5; Republic of Kenya, *Development Plan for the Period 1989 to 1993*, p. 34; and World Bank, *World Development Report 1992*, p. 220. For additional work force data and analysis, see Republic of Kenya, *Economic Management and Renewed Growth*, Sessional Paper No. 1 of 1986 (Nairobi: Government Printer, 1986), pp. 5–25, and Republic of Kenya, *Economic Survey 1990* (Nairobi: Central Bureau of Statistics, Ministry of Planning and National Development, May 1990), pp. 33–45.

11. Republic of Kenya, *Demographic and Health Survey 1989* (Nairobi: National Council for Population and Development and Ministry of Home Affairs and National Heritage, 1989), p. 22, cited in Kelley and Nobbe, *Kenya at the Demographic Turning Point?* p. 6. Education, wage employment, and the comparatively independent status of urban women seem most consistently to account for these differences in fertility rate. For convincing earlier arguments to this effect, see Susan H. Mott and Frank L. Mott, "Rapid Population Growth in Kenya," paper presented at the Twenty-Third Annual Meeting of the African Studies Association, Philadelphia, October 1980, and "Kenya's Record Population Growth," pp. 9–28.

12. Land Development Resources Centre, *Kenya: Profile of Agricultural Potential* (Surbiton, U.K.: British Overseas Development Administration, 1986), p. 1.

13. Republic of Kenya, *Statistical Abstract 1989* (Nairobi: Central Bureau of Statistics, Ministry of Planning and National Development, 1989), p. 92, and official estimates cited in Uma Lele and Steven W. Stone, *Population Pressure, the Environment, and Agricultural Intensification: Variations on the Boserup Hypothesis*, Managing Agricultural Development in Africa Discussion Paper 4 (Washington, DC: World Bank, 1989), p. 54.

14. World Bank, *World Development Report 1992*, p. 224. Continuing food dependency, albeit at lower overall levels of need (or perhaps availability), is suggested by the fact that in 1987 the ratio of purchased to donated food imports was 274,000 to 107,000 metric tons. World Bank, *World Development Report 1989* (New York: Oxford University Press, 1989), p. 170.

15. Cited in Lele and Stone, *Population Pressure*, p. 30.

16. In October 1984, these other countries were Niger and strife-torn Sudan, Ethiopia, and Mozambique. For a socioeconomic commentary on this situation, see Janet Raloff, "Africa's Famine: The Human Dimension," *Science News* 127 (May 11, 1985): pp. 299–301.

17. Two U.S. social scientists who happened to be working in Kenya as management consultants studied the 1984–1985 relief program and attributed its success to a strong presidential commitment that enabled public and private agencies to plan and execute a decisive, but limited, adaptable campaign targeted at those areas most affected by the drought. John M. Cohen and David B. Lewis,

"Role of Government in Combatting Food Shortages: Lessons from Kenya 1984–1985," unpublished paper, Ithaca, NY, and Cambridge, MA, 1985. See also Thomas E. Downing, Kangethe W. Gitu, and Crispin M. Kamau, eds., *Coping with Drought in Kenya: National and Local Strategies* (Boulder: Lynne Rienner, 1989).

18. These pilot initiatives were collectively termed the Special Rural Development Programme, and donors included the European Economic Community, the World Bank's International Development Association, Britain, the Netherlands, Norway, and the United States.

19. Steve Wiggens, "The Planning and Management of Integrated Rural Development in Drylands: Early Lessons from Kenya's Arid and Semi-Arid Lands Programmes," *Public Administration and Development* 5 (1985), p. 91.

20. ASAL development was incorporated into the 1989–1993 development plan as a heavily donor-financed component of a purportedly decentralized District Focus for Rural Development. See Republic of Kenya, *Arid and Semi-Arid Land Development in Kenya: The Framework for Implementation Programme Planning and Evaluation* (Nairobi: Prudential Printers, May 1979); Republic of Kenya, *Plan of Action for the Integration of the ASAL Programme into District Focus* (Nairobi: Rural Planning Division, Ministry of Finance and Planning, July 1985); Republic of Kenya, *Economic Management for Renewed Growth*, pp. 114–115; and Republic of Kenya, *Development Plan for the Period 1989 to 1993*, pp. 132–138 and 174–191. With financial support supplied by the Canadian-based International Fund for Agricultural Development, in 1988 the government invited the Institute for African Development at Cornell University to propose a detailed strategy for economically and environmentally sustainable ASAL development. For the initial products of this exercise, see Institute for African Development, *Development in the Arid and Semi-Arid Areas of Kenya: Report of a Workshop Convened at Cornell University, January 27–30, 1988* (Ithaca: Cornell University, 1988).

21. See, for example, National Environment and Human Settlements Secretariat (NES), *Endangered Resources for Development—Strategy Conference for the Management and Protection of Kenya's Plant Communities: Forests, Woodlands, Bushlands, Savannahs, and Aquatic Communities* (Nairobi: NES, USAID, and U.S. National Park Service, June 1984). Forested lands, the source of some 75 percent of Kenya's fuel, are being rapidly depleted. The first definitive evidence of the extent and speed of this destruction became apparent in the early 1980s from satellite images enhancing earlier aerial photographic data. It was found, for instance, that the lush Mau Forest had lost 30 percent of its cover over the previous decade. In semiarid lower Meru District, woodlands and bushlands decreased from 69 percent of total coverage in 1948 to 11 percent by 1982. NES, *Endangered Resources*, p. 4, and Land Resources Development Centre, *Kenya*, p. 24. Experts estimate that at such loss rates "Kenya will be denuded of all indigenous forests outside strictly protected areas by the end of the century" (NES, *Endangered Resources*, p. 3). A view of this predicament from the grass-roots level is offered in Mohamud Abdi Jama, *Rural Energy in an Arid Sub-Location of Meru District, Kenya*, African-Caribbean Institute African Natural Resources Working Paper (Hanover, NH: African-Caribbean Institute, 1991).

22. See Rodger Yeager and Norman N. Miller, *Wildlife, Wild Death: Land Use and Survival in Eastern Africa* (Albany: State University of New York Press,

1986), pp. 68–114. In all, 38,491 square kilometers (15,796 square miles), or 7 percent of Kenya's total land area, are set aside for thirty-three national parks and reserves in which human settlement is prohibited. Together with commercial poaching, which seems to have reached nearly uncontrollable levels, ever-higher settlement densities in the buffer zones bordering these protected areas now pose serious challenges to the survival of invaluable and irreplaceable indigenous flora and fauna. The economic costs of these trends, mainly in terms of lost tourist revenues, are discussed in Chapter 5.

23. Three factors, all related to population pressures and land abuse, may be creating a "drought-feedback" system of permanent aridity in Kenya and other African countries—a reduction in the soil's ability to retain water, alterations in land surface reflectance, and the elimination of biogenic substances in rain clouds that permit ice formation. For a summary discussion of the drought-feedback hypothesis, see Stefi Weisburd and Janet Raloff, "Climate and Africa: Why the Land Goes Dry," *Science News* 127 (May 4, 1985), p. 284.

24. For example, a large amount of coverage is annually given over to Kenya's deforestation problems in the country's leading daily newspapers, the *Standard* and the *Daily Nation*, notably to coincide with National Tree Planting Day, April 18. In the middle 1980s, the Nairobi-based Public Law Institute included environmental law reform as one of its most urgent priorities. Public Law Institute (PLI), *Policies, Programmes, and Prospects: 1984–86, A Short Term Plan* (Nairobi: PLI, April 1984), Chapter 3 and especially pp. 25–40.

25. In 1984, a study was conducted in preparation for the development of a national conservation strategy for Kenya as part of a movement led by the Swiss-based International Union for Conservation of Nature and Natural Resources (IUCN). In its survey of relevant institutional resources, the report identified seventeen government ministries and agencies, two universities, nine multilateral development organizations, ten bilateral donors, twenty-three national non-governmental organizations (NGOs), and twenty-one international NGOs. Since that time, the number of such organizations has increased (for NGOs, significantly) in each of these categories. World Wildlife Fund/IUCN Regional Office for Eastern Africa, *Kenya: Natural Resources Expertise Profile* (Geneva: Conservation for Development Centre, IUCN, August 1984), pp. 13–35.

26. J. B. Ojwang, *Constitutional Development in Kenya: Institutional Adaptation and Social Change* (Nairobi: African Centre for Technology Studies Press, 1990), p. 169.

27. John Lonsdale, "Mau Maus of the Mind: Making Mau Mau and Remaking Kenya," *Journal of African History* 31 (1990), p. 417.

28. For an excellent case study of this problem in Western Province, see David K. Leonard, *Reaching the Peasant Farmer: Organization Theory and Practice in Kenya* (Chicago: University of Chicago Press, 1977), especially pp. 173–194.

29. One instance of such assistance involves a compensation scheme for Maasai herders in the vicinity of Amboseli National Park. To encourage conservation of Amboseli's grazing land and game animals, the government has shared some of the park's tourist earnings with the Maasai and compensated them for cattle lost to wild predators. Watering points have been established outside the park to lessen livestock pressures within. In the early years of the program, these

measures contributed to a doubling of the Amboseli rhinoceros population and to further increases in elephant, buffalo, and migratory ungulates. See Lloyd Timberlake, "Guarding Africa's Renewable Resources," in Robert J. Berg and Jennifer Seymour Whitaker, eds., *Strategies for African Development* (Berkeley: University of California Press, 1986), p. 124. Ironically, some of this growth is now reviving serious human/wildlife competition.

30. Local editorial opinion has somewhat derisively captured the central reason for this decision: "At the very heart of the matter is a subject we hold dear: the country's vaunted foreign exchange earner, tourism. Should the country be rid of its wildlife, especially the exotic elephant and rhinoceros, we would only have agriculture to turn to. In other words we would become strictly a one-legged economy. God forbid!" (*Daily Nation* [Nairobi], May 25, 1989).

31. Garrett Hardin, "The Tragedy of the Commons," *Science* 162 (December 13, 1968), pp. 1243–1248.

32. For examples drawn from partly semiarid Machakos District, see Betty Nafuna Wamalwa, *Learning from the Past: Traditional Land Management Systems in Kenya,* African-Caribbean Institute African Natural Resources Working Paper (Hanover, NH: African-Caribbean Institute, 1991). For empirical evidence of factors working against such adaptations, see Frank E. Bernard and Derrick J. Thom, "Population Pressure and Human Carrying Capacity in Selected Locations of Machakos and Kitui Districts," *Journal of Developing Areas* 15 (1981), pp. 381–406. These limits are placed in historical perspective in Douglas Johnson and David Anderson, eds., *The Ecology of Survival: Case Studies from Northeastern African History* (London and Boulder: Lester Crock Academic Publishing and Westview Press, 1988), pp. 193–260.

33. *Daily Nation* (Nairobi), April 18, 1986.

34. In an economic sense, ASAL dwellers have much in common with urban residents in that both groups must rely on cash incomes to make ends meet.

35. For recent indicators of these advances, see World Bank, *World Development Report 1992,* pp. 272 and 280.

36. U.S. Bureau of the Census, *Recent HIV Seroprevalence Levels by Country: February 1991,* Research Notes 3 (Washington, DC: Center for International Research, U.S. Bureau of the Census, 1991), p. 9.

37. Based on information collected by the U.S. Census Bureau and cited in USAID, *HIV Infection and AIDS: Report to Congress on the USAID Program for Prevention and Control* (Washington, DC: USAID, May 1991), pp. 30, 32, and 33. In Uganda, 76 percent of high-risk rural populations are estimated to be HIV-seroprevalent, while in Tanzania the rate of high-risk rural infection is 38.7 percent. Most rural residents are less susceptible to HIV, although seroprevalence rates in this group have risen to 12.3 percent in Uganda and 5.4 percent in Tanzania. In Kenya, rural HIV seroprevalence is still only about 1 percent.

38. Republic of Kenya, *Development Plan for the Period 1989 to 1993,* p. 244. An exception to this inaction is what has been termed one of Africa's "earliest and best publicised AIDS education programmes with women prostitutes" in Nairobi. Panos Institute, *AIDS and the Third World* (London: Panos Institute, 1988), p. 162. Amid much fanfare, in 1990 the government announced the

development by the Kenya Medical Research Institute of a new drug, Kemron, to reverse AIDS symptoms. Despite considerable skepticism on the part of the international medical community, clinical trials were planned in Cameroon, Tanzania, Zambia, and Zimbabwe. Under strong pressure from African-American HIV/AIDS patients and health practitioners, in late 1992 the U.S. National Institutes of Health announced that they too would test Kemron.

39. The United States, for example, spent slightly more than $1 million on HIV/AIDS education and prevention projects in 1990, up from an allocation of about $712,000 in 1989. USAID, *HIV Infection and AIDS*, p. 30, and *USAID Support for Community-Based HIV/AIDS Prevention Activities: Report to the Senate Appropriations Committee* (Washington, DC: USAID, May 1991), Appendix B, pp. 2–3.

40. Peter O. Way and Karen Stanecki, *The Demographic Impact of AIDS in Sub-Sahara Africa* (Washington, DC: Center for International Research, U.S. Bureau of the Census, 1990), p. 1. This model was devised by a research team sponsored by the U.S. State Department's Interagency Working Group on AIDS Models and Methods. The team was composed of mathematicians, systems analysts, and demographers from Los Alamos National Laboratories, Merriam Laboratories, the University of Illinois, and the Census Bureau.

41. For further discussion of these contingencies, see Anne V. Akeroyd, "Sociocultural Aspects of AIDS in Africa: Topics, Methods, and Some Lacunae," paper presented at the conference "AIDS in Africa and the Caribbean: The Documentation of an Epidemic," Columbia University, New York, November 1990; Barbara Boyle Torrey et al., "Epidemiology of HIV and AIDS in Africa: Emerging Issues and Social Implications," in Norman Miller and Richard C. Rockwell, eds., *AIDS in Africa: The Social and Policy Impact* (Lewiston, NY: Edwin Mellen Press, 1988), pp. 31–54; Norman Miller and Manuel Carballo, "AIDS: A Disease of Development?" *AIDS and Society: International Research and Policy Bulletin* 1 (1989), pp. 1 and 21; and Rodger Yeager, "Historical and Ecological Ramifications for AIDS in Eastern and Central Africa," in Miller and Rockwell, *AIDS in Africa*, pp. 71–83.

42. Hyden and Lanegran correctly attribute the current absence of organized power sharing in Kenya and other African countries to a lack of class-based "civic activism" in the demand structures of African political systems: "The predominant pattern of articulating issues has been through informal, patron-client relations rather than organizations representing specific interests. The result is that politics in African countries have lost much of a public character, a tendency often exacerbated by the presence of only one political party which regards itself as above public criticism. The rulers, their ideology and their organization have typically been spared open public criticism" (Goran Hyden and Kim Lanegran, "Mapping the Politics of AIDS in Eastern Africa," *AIDS and Society: International Research and Policy Bulletin* 2 [1991], p. 12).

43. See John D. Kesby, *The Cultural Regions of East Africa* (London: Academic Press, 1977), Chapters 1–5.

44. The largest groups in the Abaluhya cluster are the Bukusu, the Maragoli, and the Bunyore. Others include the Isukha, the Idakho, the Kabras, the Bunyala, the Marama, the Wanga, the Kisa, the Bukhayo, the Marach, the Butsotso, the Tiriki, the Nyangore, and the Itesio.

45. In addition to the Tugen, the Kalenjin ethnic complex consists of the Nandi, the Kipsigis, the Elgeyo, the Marakwet, the Pokot, the Kamasya, the Sapei, and the Koney.

46. This generalization is qualified by the over-representation of some pastoral groups in parliament as a result of district and constituency boundaries drawn at independence. See Charles Hornsby, "The Social Structure of the National Assembly in Kenya, 1963–83," *Journal of Modern African Studies* 27 (1989), pp. 283–285.

47. Ouko's death touched off a political firestorm that fundamentally altered the presidency of Daniel arap Moi. (See Chapter 4).

48. For a firsthand account of the trial, see Blaine Harden's coverage in *The Washington Post National Weekly Edition*, March 2, 1987.

49. These attacks were led by ex-soldiers and civilians fleeing a clan-based civil war in Somalia that finally led to the downfall of President Siad Mohamed Barre. In addition to highway robberies and murders, the bandits turned to commercial game poaching. Reacting against this highly visible threat to international tourism, the Kenya government mounted an antipoaching offensive in which more than two dozen *shifta* were killed. The antipoaching effort had the undesirable side effect of forcing *shifta* out of the northeastern game areas and closer to human settlements.

50. *Daily Nation* (Nairobi), October 22, 1990. The official justification for this hard line was that foreigners were engaging in illegal activities and using Kenya as a base of operations for attempts to overthrow the Rwandese government of Major General Juvenal Habyarimana.

51. *News from Africa Watch* (Washington, New York, and London), December 11, 1990.

52. Kenya is a party to the United Nations Convention Relating to the Status of Refugees. Articles 32 and 33 of this treaty forbid the expulsion of refugees without due process of law. In spite of Kenyan attempts to prevent further inflows from Somalia, victims of the Somali civil war continued to arrive and were placed in hastily constructed border camps. In early 1992, the Kenya government informed the resident UN High Commissioner for Refugees that it lacked the resources to assist these displaced people. After a June visit to Wajir and El-Wak, U.S. Ambassador Smith Hempstone confirmed the presence in northeastern Kenya of more than four hundred thousand starving refugees. See Smith Hempstone, "Misery and Death, This Time in Kenya," *The Washington Post National Weekly Edition*, August 31–September 6, 1992.

As for Kenya citizens of Somali ethnic origin, the government began a campaign in November 1989 to screen all such persons above the age of eighteen. They were instructed to report to screening centers with proof of citizenship or permission to reside in Kenya. Roadblocks were set up to ratify and extend these identity checks.

53. Bethwell Ogot, *Historical Dictionary of Kenya* (Metuchen, NJ, and London: Scarecrow Press, 1981), p. 63.

54. Simeon W. Chilungu, "Kenya—Recent Developments and Challenges," *Cultural Survival Quarterly* 9 (1985), p. 17.

55. Hornsby, "The Social Structure of the National Assembly," p. 294.

56. World Bank, *World Development Report 1992*, pp. 218 and 285. In this assessment, poverty is measured according to comparisons of estimated per capita gross national product.

57. UN International Comparison Program estimates of GDP per capita, cited in ibid., p. 262.

58. Irving Kaplan, ed., *Area Handbook for Kenya* (Washington, DC: American University, 1976), p. 114.

59. KShs. stands for Kenya shillings. Twenty KShs. equal one K£.

60. Based on the results of Kenya's 1986 Urban Labour Force Survey, reported in Republic of Kenya, *Economic Survey 1990*, p. 36.

61. *New York Times*, December 2, 1990.

62. Republic of Kenya, *Statistical Abstract 1989*, p. 99.

63. For background information and analysis on these continuing problems, see Marc H. Ross, "Political Alienation, Participation, and Ethnicity in the Nairobi Urban Area," in John N. Paden, ed., *Values, Identities, and National Integration* (Evanston: Northwestern University Press, 1980), pp. 173–181, and Herbert H. Werlin, *Governing an African City: A Study of Nairobi* (New York: Africana Publishing House, 1974).

64. Men's control over agricultural incomes extends to the estimated 40 percent of farm holdings that are managed by women because of male labor migration.

65. Julius Gould and William L. Kolb, eds., *A Dictionary of the Social Sciences*. (New York: Free Press, 1964), p. 60.

66. The government has reported that between 1985 and 1989 the enrollment of girls in primary schools increased by 12.5 percent and in secondary schools by 36 percent. In 1989–1990, 6,550 females, or 42.4 percent of the total, were enrolled in primary teacher–training colleges. At other postsecondary levels the ratios of females to males were as follows: diploma programs, 410 to 1,123 (36.5 percent); undergraduate programs, 7,264 to 17,000 (42.7 percent); and graduate programs, 444 to 1,331 (33.3 percent). Republic of Kenya, *Economic Survey 1990*, pp. 173–177.

67. Ibid., p. 181.

68. Daphne Topouzis, "Wangarí Maathai: Empowering the Grass Roots," *Africa Report* 35 (November–December 1990), p. 31.

69. *New York Times*, November 26, 1989.

70. Ibid., February 11, 1990.

71. These groups include the Maendeleo ya Wanawake and the National Council of Women of Kenya, together with the Young Women's Christian Association, Media Women of Kenya, the East African Women's League, the Kenya Association of University Women, the Business and Professional Women's Association, the Kenya Women's Trust, and the Development Land Committee. Bessie House-Midamba, "The United Nations Decade: Political Empowerment or Increased Marginalization for Kenyan Women?" *Africa Today* 37 (1990), pp. 42–44.

72. Ibid., p. 40. In the 1992 general election, six women were elected to parliament. The potential implications of this increase are discussed in Chapter 4.

73. Republic of Kenya, *Economic Survey 1990*, p. 172. Since the first edition of this book was written, Kenyatta College has been separated from the

University of Nairobi and granted full university status with an emphasis on teacher preparation. Egerton College of Agriculture, located at Njoro, near Nakuru, has been expanded and renamed Egerton University. Moi University was established in 1984 in the Rift Valley town of Eldoret, about 40 kilometers (24 miles) from President Moi's birthplace. By 1990 it housed 3,173 students, as compared with 12,428 at the University of Nairobi, 7,360 at Kenyatta University, and 3,841 at Egerton University. Ibid., pp. 175 and 177. At the same time, "constituent" colleges are being attached to major public institutions. The Jomo Kenyatta University College of Agriculture and Technology has become a constituent of Kenyatta University and Maseno University College a part of Moi University. Formed by merging Siriba Teachers' College and Maseno Government Training Institute, the Maseno campus was established near Kisumu in 1990 to provide higher-education facilities for the Luo and Abaluhya areas of western Kenya. In its first year of operation, Maseno enrolled 1,600 Bachelor of Education students in sixteen academic departments staffed by ninety-one lecturers and professors. *Equator News* (Maseno University College), No. 1, November 1991, pp. 8, 13, and 16–17. By the early 1990s, the only populous part of the country without a university or a constituent college was the coastal region—an omission highly irritating to the largely Muslim residents of Kenya's second-largest city, Mombasa.

74. Republic of Kenya, *Economic Survey 1985* (Nairobi: Central Bureau of Statistics, Ministry of Finance and Planning, May 1985), p. 192, and Republic of Kenya, *Economic Survey 1990*, p. 175.

75. Republic of Kenya, *Development Plan for the Period 1989 to 1993*, p. 212.

76. For historical perspectives on the emergence and growth of these problems, see David Court and Dharam P. Ghai, eds., *Education, Society, and Development: New Perspectives from Kenya* (Nairobi: Oxford University Press, 1974), especially Kenneth Prewitt, "Education and Social Equality in Kenya," pp. 199–216. See also James R. Sheffield, *Education in Kenya: An Historical Study* (New York: Columbia University Teachers College Press, 1973). For national comparisons in eastern Africa, see David Court, "The Education System as a Response to Inequality in Tanzania and Kenya," *Journal of Modern African Studies* 14 (1976), pp. 661–690.

77. Republic of Kenya, *Development Plan for the Period 1989 to 1993*, p. 259.

78. Ibid., p. 237.

79. World Bank, *World Development Report 1985* (New York: Oxford University Press, 1985), p. 220; Republic of Kenya, *Economic Survey 1985*, p. 195; and Republic of Kenya, *Economic Survey 1990*, pp. 178–179. On a more favorable note, the number of first visits to family planning clinics rose from about 65,000 in 1981 to almost 340,000 by 1987. Republic of Kenya, *Statistical Abstract 1989*, p. 200.

80. Extrapolated from UNICEF, *Country Profile: Kenya 1981*, p. 20. Also see Norman N. Miller, *Traditional Medicine in East Africa*, American Universities Field Staff Reports 1980/22 (Hanover, NH: American Universities Field Staff, 1980).

81. Republic of Kenya, *Economic Survey 1981* (Nairobi: Central Bureau of Statistics, Ministry of Finance and Economic Planning, May 1981), p. 207, and Republic of Kenya, *Economic Survey 1990*, p. 179. Other medical personnel include more than thirty thousand nurses, clinical officers, and public health technicians collectively arrayed against an imposing number of serious diseases. Malaria,

carried by mosquitos, is the country's leading malady and is thought to be hyper-endemic at altitudes below 1,500 meters (5,000 feet). Pneumonia and similar upper respiratory ailments account for the highest rates of hospitalization. Venereal diseases are among the most difficult to treat because of the frequent movement of truck drivers, soldiers, migratory workers, and other carriers. Diarrheal diseases and intestinal disorders are common among children, while the main causes of childhood death are measles, gastroenteritis, colitis, kwashiorkor, tetanus, scabies, and whooping cough. Schistosomiasis, transmitted by freshwater snails, affects people living near lakeshores and irrigation projects. Leprosy is still of major concern in western Kenya and along the Indian Ocean coast. Nomadic peoples are susceptible to eye infections such as trachoma and to trypanosomiasis (sleeping sickness), which is carried by the bush-dwelling tsetse fly. Endemic to coastal areas, filariasis is spread by black flies, mosquitos, and mangrove flies. In recent years, tuberculosis has become a major urban problem.

82. Republic of Kenya, *Development Plan for the Period 1989 to 1993*, p. 244.

83. Instead of merely projecting targets and expenditures for the justice system, the 1989–1993 plan admonishes: "As the nation develops both socially and economically, it faces challenges from new types of criminal activity and juvenile delinquency arising from social and economic forces. While the police force has the normal responsibility for the prevention and elimination of criminal activities, it should be appreciated that crime prevention must begin both at the home and community levels, for it is only there that early tendencies to crime can be curbed" (Ibid., p. 250).

84. As many as fifty thousand juveniles belong to Nairobi's street society. Girls are often organized into groups of prostitutes, and boys band together for petty jobs and begging, scavenging food, and minor crime. The United Nations has identified the breakdown of traditional family structures as part of the problem in its estimate that up to 75 percent of the city's squatter families are headed by single women. *New York Times*, January 2, 1991.

85. B. E. Kipkorir, "Towards a Cultural Policy for Kenya: Some Views," unpublished Discussion Paper No. 131, Institute of African Studies, University of Nairobi, 1980, p. 34. See also Kivuto Ndeti, *Cultural Policy in Kenya* (Paris: UNESCO Press, 1975), and Ngugi wa Thiong'o, *Decolonising the Mind: The Politics of Language in African Literature* (London: Heinemann, 1986).

86. See, for example, *The Weekly News* (Nairobi), January 4, 1991.

87. Republic of Kenya, *Economic Survey 1990*, p. 170.

88. *Detained: A Writer's Prison Diary* (London: Heinemann, 1981) and *Devil on the Cross* (London: Heinemann, 1982).

89. That is, they are losing what Hyden has termed the "exit option" of African rural dwellers—the choice of returning to subsistence production on land secure under traditional tenure to avoid the imposition of unacceptable social, political, and economic conditions from above. See Goran Hyden, *Beyond Ujamaa in Tanzania: Underdevelopment and an Uncaptured Peasantry* (Berkeley: University of California Press, 1980) and *No Shortcuts to Progress: African Development Management in Perspective* (Berkeley: University of California Press, 1983).

CHAPTER 4

1. According to these amendments, presidential elections would eventually be "by direct, universal and equal suffrage." The candidate who received 25 percent of the vote in each of at least five provinces and amassed the largest number of votes would be declared president, no matter which party won the majority of seats in parliament. This raised the possibility of a parliamentary vote of no confidence if a sitting president were to opt to appoint a cabinet from one or more minority parties.

Perhaps to offset the rising tide of public alienation from KANU and from Moi, the amendments also limited a president to two five-year terms and proposed the replacement of the vice president by a prime minister, appointed by the president, to share power with him. The prime minister was to "keep the president fully informed concerning the general conduct of the government of Kenya and . . . furnish him with such information as he may require with respect to any particular matter relating to the government of Kenya." Unless also an MP, the president would be unable to intervene in parliamentary affairs. The idea of two executive offices was originally proposed by Attorney General Amos Wako and endorsed by President Moi as a way of defusing complaints about excessive concentration of power. Taken together, the amendments were seen as offering a more balanced power structure by limiting presidential power over domestic affairs and subjecting presidential candidates to public scrutiny on a nationwide basis. *Weekly Review* (Nairobi), March 6, 1992. After several prominent KANU leaders opposed the plan, presumably because of aspirations to the vice presidency, the president withdrew his support, and the motion apparently died.

2. A thorough study of this transition is provided in Joseph Karimi and Phillip Ochieng, *The Kenyatta Succession* (Nairobi: Transafrica Book Distributors, 1980).

3. Seven of Kenyatta's ministers and fifteen assistant ministers lost their parliamentary seats in the 1978 election.

4. For further notes on Daniel arap Moi's rise to power, see John Dickie and Alan Rake, *Who's Who in Africa* (London: African Buyer and Trader, 1973), p. 203.

5. A new religious atmosphere permeated Kenya. Church music filled the radio waves, meetings were opened with prayers, and MPs handed out bibles (or, if constituents suspected them of being less than Christian or less than always sober, received them).

6. In addition, oil prices rose dramatically between 1979 and 1980, from K£145.7 million ($383.4 million) to K£220 million ($579 million). About half of the difference was recouped from sales of refined petroleum products to other countries, but the balance equaled total earnings from coffee exports. Guy Arnold, *Modern Kenya* (London: Longman, 1981), p. 32.

7. *Standard* (Nairobi), December 22, 1981.

8. For additional information on the unsettled politics of this period, see Colin Legum, ed., *Africa Contemporary Record: Annual Survey and Documents, 1980–1981* (New York: Africana Publishing House, 1981), pp. B215–B238.

9. *Africa News* (Durham, NC), August 30 and October 18, 1982, and *New York Times*, September 1, 12, 16, 23, and 24, 1982.

10. Smith Hempstone, quoted in the *Globe Democrat* (St. Louis), August 20, 1982.

11. *Africa Now* (London), September 1982, pp. 14–19.

12. Dirk Berg-Schlosser and Rainer Siegler, *Political Stability and Development: A Comparative Analysis of Kenya, Tanzania, and Uganda* (Boulder: Lynne Rienner, 1990), p. 55.

13. Njonjo's national strength was somewhat exceptional among professional politicians. Kenyan politics has had a spatial dimension since before independence. Nairobi is the seat of power, the national epicenter. Outside the capital the political map is an intricate mosaic of ethnic and regional support and competition. There is a middle zone that encompasses forty administrative districts, each with its urban center. District headquarters are usually also market towns and, as such, serve as central places for economic exchanges, the dissemination of political information, and the making of decisions on who gets what, when, and how. In the rural hinterlands lie more than six thousand small communities, each typically located near a market or a school, a church, a medical dispensary, or a subchief's office. Home to well over half of the Kenyan population, these settlements form micropolitical enclaves that are often unrelated to the central establishment except through local notables who attach themselves to their district and provincial patrons and to their respective MPs.

14. Troon further testified that one of his witnesses had been beaten by police and that interference originating at the highest levels had prevented his team from finishing its investigation.

15. *Kenya: Taking Liberties* (New York, Washington, DC, and London: Africa Watch, July 1991), p. 28. The Moi regime had consistently defended Kenya's single-party system as the only way to promote national unity and avoid ethnic strife. Despite the possibility that the new parties might simply evolve into opposing communal factions, by 1990 the Moi argument had become anachronistic both within and outside Kenya. For further discussion of this controversy, see "Kenya Defends One Party Rule," *Africa News* (Durham, NC), April 30, 1990.

16. *Society* (Nairobi), May 25, 1992. The survey was published even though police had earlier raided the offices of *Society* and impounded thirty thousand copies of the magazine's inaugural issue. The attorney general's office justified the ban on the basis of a picture portraying President Moi as looking "dejected" and therefore "rejected" by the Kenyan people. Soon after this warning, the editor of *Society*, his wife, and three staff members were detained without charge. Following an international protest, they were formally charged with publishing articles that caused public "disaffection." This episode occurred after several other direct attacks on Kenya's opposition press, including Gitobu Imanyara's *Nairobi Law Monthly*.

17. The divisions within FORD's leadership became so deep that individual factions later registered separately as semi-independent political parties.

18. *Monthly News* (Nairobi), August 1992.

19. Ibid.

20. *Daily Nation* (Nairobi), May 23, 1992.

21. *Society* (Nairobi), June 1, 1992.

22. The Matiba/Shikuku faction boycotted the FORD party election, arguing that Muite and Imanyara had rigged it to favor Odinga. Matiba, Shikuku and their supporters were then excluded from the party's national congress, which resulted in Odinga's being elected chairman and Muite vice chairman. On October 3, Muite and Shikuku held their own national congress, leaving it for the attorney general to decide which group to recognize as representing FORD. As expected, the KANU government eventually recognized both. For an analysis of this episode, see Makau wa Mutua, "The Changing of the Guard," *Africa Report* 37 (November-December 1992), pp. 56–58.

23. Moi also encountered some opposition to his reelection from within his own party. The one-time manpower development minister, Paul Ngei, announced in July that he would challenge the president on the KANU ticket. Ngei was disqualified by a personal bankruptcy order, however, and could not run unless the high court was prepared to dismiss it. Moi saw to it that the order remained in effect. The KANU parliamentary group endorsed Moi for both his Baringo seat and the presidency. It also backed Vice President George Saitoti for the seat representing Kajiado North in Maasailand. Saitoti had never before run for elective office and faced stiff competition from several popular candidates, including the FORD interim branch chairman Oliver Seki and the DP interim secretary-general and former MP John Keen.

24. *Monthly News* (Nairobi), August 1992. Speaking in parliament, Agriculture Minister Elijah Mwangale tried to deflect criticism away from the government by holding opposition parties responsible for the food shortages. According to his contorted logic, "Donors have not been able to support us this year because of the dirty politics of the day. If there are people who have demonstrated their disloyalty to this nation, they are the opposition parties."

25. Other interested parties urged that the date for elections be pushed even beyond the March 1993 constitutional deadline. Members of the press, the clergy, and a group calling itself the Coalition for a National Convention (CNC) argued that early elections would inevitably favor KANU and that a KANU win would result in mass outrage and political disintegration. Made up of local NGOs and minor parties, the CNC went on to advocate a constituent assembly and an interim government that would provide guidance in the transition to representative government.

26. *New York Times,* December 27, 1992.

27. The election results were released on January 1, 1993, and the opposition immediately expressed doubts as to their veracity and questioned the reported numbers of registered voters and turnout percentages. For a breakdown of presidential and parliamentary totals by constituency, see *Weekly Review* (Nairobi), January 1, 1993.

28. Since the attempted coup of 1982, Moi has maintained control over the military through a number of trusted senior officers representing Kalenjin and other ethnic minorities, notably General M. H. Mohammed, a Kenya Somali who had led the counterattack on the rebellious air force personnel. The military's

noninvolvement in politics has been reinforced by the appeal for many Kenyans of secure careers in the armed forces. Officers and enlisted men are well paid and provided with food, housing, medical services, and recreational facilities. Authorized spheres of military activity are well defined; the army's paramilitary General Services Unit (GSU) specifically trained for civil control, is self-contained, and other units are kept out of domestic police actions.

29. Chandra D. Watkins, *Marketing in Kenya*, Overseas Business Reports OBR 92-06 (Washington, DC: International Trade Administration, U.S. Department of Commerce, September 1992), p. 33.

30. The Harambee movement is the clearest institutional manifestation of this grass-roots system of patronage distribution.

31. The occasion for this change was Moi's 1991 replacement of an inept and unpopular attorney general, Mathew Mule, with the more competent and respected Amos Wako. Legally, Moi could not force Mule's resignation. Instead, he simply "transferred" him to an obscure judgeship on the Kenya Court of Appeal. This allowed Mule to save face and to prepare for retirement while nullifying the attorney general's guaranteed tenure. See *Weekly Review* (Nairobi), May 17, 1991.

32. Quoted in ibid. The Law Society's resolution included several allegations of judicial malfeasance, including the high court's dismissal of suits by Wangarí Maathai and Herma Muge. Maathai's suit had dealt with the government's attack on her Green Belt movement during and after the Kenya Times Media Trust building controversy. Muge, the widow of CPK Bishop Alexander Muge, had applied for an official inquest into the accidental death of her politically influential husband, suspecting an official cover-up in the trial and conviction of the truck driver charged with reckless driving in the case.

33. The Law Society was itself divided into radical and proestablishment wings, the first led by Muite and the second by Fred Ojiambo, whom Muite replaced as chairman in an election in March 1991.

34. The reformers received significant outside help in their final drive to end one-party rule. In October 1990, the U.S. Congress voted to suspend military assistance to Kenya, totaling about $15 million, until the government met four conditions: the release or formal charging of all political detainees, the restoration of an independent judiciary, an end to the physical abuse of prisoners, and the reinstatement of freedom of speech and of the press. This ultimatum was followed in 1991 by the American-led moratorium on most economic aid. The moratorium was reviewed after six months on the basis of political, economic, and human-rights reforms that the Moi regime had set in motion. Finding some progress on these fronts, the foreign donors restored some of their economic assistance.

35. For earlier analyses of the requirements for stability in Kenya, see M. Tamarkin, "The Roots of Political Stability in Kenya," *African Affairs* 77 (1978), pp. 297–320, and Emmet B. Evans, Jr., "Sources of Socio-Political Instability in an African State: The Case of Kenya's Educated Unemployed," *African Studies Review* 20 (1977), pp. 37–52.

36. Tamarkin, "The Roots of Political Stability," p. 300.

CHAPTER 5

1. Rothchild and Curry have observed three central tendencies in African development policy: a conservative "accommodation strategy," which preserves an open and largely unfettered relationship with Western capitalism; a radical "transformation strategy," which attempts to create a relatively closed, self-reliant economy and to limit the penetration of foreign capital; and a "reorganization strategy," which falls somewhere in between and is guided by the following rationale: "Having accomplished rapid economic growth through their association with the West . . . leaders wish to avert any rupture in this basic relationship—only to liberalize it. Thus they hope to harness the strengths of the current international order to their immediate benefit, and leave open until later the possibility of more fundamental adjustment." (Donald Rothchild and Robert L. Curry, Jr., *Scarcity, Choice, and Public Policy in Middle Africa* [Berkeley: University of California Press, 1978], p. 118.) Two mechanisms for pursuing these goals are the localization of key positions and, eventually, controlling interests in foreign-owned enterprises.

2. World Bank, *World Development Report 1987* (New York: Oxford University Press, 1987), p. 244, *World Development Report 1989* (New York: Oxford University Press, 1989), p. 170, and *World Development Report 1992* (New York: Oxford University Press, 1992), pp. 220, 224, and 256.

3. The term "peasants" is used here in the general sense of subsistence farmers and herders who live in poverty at the periphery of the formal economy, whether or not they own their fields and grazing lands. A decade ago, Christopher Leo also stressed the central importance of small-scale agricultural producers to Kenyan development. See *Land and Class in Kenya* (Toronto: University of Toronto Press, 1984), pp. 169–170. From a broader perspective, Robert Chambers sheds light on how the biases, ignorance, and neglect of policy elites and outside "experts" help perpetuate rural poverty by stifling the productive potentials of peasant communities. See *Rural Development: Putting the Last First* (London: Longman Scientific and Technical, 1983).

4. For a detailed economic analysis of this period, see Arthur Hazlewood, *The Economy of Kenya: The Kenyatta Era* (London: Oxford University Press, 1979).

5. World Bank, *World Development Report 1981* (New York: Oxford University Press, 1981), pp. 136 and 138. The demise of the East African Community is discussed later in this chapter and in Chapter 6. Industrial development in eastern Africa was further retarded by Tanzania's economically enervating commitment to state socialism and by the devastation of a once-thriving Ugandan economy during Idi Amin's eight-year reign of terror (1971–1979). See Rodger Yeager, *Tanzania: An African Experiment*, 2d ed. (Boulder: Westview Press, 1989), Chapter 4, and G. N. Uzoigwe, ed., *Uganda: The Dilemma of Nationhood* (New York: NOK, 1982).

6. Republic of Kenya, *Development Plan for the Period 1979 to 1983* (Nairobi: Government Printer, 1978), Parts 1 and 2.

7. U.S. Census Bureau estimates and Republic of Kenya, *Development Prospects and Policies*, Sessional Paper No. 4 (Nairobi: Government Printer, 1982), p. 5.

8. *Institutional Investor* (New York), September 1982, p. 304.

9. Interestingly, within about a week business had returned to normal in Nairobi. The immediate restocking of city shops suggests that merchants had kept many high-priced goods hidden as a hedge against import restrictions and had been practicing a form of price rigging by releasing them only a few at a time.

10. Republic of Kenya, *Working Party on Government Expenditure: Report and Recommendations of the Working Party* (Nairobi: Government Printer, 1982), p. 15.

11. Republic of Kenya, *Development Plan for the Period 1984 to 1988* (Nairobi: Government Printer, 1983), p. xi.

12. Bill Freund, *The Making of Contemporary Africa: The Development of African Society since 1800* (Bloomington: Indiana University Press, 1984), pp. 244–245. Freund draws parallels between these trends and the emergence of a politically and economically advantaged "new class" in the former Soviet Union and other communist states. For a now-classic critique of this phenomenon, see Milovan Djilas, *The New Class: An Analysis of the Communist System* (New York: Praeger, 1957).

13. Republic of Kenya, *Statistical Abstract 1989* (Nairobi: Central Bureau of Statistics, Ministry of Planning and National Development, 1989), p. 94.

14. Republic of Kenya, *Economic Survey 1990* (Nairobi: Central Bureau of Statistics, Ministry of Planning and National Development, May 1990), pp. 104–107.

15. Officially defined as agricultural holdings of between 0.2 and 12 hectares (0.5 and 30 acres).

16. Republic of Kenya, *Statistical Abstract 1989*, pp. 84, 95, and 99.

17. Uma Lele and L. Richard Meyers, *Growth and Structural Change in East Africa: Domestic Policies, Agricultural Performance, and World Bank Assistance, 1963–1986*, Managing Agricultural Development in Africa Discussion Paper 3 (Washington, DC: World Bank, 1989), p. 11. Registered smallholdings are defined as plots of less than 20 hectares (50 acres), although about 75 percent of these are less than 2 hectares (5 acres). Ibid., p. 26.

18. Ibid., p. 13, and Uma Lele, "Sources of Growth in East African Agriculture," in Uma Lele, ed., *Managing Agricultural Development in Africa: Three Articles on Lessons from Experience*, Managing Agricultural Development in Africa Discussion Paper 2 (Washington, DC: World Bank, 1989), p. 23. These averages require some interpretation. In contrast to other eastern African countries, Kenya has generally managed to meet its minimal needs in food staples during years of abundant rainfall. Then the problem is more one of distribution than of production, partly because so much of the annual maize crop is marketed outside the formal economy. During dry years, however, the country is immediately plunged into a food-deficit situation. For the period under review, food imports remained low between 1970 and 1978 and then advanced dramatically in successive years of low rainfall. Since 1985, uncertainty and periodic shortfalls have become commonplace in the production and distribution of maize and other staples. At the same time, population growth and urbanization, small farmers' shift to export crops and off-farm employment, and slowly rising rural and urban incomes have all stimulated demand. In this sense Kenya suffers from a structural

dependence on imported food even though, thanks to hybridization, maize yields have increased at an average annual rate of about 5 percent since 1970. Moreover, "given the instability of and the stagnant or declining dollar-denominated value of [Kenya's] export earnings, policymakers cannot be certain that foreign exchange will be available to meet the increased food import bill" (Lele, *Managing Agricultural Development*, p. 25). In 1991, maize consumption outstripped domestic production by 2.5 million bags, forcing the parastatal National Cereals and Produce Board to import 1.1 million bags before the end of February 1992—at more than twice the cost of maize grown and sold locally. *Weekly Review* (Nairobi), February 14, 1992, pp. 22–23.

19. Republic of Kenya, *Statistical Abstract 1989*, p. 110, and Republic of Kenya, *Economic Survey 1990*, p. 116. For an earlier analysis of the socioeconomic impact of livestock in Kenya, see Harold Schneider, *Livestock and Equality in East Africa: Basis for Social Structure* (Bloomington: Indiana University Press, 1979), Chapter 4.

20. Republic of Kenya, *District Focus for Rural Development*, rev. ed., (Nairobi: Government Printer, March 1987), p. 1.

21. Republic of Kenya, *Development Plan for the Period 1984 to 1988*, pp. 91–98; Republic of Kenya, *Economic Management for Renewed Growth*, Sessional Paper No. 1 of 1986 (Nairobi: Government Printer, 1986), p. 114; and Republic of Kenya, *Development Plan for the Period 1989 to 1993* (Nairobi: Government Printer, 1988), pp. 33–37.

22. For a study of this transitional period, see Joel D. Barkan and Michael Chege, "Decentralising the State: District Focus and the Politics of Reallocation in Kenya," *Journal of Modern African Studies* 27 (1989), pp. 438–446.

23. Chaired by the district commissioners, DDCs are composed of the DDOs, district KANU chairmen, district heads of central ministries, members of parliament, chairmen and clerks of local government authorities, chairmen of divisional development committees, and representatives of development-related parastatal corporations and nongovernmental organizations. DDC executive committees are made up of district commissioners and development officers, clerks of local authorities, and local ministerial and parastatal officials.

24. In addition to the RDF, District Focus funding is drawn from ministerial budgets, local government revenues, Harambee self-help contributions, and earmarked donor assistance.

25. Barkan and Chege, "Decentralising the State," p. 6. For earlier predictions along these lines, see John W. Harbeson, *Structural Adjustment and Development Reform in Kenya—The Missing Dimension*, UFSI Reports 1984/7 (Hanover, NH: Universities Field Staff International, 1984), p. 6. Some degree of local control over development activities is strongly recommended by international financial institutions such as the World Bank and the International Monetary Fund, and this factor also weighed heavily in the Moi government's decision to proceed with the District Focus policy, if not to the point of actual decentralization.

26. Republic of Kenya, *Economic Management for Renewed Growth*, p. 107. See also Republic of Kenya, *Development Plan for the Period 1989 to 1993*, pp. 132–138.

27. Republic of Kenya, *Plan of Action for the Integration of the ASAL Pro-*

gramme into District Focus (Nairobi: Rural Planning Division, Ministry of Finance and Planning, July 1985), p. 18.

28. In 1987, the UN Food and Agriculture Organization (FAO) estimated that even at home more than 50 percent of ASAL dwellers were engaged in nonfarm productive activities including petty trading, beer brewing, crafts, and charcoal making. These enterprises contributed more than half of household earnings east of the Rift Valley and one-third of earnings west of the Rift. FAO, *Kenya: Arid and Semi-Arid Lands (ASAL) Development, Issues and Options,* Volume 1 (Rome: FAO, 1987), p. 5.

29. For discussion of these possibilities, see Institute for African Development, *Development in the Arid and Semi-Arid Lands of Kenya: Report of a Workshop Convened at Cornell University, January 27–30, 1988* (Ithaca: Cornell University, 1988), p. 8.

30. The Institute for African Development workshop at Cornell University identified five essential policy guidelines for such efforts: (1) that areas selected for assistance should be kept relatively small, (2) that economic inputs should belong to local users, (3) that the level of economic and ecological stress should be high enough to motivate behavior change but not overwhelming, (4) that status distinctions between resource users and change agents should be minimized, and (5) that the boundaries of the rural development management system should remain clear. Ibid., p. 5. According to the FAO, "Projects which deliver inputs to groups (self-help groups, women's groups) as opposed to individuals have wider outreach, lower overhead costs per beneficiary, and better spread effects to the poor. There is a direct positive correlation between self-help mobilization and sustainability. . . . Willingness to provide self-help labour depends on whether the participants see tangible benefits (such as food security, higher income, reduced drudgery). Strengthening groups' self-reliance and ability to continue activities, maintain/repair works, and solve routine technical problems on their own takes the burden off line ministry staff, saves time and transport costs, and improves sustainability" (FAO, *Kenya,* p. 7).

31. York W. Bradshaw, "Perpetuating Underdevelopment in Kenya: The Link between Agriculture, Class, and State," *African Studies Review* 33 (1990), pp. 13 and 15.

32. For descriptions of the many public and private agencies concerned with these efforts in Kenya, see Environmental Liaison Centre (ELC), *Directory of NGOs Working on Renewable Energy and Fuelwood Projects in Africa* (Nairobi: ELC, 1982), pp. 5–10, and Republic of Kenya, *Proceedings of a National Workshop on Strengthening Forestry Research in Kenya* (Nairobi: Ministry of Environment and Natural Resources and USAID, 1983), Appendix 2.

33. UN Development Programme and World Bank estimates, reported in *Africa Recovery Briefing Paper 5* (New York: United Nations Department of Public Information, Communication and Project Management Division, June 1992), p. 2.

34. Republic of Kenya, *Economic Survey 1990,* p. 132.

35. World Bank estimate, reported in *New York Times,* September 9, 1990.

36. In 1985, Kenya exported 611.9 thousand metric tons of refined petroleum products valued at K£118.03 million ($144.96 million at current exchange rates). By 1989, these exports had fallen to 187.6 thousand metric tons valued at

K£34.6 million (about $36.42 million). Republic of Kenya, *Economic Survey 1990*, p. 128.

37. Ibid.; *Weekly Review* (Nairobi), September 14, 1990; and World Bank, *World Development Report 1992*, p. 226. All dollar and cent figures are approximate because of frequent fluctuations in the exchange-rate value of the Kenya shilling.

38. *Weekly Review*, September 14, 1990.

39. Republic of Kenya, *Economic Survey 1990*, pp. 164–165, 167.

40. Ibid.; Republic of Kenya, *Statistical Abstract 1989*, p. 171; and Republic of Kenya, *Development Plan for the Period 1989 to 1993*, p. 79.

41. Republic of Kenya, *Working Party on Government Expenditure*, p. 92.

42. Republic of Kenya, *Development Plan for the Period 1989 to 1993*, p. 139.

43. Public-sector involvement in industry is further assisted by several other governmental and parastatal organizations, including official tender boards, the Price Controller and Bureau of Standards, the Central Bank, the Kenya Industrial Research and Development Institute, the Ministry of Commerce and Industry and its New Projects Committee, and the commerce and planning ministries' Investment Advisory Centre. With their help and that of the parastatal finance institutions, lucrative ownership arrangements have been concluded with a variety of foreign corporations. An example is Leyland Kenya Ltd., of which 45 percent is owned by British Leyland International, 35 percent by the Kenya Treasury, and 20 percent by the local product distributor, CMC Holdings. Leyland Kenya assembles and distributes British Leyland vehicles and also, under contract, Volkswagen, Mitsubishi, and Suzuki vehicles. Government also owns 51 percent of General Motors Kenya and 50 percent of Kenya Oil Refineries.

44. Peter Coughlin and Gerrishon K. Ikiara, eds., *Industrialization in Kenya: In Search of a Strategy* (Nairobi: Heinemann Kenya, and London: James Currey, 1988), p. 1.

45. World Bank, *World Development Report 1992*, pp. 228, 230, and 250.

46. P. Anyang' Nyong'o, "The Possibilities and Historical Limitations of Import-Substitution Industrialization in Kenya," in Coughlin and Ikiara, *Industrialization in Kenya*, p. 42.

47. Peter Coughlin, "Toward a New Industrial Strategy in Kenya?" in ibid., p. 282.

48. Ibid., p. 285.

49. For further details on events leading up to and following the EAC's collapse, see Yeager, *Tanzania*, pp. 133–139.

50. Republic of Kenya, *Development Plan for the Period 1989 to 1993*, pp. 154 and 157–158. Besides Kenya, PTA member countries include Burundi, Comoros, Djibouti, Ethiopia, Lesotho, Malawi, Mauritius, Namibia, Rwanda, Somalia, Swaziland, Tanzania, Uganda, Zambia, and Zimbabwe. As of late 1992, the governments of Angola, Botswana, Madagascar, and Mozambique had signed the PTA treaty but had not yet ratified it.

51. Despite these controls, inflation is still nearly 10 percent per annum.

52. Coughlin, "Toward a New Industrial Strategy," p. 293. Coughlin also raises the perennial specter of land shortage: "The goal must be to achieve a well complemented, interlinked industrial base so that in twenty years industry will

be able to create a larger share of the needed jobs for Kenyans as population pressure on the land increases" (Ibid., p. 302).

53. World Bank, *World Development Report 1982* (New York: Oxford University Press, 1982), p. 124, and *World Development Report 1992*, p. 244.

54. World Bank, *World Development Report 1992*, p. 252.

55. S. K. Adjala, in the *Standard* (Nairobi), April 29, 1981.

56. Under the Moi regime, domestic and multinational firms alike have been subjected to trade-restricting political manipulation and corruption, which have exerted a negative impact on international investment as well as on local industrial growth. A case in point is Firestone Tire and Rubber Company, which for years endured long delays in receiving licenses for imported raw materials and work permits for expatriate technicians. Firestone was also unsuccessful in several requests for price increases, had a $25 million expansion project indefinitely deferred, and received no protection against the smuggling of tires into Kenya for sale at below Firestone's production costs. Finally deciding to cut its losses, in 1985 the company sold all but 19 percent of its 70 percent interest in the Kenya subsidiary and entered into a management contract with the new controlling interest, Sameer Investments. Sameer, a holding company enjoying close ties to President Moi, had similarly acquired majority interests in the Kenya subsidiaries of Eveready Batteries and the Bank of America. Not surprisingly in light of this experience, the number of U.S. firms operating in Kenya declined from approximately two hundred in the early 1980s to about half that number at decade's end. Another, more objective constraint affecting foreign investors is Kenya's chronic foreign-exchange shortages, which themselves cause delays in the issuance of import licenses and in the repatriation of corporate profits. In general, however, Bradshaw's conclusion still holds: "Future development research should continue to examine the relationship of foreign capital, local capital, and the domestic state. Although these actors may be relatively equal partners in strong semi-peripheral countries (e.g., Brazil), they do not exhibit equal strength in most peripheral societies. In Kenya, for instance, local capital is not yet sufficiently developed to become an equal partner with foreign capital and the state" (York W. Bradshaw, "Reassessing Economic Dependency and Uneven Development: The Kenyan Experience," *American Sociological Review* 53 [1988], p. 706).

57. Republic of Kenya, *Development Plan for the Period 1984 to 1988*, p. 217. U.S. dollar equivalents are expressed in terms of current exchange rates for 1963 and 1982.

58. Ibid.

59. See Allan Frank, "The Market's Discipline," *Forbes*, November 22, 1982, pp. 102–106, and the *Standard* (Nairobi), February 12, 1981, and January 23, 1983.

60. Estimates provided by the African Wildlife Foundation and the International Union for Conservation of Nature and Natural Resources. For additional information, see "African Elephants: A Dying Way of Life," *Science News* 133 (May 21, 1988), p. 333.

61. *Sunday Standard* (Nairobi), May 21, 1989.

62. Republic of Kenya, *Development Plan for the Period 1989 to 1993*, pp. 183 and 184.

63. For perspectives on this program, see *Daily Nation* (Nairobi), April 21 and 23, 1986. Reckoning the costs and benefits of tourism is further complicated by continuing uncertainty over just how much the industry's international component contributes to Kenyan foreign earnings and society at large. Berry and other skeptics once suggested that the direct value of international tourism might not exceed 10 percent of gross receipts, while the Ministry of Tourism set the remitted proportion at 80 percent. The official profit-share estimate may be more accurate now that the country has gone farther with the localization of private enterprise, but reliable figures are still unavailable, and, in any case, gains from tourism remain heavily concentrated in the higher political and economic strata of Kenyan society. See L. Berry, *East Africa Country Profiles: Kenya* (Worcester, MA: Program for International Development, Clark University, 1980), p. 54.

64. See Hazlewood, *Economy of Kenya*, pp. 59 and 69, and Nicola Swainson, *The Development of Corporate Capitalism in Kenya, 1918–1977* (London: Heinemann, 1980), pp. 236–249.

65. See Republic of Kenya, *Working Party on Government Expenditure*, pp. 93–101.

66. World Bank estimates.

67. Kenya Department of Personnel Management estimates.

68. World Bank, *World Development Report 1992*, p. 232. To enhance their comparability with those for Kenya, all Third World averages exclude China and India.

69. Ibid., p. 258. All dollar figures are expressed at current exchange rates.

70. Ibid., p. 264.

71. It should be noted that twelve other African economies have much more precarious ratios of external debt to GNP and export earnings, including impoverished Mozambique, Tanzania, and Somalia, and middle-income Côte d'Ivoire and Congo. At the other end of the scale is mineral-rich Botswana, whose external debt is less than 25 percent of both GNP and sales from exports. Ibid., pp. 264–265.

72. As this goal was announced, estimated revenue collections by the central government totaled K£515 million ($573.7 million) from progressive income taxes but K£730.6 million ($769 million) from excise and sales levies. Republic of Kenya, *Statistical Abstract 1989*, p. 208.

73. Republic of Kenya, *Development Plan for the Period 1989 to 1993*, pp. 33–41 and 63–64.

74. International Bank for Reconstruction and Development (IBRD; World Bank), *Accelerated Development in Africa: An Agenda for Action* (Washington, DC: IBRD, 1981), and Republic of Kenya, *Working Party on Government Expenditure*.

75. Harbeson, "Structural Adjustment and Development Reform," p. 6.

76. Norman N. Miller, *Kenya: The Quest for Prosperity*, 1st ed. (Boulder: Westview Press, 1984), p. 127.

77. Goran Hyden, *No Shortcuts to Progress: African Development Management in Perspective* (Berkeley: University of California Press, 1983).

78. Republic of Kenya, *Statistical Abstract 1989*, pp. 35 and 36, and Republic of Kenya, *Economic Survey 1990*, p. 21.

79. Kenya Central Bureau of Statistics estimate.

80. Keith Marsden, *African Entrepreneurs: Pioneers of Development*, International Finance Corporation Discussion Paper 9 (Washington, DC: World Bank, 1990), p. 6.

81. Ibid., p. 7. Marsden adds: "In addition, from 4,088 to 5,240 new business names were registered annually. These are new businesses without limited liability status, but they are still formal enough to require a registered name and office, both for regulatory purposes and to facilitate business operations."

82. For example, official transfers to households and unincorporated enterprises declined by nearly 20 percent in the last half of the 1980s, while transfers to larger incorporated enterprises increased by almost 575 percent and to government itself by slightly under 70 percent. Republic of Kenya, *Economic Survey 1990*, p. 79.

83. Marsden, *African Entrepreneurs*, p. 21.

84. Marsden drew on four case studies of Kenya to make his case for Kenyan small business. Perhaps ironically, one of these firms is headed by a former senior civil servant.

85. Blane D. Lewis, "Growth Linkages in Regional Economic Development in Africa," *Africa Notes* (Institute for African Development, Cornell University), May 1991, p. 1, emphasis added. Co-authored with Erik Thorbeck, the larger study is titled "District-Level Economic Linkages in Kenya: Evidence Based on a Small Region Social Accounting Matrix."

CHAPTER 6

1. U.S. Arms Control and Disarmament Agency (USACDA), *World Military Expenditures and Arms Transfers, 1985* (Washington, DC: Defense Program and Analysis Division, USACDA, August 1985), p. 69. During this period, Kenya's military budget increased from $57 million to $235 million in constant 1982 U.S. dollars, and the military establishment was expanded from eight thousand to nineteen thousand officers and enlisted personnel. In both respects, an interesting comparison can be made with neighboring Tanzania. In that country, military expenditures rose from $87 million to $143 million beween 1973 and 1982, an increase of 64 percent in constant terms, and the Tanzanian armed forces grew by 72 percent, from twenty-five thousand to forty-three thousand troops. Ibid., p. 83. This means that, although smaller than its Tanzanian counterpart, the Kenyan military experienced much faster growth while receiving relatively lavish financial support. Perhaps ironically, these advantages failed to prevent the attempted coup of August 1982.

2. *Standard* (Nairobi), January 1, 1980.

3. For an analysis of the Kenyan attempt to resolve the crisis between Tanzania and Uganda, see Donald Rothchild and Robert L. Curry, Jr., *Scarcity, Choice, and Public Policy in Middle Africa* (Berkeley: University of California Press, 1978), pp. 236–238.

4. For a summary of the factors involved in this conflict, see Rodger Yeager, *Tanzania: An African Experiment*, 2d ed. (Boulder: Westview Press, 1989), pp. 135–137.

5. Libyan pilots had been operating in southern Sudan against the Sudanese People's Liberation Army (SPLA), which was receiving food and probably other assistance from Kenya. Since Lokichoggio was a key point of disbursement for this aid, little doubt remained that Uganda was innocent of the bombing. Some weeks later, the government-owned *Kenya Times* admitted as much to the nation, but Moi continued to blame the Ugandans—evidently in an attempt to embarrass the Museveni government and disguise Kenya's support for the SPLA.

6. For further information about recent Kenya-Uganda relations, see *African Recorder* 30 (March 12–25, 1991), p. 8334.

7. Kenya and Sudan experienced one minor crisis in 1978, during the transition from the Kenyatta to the Moi presidency. When a Kikuyu plot to remove Moi misfired, one of its principals fled to Sudan and then to Britain. Although the fugitive was eventually pardoned and returned home, his having been granted asylum in Sudan continued to irritate the Kenyan governing elite.

8. See *African Research Bulletin* 29 (March 1–3, 1992), p. 10485.

9. For a conceptual discussion of Afro-Marxism and its application in Ethiopia, see Crawford Young, *Ideology and Development in Africa* (New Haven: Yale University Press, 1982), pp. 22–96, especially pp. 69–83. See also Mulatu Wubneh and Yohannis Abate, *Ethiopia: Transition and Development in the Horn of Africa* (Boulder: Westview Press, 1987).

10. See Norman N. Miller, *The Other Somalia: Illicit Trade and the Hidden Economy,* Part 1, American Universities Field Staff Reports 1981/29 (Hanover, NH: American Universities Field Staff, 1981), and *The Indian Ocean: Traditional Trade on a Smuggler's Sea,* American Universities Field Staff Reports 1980/7 (Hanover, NH: American Universities Field Staff, 1980).

11. UN High Commissioner for Refugees estimates and *The Washington Post National Weekly Edition,* November 30–December 6, 1992.

12. *Weekly Review* (Nairobi), February 1, 1991.

13. For an excellent analysis of the background of this ongoing struggle, see Allen Isaacman and Barbara Isaacman, *Mozambique: From Colonialism to Revolution, 1900–1982* (Boulder: Westview Press, 1983).

14. For a useful overview of Southern Rhodesia's fitful transition to an independent Zimbabwe, see Christine Sylvester, *Zimbabwe: The Terrain of Contradictory Development* (Boulder: Westview Press, 1991).

15. *Africa Report* 33 (March–April 1988), p. 8.

16. Although its authenticity cannot be confirmed, this memorandum was printed verbatim in *Finance* (Nairobi), July 31, 1992. In one passage: "There is reason to believe we influence Moi. After all, he has done, largely against his own instincts, everything we set ourselves to persuade him to do two years ago [involving economic and political reforms]. He may have done it for quite other reasons but it is an advantage that we have a dialogue with him in which we can and do tell him some truths. The American Ambassador has no effective understanding with him at all."

17. U.S. Department of State, "Sub-Saharan Africa and US Policy," in *Gist: A Quick Reference Aid on US Foreign Policy* (Washington, DC: Bureau of Public Affairs, U.S. Department of State, October 1990), pp. 1–2.

18. Ibid., p. 2.

19. For references to these rancorous exchanges and fitful attempts to moderate them, see *New York Times*, May 6, 9, and 12, 1990, and *Weekly Review* (Nairobi), January 11, 1991.

20. The senatorial delegation included Patrick Leahy (Democrat of Vermont), chairman of the influential Foreign Operations Subcommittee of the Senate Appropriations Committee, the future vice president, Al Gore (Democrat of Tennessee), and outspoken Barbara Mikulski (Democrat of Maryland). The Kenyan reaction to their proposed ultimatum was predictable. Speaking in parliament, Vice President Saitoti declared that "Kenyans will not allow themselves to be dictated as to what changes to undertake. . . . We shall not do anything to appease anybody."

21. Chandra D. Watkins, *Marketing in Kenya*, Overseas Business Reports OBR 92-06 (Washington, DC: International Trade Administration, U.S. Department of Commerce, September 1992), p. 3.

22. Two and one-half years earlier, the U.S. government had tried one more time to lure Kenya into political and economic reform by converting a $10-million food-aid loan into an outright grant. Ambassador Hempstone presided at a public signing of this agreement.

23. Republic of Kenya, *Economic Survey 1990* (Nairobi: Central Bureau of Statistics, Ministry of Planning and National Development, 1990), pp. 96 and 97.

24. The Yaoundé and Lomé conventions and their application to Kenya and other African states are summarized in Peter Calvocoressi, *World Politics since 1945*, 6th ed. (London and New York: Longman, 1991), pp. 157–160.

25. Arthur Hazlewood, *The Economy of Kenya: The Kenyatta Era* (London: Oxford University Press, 1979), p. 122.

26. U.S. Agency for International Development sources in Nairobi, March 1983. For information on the immediately preceding period, see Republic of Kenya, *Development Estimates for the Year 1981–1982* (Nairobi: Government Printer, 1981), p. 88.

27. Uma Lele and L. Richard Meyers, *Growth and Structural Change in East Africa: Domestic Policies, Agricultural Performance, and World Bank Assistance, 1963–1986,* Managing Agricultural Development in Africa Discussion Paper 3 (Washington, DC: World Bank, 1989), pp. 23–24. According to Lele and Meyers, bilateral donors had granted the bank this leadership role because of its presumed competence, its increasing willingness to cofinance projects with them, and its leadership in promoting macroeconomic and sectoral policy reforms.

28. Republic of Kenya, *Development Plan for the Period 1989 to 1993* (Nairobi: Government Printer, 1988), p. 72.

29. See John M. Cohen, *Expatriate Advisors in the Government of Kenya: Why They Are There and What Can Be Done About It*, Development Discussion Paper 376 (Cambridge: Harvard Institute for International Development, Harvard University, June 1991), p. 4, and Lele and Myers, *Growth and Structural Change in East Africa*, p. 24.

30. David B. Abernethy, "The Informal Governance of Africa by Aid Agencies," unpublished paper, Stanford University, Stanford, CA, n.d., p. 5.

31. According to Crawford Young, "At issue here is certainly not total

economic autonomy, which no state can achieve in an interdependent world, much less an impossible autarchy. Positive performance consists in enlarging the scope of choice and reducing the impact of external constraints on policy options. The essence of autonomy is the possibility of designing a development strategy that is responsive solely to internal value preferences and images of desired future societal arrangements" (Young, *Ideology and Development in Africa*, p. 308). In the present context, autonomy means freedom of political as well as socio-economic choice.

32. For case studies of this phenomenon and its vicissitudes, see Larry Diamond, Juan J. Linz, and Seymour Martin Lipset, eds., *Democracy in Developing Countries, Volume 2, Africa* (Boulder: Lynne Rienner, 1988).

33. These schools of thought are concisely described in Naomi Chazan et al., *Politics and Society in Contemporary Africa*, 2d. ed. (Boulder: Lynne Rienner, 1992), pp. 14–22. See also David E. Apter, *Rethinking Development: Modernization, Dependency, and Postmodern Politics* (Newbury Park, CA: Sage, 1987), and Alvin Y. So, *Social Change and Development: Modernization, Dependency, and World-System Theories* (Newbury Park, CA: Sage, 1990).

CHAPTER 7

1. World Bank, *World Development Report 1992* (New York: Oxford University Press, 1992), pp. 224, 268, 272, 274, and 280.

2. Neighboring Tanzania offers perhaps the best example of this disparity.

3. See, for example, York W. Bradshaw, "Perpetuating Underdevelopment in Kenya: The Link between Agriculture, Class, and State," *African Studies Review* 22 (1990), pp. 1–28; Kate Currie and Ray Barry, "State and Class in Kenya: Notes on the Cohesion of a Ruling Class," *Journal of Modern African Studies* 22 (1984), pp. 559–593; Raphael Kaplinsky, "Capitalist Accumulation in the Periphery: Kenya," in Martin Fransman, ed., *Industry and Accumulation in Africa* (London: Heinemann, 1982), pp. 193–221; Gavin Kitching, *Class and Economic Change in Kenya: The Making of an African Petite Bourgeoisie, 1905–1970* (New Haven: Yale University Press, 1980); Christopher Leo, *Land and Class in Kenya* (Toronto: University of Toronto Press, 1984); Colin Leys, *Politics in Kenya: The Political Economy of Neo-Colonialism, 1964–1971* (Berkeley: University of California Press, 1974, and London: Heinemann, 1975); Leys, "State and Capital in Kenya: A Research Note," *Canadian Journal of African Studies* 14 (1980), pp. 307–318; Leys, "Accumulation, Class Formation and Dependency: Kenya," in Fransman, *Industry and Accumulation in Africa*, pp. 170–192; Scott MacWilliam and M. P. Cowan, eds., *Essays on Capital and Class in Kenya* (London: Longman, 1976); and Nicola Swainson, *The Development of Corporate Capitalism in Kenya, 1918–1977* (London: Longman, 1980).

4. For instance, Peter Coughlin and Gerrishon K. Ikiara, eds., *Industrialization in Kenya: In Search of a Strategy* (Nairobi: Heinemann Kenya, and London: James Curry, 1988), and, more generally, Goran Hyden, *No Shortcuts to Progress: African Development Management in Perspective* (Berkeley: University of California Press, 1983), and Robert H. Jackson and Carl G. Rosberg, *Personal Rule in Black Africa: Prince, Autocrat, Prophet, Tyrant* (Berkeley: University of California Press,

1984). For a countervailing view praising Kenya for a "policy-induced agrarian success," see Michael F. Lofchie, *The Policy Factor: Agricultural Performance in Kenya and Tanzania* (Boulder: Lynne Rienner, and Nairobi: Heinemann Kenya, 1989).

5. In an essay completed on the eve of the 1992 U.S. presidential election, the U.S. permanent representative to the United Nations, Ambassador Edward J. Perkins, set forth a similar agenda for good global citizenship among the world's nations. In addition to arms control and the protection of minority rights, he identified the following as basic requisites for a global democratic community: open markets with attention paid to social equity, open access to political participation through free elections, and environmentally sustainable economic development. Edward J. Perkins, "The United States as a Global Citizen," *Presidential Studies Quarterly* 23 (1993), pp. 17–22.

6. A metaphor drawn from Chinua Achebe's powerful novel about early colonial Nigeria. Chinua Achebe, *Things Fall Apart* (London: Heinemann, 1965).

Selected Bibliography

REFERENCE WORKS

Howell, John B. *Kenya: Subject Guide to Official Publications*. Washington, DC: Library of Congress, 1978.

Kaplan, Irving, et al. *Area Handbook for Kenya*. 3d ed. Washington, DC: American University, 1984.

Killick, Tony. *The Economies of East Africa*. Boston: G. K. Hall, 1976.

Thurston, Anne. *Guide to Archives and Manuscripts Relating to Kenya and East Africa in the United Kingdom*. Volume 1, *Official Records*. Volume 2, *Unofficial Records/Index*. Oxford: Hans Zell, 1990.

Webster, John B., et al. *A Bibliography on Kenya*. Syracuse: Program of Eastern African Studies, Syracuse University, 1967.

HISTORY

Ambler, Charles H. "Population Movement, Social Formation, and Exchange: Central Kenya in the Nineteenth Century." *International Journal of African Historical Studies* 18 (1985):201–222.

———. *Kenyan Communities in the Age of Imperialism: The Central Region in the Late Nineteenth Century*. New Haven: Yale University Press, 1988.

Anderson, David, and David Throup. "Africans and Agricultural Production in Colonial Kenya: The Myth of War as a Watershed." *Journal of African History* 26 (1985):327–345.

Barnett, Donald L., and Njama Karari. *Mau Mau from Within*. New York: Praeger, 1966.

Bennett, George. *Kenya, a Political History: The Colonial Period*. London: Oxford University Press, 1963.

Bennett, George, and Carl Rosberg. *The Kenyatta Election: Kenya 1960–1961*. London: Oxford University Press, 1961.

Berman, Bruce. *Control and Crisis in Colonial Kenya: The Dialectic of Domination*. Athens, OH: Ohio University Press, 1990.

Berman, Bruce, and J. M. Lonsdale. "Crises of Accumulation, Coercion and the Colonial State: The Development of the Labor Control System in Kenya, 1919–29." *Canadian Journal of African Studies* 14 (1980):55–82.

Brett, E. A. *Colonialism and Underdevelopment in East Africa: The Politics of Economic Change, 1919–39.* New York: NOK, 1973.

Clark, J. Desmond *The Prehistory of Africa.* Baltimore: Penguin Books, 1963.

Clayton, Anthony, and Donald C. Savage. *Government and Labour in Kenya, 1895–1963.* London: Frank Cass, 1974.

Clough, Marshall S. *Fighting Two Sides: Kenyan Chiefs and Politicians, 1918–1940.* Niwot, CO: University Press of Colorado, 1991.

Coldham, Simon. "The Settlement of Land Disputes in Kenya: An Historical Perspective." *Journal of Modern African Studies* 22 (1984):59–71.

Cone, L. W., and J. F. Lipscomb. *The History of Kenya Agriculture.* Nairobi: University Press of Africa, 1972.

Fearn, H. *An African Economy: A Study of the Economic Development of Nyanza Province of Kenya, 1903–1953.* London: Oxford University Press, 1961.

Freeman-Grenville, G.S.P. *The East African Coast: Select Documents from the First to the Earlier Nineteenth Century.* Oxford: Clarendon Press, 1962.

Furedi, Frank. *The Mau Mau War in Perspective.* Athens, OH: Ohio University Press, 1989.

Huxley, Elspeth. *White Man's Country: Lord Delamere and the Making of Kenya.* Two volumes. London: Macmillan, 1935.

———. *The Flame Trees of Thika: Memories of an African Childhood.* London: Chatto and Windus, 1959.

———. *The New Earth: An Experiment in Colonialism.* London: Chatto and Windus, 1960.

Kanogo, Tabitha. *Squatters and the Roots of Mau Mau: 1905–63.* London, Nairobi, and Athens, OH: James Currey, Heinemann Kenya, and Ohio University Press, 1987.

King, Kenneth. "The Kenya Maasai and the Protest Phenomenon, 1900–1960." *Journal of African History* 13 (1971):117–137.

Kitching, Gavin. *Class and Economic Change in Kenya: The Making of an African Petite Bourgeoisie, 1905–1970.* New Haven: Yale University Press, 1980.

Lamphear, John. "The People of the Grey Bull: The Origins and Expansion of the Turkana." *Journal of African History* 29 (1987):27–39.

Leo, Christopher. "Who Benefited from the Million Acre Scheme? Toward a Class Analysis of Kenya's Transition to Independence." *Canadian Journal of African Studies* 15 (1981):201–222.

Lonsdale, J. M. "The Politics of Conquest: The British in Western Kenya, 1894–1908." *Historical Journal* 20 (1977):841–870.

———. "Mau Maus of the Mind: Making Mau Mau and Remaking Kenya." *Journal of African History* 31 (1990):393–421.

Maxon, Robert M. "A Kenya Petite Bourgeoisie Enters Local Politics: The Kisii Union, 1945–1949." *International Journal of African Historical Studies* 19 (1986):451–462.

Miller, Charles. *The Lunatic Express.* New York: Macmillan, 1971.

———. *Battle for the Bundu.* New York: Macmillan, 1974.

Morton, Fred. *Children of Ham: Freed Slaves and Fugitive Slaves on the Kenya Coast, 1873–1907.* Boulder: Westview Press, 1990.

Mosley, Leonard. *Duel for Kilimanjaro: An Account of the East African Campaign, 1914–1918.* London: Weidenfeld and Nicolson, 1960.

Mungeam, G. H. "Masai and Kikuyu Responses to the Establishment of British Administration in the East Africa Protectorate." *Journal of African History* 11 (1970):127–143.

———. *British Rule in Kenya, 1895–1912.* London: Oxford University Press, 1974.

Muriuki, Godfrey. *A History of the Kikuyu, 1500–1900.* Nairobi: Oxford University Press, 1974.

Murphy, John. "Legitimation and Paternalism: The Colonial State in Kenya." *African Studies Review* 29 (1986):55–66.

Ochieng', William R. *Themes in Kenyan History.* Athens, OH: Ohio University Press, 1991.

Ogot, Bethwell A. *Historical Dictionary of Kenya.* Metuchen, NJ, and London: Scarecrow Press, 1981.

Oliver, Roland, and Gervase Mathew. *History of East Africa.* Three volumes. Oxford: Clarendon Press, 1963, 1965, and 1976.

Prins, A.H.J. *The Swahili-speaking Peoples of Zanzibar and the East African Coast: Arabs, Shirazi, and Swahili.* London: International African Institute, 1961.

Rosberg, Carl G., Jr., and John Nottingham. *The Myth of "Mau Mau": Nationalism in Kenya.* New York: Praeger, 1966.

Sorrenson, M.P.K. *Origins of European Settlement in Kenya.* Nairobi and London: Oxford University Press, 1968.

Spear, Thomas. *Kenya's Past: An Introduction to Historical Method in Africa.* London: Longman, 1981.

Stamp, Patricia. "Government in Kenya: Ideology and Political Practice, 1895–1974." *African Studies Review* 29 (1986):17–42.

Throup, David. *Economic and Social Origins of Mau Mau: 1944–1952.* Athens, OH: Ohio University Press, 1988.

Tignor, R. L. *The Colonial Transformation of Kenya.* Princeton: Princeton University Press, 1976.

Turton, E. R. "Somali Resistance to Colonial Rule and the Development of Somali Political Activity in Kenya, 1893–1960." *Journal of African History* 13 (1972):117–143.

Wanjau, Gakaara wa. *Mau Mau Author in Detention: An Author's Detention Diary.* London: Heinemann, 1989.

Wolff, Richard D. *The Economics of Colonialism: Britain and Kenya, 1870–1930.* New Haven: Yale University Press, 1974.

Zwanenburg, Roger van. *The Agricultural History of Kenya to 1939.* Nairobi: East African Publishing House, 1972.

ECOLOGY, SOCIETY, AND CULTURE

Cable, Vincent. "The Asians of Kenya." *African Affairs* 68 (1969):218–231.

Cameron, John. *The Development of Education in East Africa.* New York: Columbia University Teachers College Press, 1970.

Court, David, and Dharam P. Ghai, eds. *Education, Society, and Development: New Perspectives from Kenya*. Nairobi: Oxford University Press, 1974.

Davison, Jean. *Voices from Mutira: Lives of Rural Gikuyu Women*. Boulder: Lynne Rienner, 1989.

De Blij, Harm J. *Mombasa: An African City*. Evanston: Northwestern University Press, 1968.

Downing, Thomas E., Kangethe W. Gitu, and Crispin M. Kamau, eds. *Coping with Drought in Kenya: National and Local Strategies*. Boulder: Lynne Rienner, 1989.

Evans, Emmet B., Jr. "Education, Unemployment, and Crime in Kenya." *Journal of Modern African Studies* 13 (1975):55–66.

————. "Sources of Socio-Political Instability in an African State: The Case of Kenya's Educated Unemployed." *African Studies Review* 20 (1977):37–52.

Fratkin, Elliot. *Surviving Drought and Development: The Ariaal of Northern Kenya*. Boulder: Westview Press, 1991.

Hickman, G. M., and W.H.G. Dickens. *The Lands and Peoples of East Africa*. London: Longman, 1960.

House-Midamba, Bessie. "The United Nations Development Decade: Political Empowerment or Increased Marginalization for Kenyan Women?" *Africa Today* 1st Quarter (1990):37–48.

Johnson, Douglas H., and David M. Anderson, eds. *The Ecology of Survival: Case Studies from Northeast African History*. London and Boulder: Lester Crook Academic Publishing and Westview Press, 1988.

Keller, Edmond. "Education, Ethnicity, and Political Socialization in Kenya." *Comparative Political Studies* 12 (1980):442–469.

Kenyatta, Jomo. *Facing Mount Kenya*. London: Secker and Warburg, 1938.

Kercher, Leonard C. *The Kenya Penal System: Past, Present, and Prospect*. Washington, DC: University Press of America, 1981.

Kesby, John D. *The Cultural Regions of East Africa*. London: Academic Press, 1977.

King, Kenneth. *The African Artisan: Education and the Informal Sector in Kenya*. London: Heinemann, 1979.

Lele, Uma, and Steven W. Stone. *Population Pressure, the Environment, and Agricultural Intensification: Variations on the Boserup Hypothesis*. Managing Agricultural Development in Africa Discussion Paper 4. Washington, DC: World Bank, 1989.

Lura, Russell. "Population Change in Kericho District, Kenya: An Example of Fertility Increase." *African Studies Review* 28 (1985):45–56.

Mackenzie, Fiona. "Local Initiatives and National Policy: Gender and Agricultural Change in Murang'a District, Kenya." *Canadian Journal of African Studies* 20 (1986):377–401.

Morgan, W.T.W., ed. *East Africa: Its People and Resources*. 2d ed. Nairobi: Oxford University Press, 1972.

Mutiso, G.C.M. "Technical Education and Change in Kenya." *East Africa Journal* 7 (1971):28–39.

Ndeti, Kivuto. *Cultural Policy in Kenya*. Paris: UNESCO Press, 1975.

Ojany, Francis F., and Reuben B. Ogendo. *Kenya: A Study in Physical and Human Geography*. Nairobi: Longman, 1973.

Ominde, Simeon H. *Land and Population Movements in Kenya*. London: Heinemann, 1968.

————. *Studies in East African Geography and Development.* Berkeley: University of California Press, 1971.

————, ed. *Population and Development in Kenya.* Portsmouth, NH: Heinemann Educational Books, 1985.

Parkin, David. *The Sacred Void: Spatial Images of Work and Ritual among the Giriama of Kenya.* Cambridge and New York: Cambridge University Press, 1991.

Presley, Cora Ann. *Kikuyu Women, the "Mau Mau" Rebellion, and Social Change in Kenya.* Boulder: Westview Press, 1992.

Sandgren, David. "Twentieth Century Religious and Political Division among the Kikuyu of Kenya." *African Studies Review* 25 (1982):195–208.

Sindiga, Isaac. "Land and Population Problems in Kajiado and Narok, Kenya." *African Studies Review* 27 (1984):23–40.

Sobiana, Neal. "Fisherman Herders: Subsistence, Survival, and Cultural Change in Northern Kenya." *Journal of African History* 29 (1988):41–56.

Soja, Edward W. *The Geography of Modernization in Kenya: A Spatial Analysis of Social, Economic, and Political Change.* Syracuse: Syracuse University Press, 1968.

Sorrenson, M.P.K. *Land Reform in the Kikuyu Country: A Study in Government Policy.* Nairobi: Oxford University Press, 1967.

Tamarkin, M. "Tribal Associations, Tribal Solidarity, and Tribal Chauvinism in a Kenya Town." *Journal of African History* 14 (1973):257–274.

Thiong'o, Ngugi wa. *Weep Not, Child.* London: Heinemann, 1964.

————. *Detained: A Writer's Prison Diary.* London: Heinemann, 1981.

————. *Devil on the Cross.* London: Heinemann, 1982.

————. *Decolonising the Mind: The Politics of Language in African Literature.* London: Heinemann, 1986.

Vogel, L. C., et al., eds. *Health and Disease in Kenya.* Nairobi: East African Literature Bureau, 1974.

Wipper, Audrey. "Equal Rights for Women in Kenya." *Journal of Modern African Studies* 9 (1971):429–442.

Whiteley, W. H., ed. *Language in Kenya.* Nairobi: Oxford University Press, 1974.

Yeager, Rodger. *Africa's Conservation for Development: Botswana, Kenya, Tanzania, and Zimbabwe.* Hanover, NH: African-Caribbean Institute, 1987.

————. "Historical and Ecological Ramifications for AIDS in Eastern and Central Africa." in Norman Miller and Richard C. Rockwell, eds. *AIDS in Africa: The Social and Policy Impact,* pp. 71–83 Lewiston, NY: Edwin Mellen Press, 1988.

————, ed. *Conservation for Development in Botswana, Kenya, Somalia, and Sudan.* Hanover, NH: African-Caribbean Institute, 1990.

Yeager, Rodger, and Norman N. Miller. *Wildlife, Wild Death: Land Use and Survival in Eastern Africa.* Albany: State University of New York Press, 1986.

POLITICS AND GOVERNMENT

Arnold, Guy. *Kenyatta and the Politics of Kenya.* London: J. M. Dent, 1974.

Barkan, Joel D. "Further Reassessment of 'Conventional Wisdom': Political Knowledge and Voting Behavior in Rural Kenya." *American Political Science Review* 30 (1976):452–456.

————. "The Rise and Fall of a Governance Realm in Kenya," in Goran Hyden and Michael Bratton, eds., *Governance and Politics in Africa*, pp. 167–192. Boulder: Lynne Rienner, 1992.

Barkan, Joel, and John D. Okumu, eds. *Politics and Public Policy in Kenya and Tanzania*. Rev. ed. New York: Praeger, 1982.

Berg-Schlosser, Dirk, and Reiner Siegler. *Political Stability and Development: A Comparative Analysis of Kenya, Tanzania, and Uganda*. Boulder: Lynne Rienner, 1990.

Bienen, Henry. *Kenya: The Politics of Participation and Control*. Princeton: Princeton University Press, 1974.

Burke, Fred G. "Political Evolution in Kenya," in Stanley Diamond and Fred G. Burke, eds. *The Transformation of East Africa: Studies in Political Anthropology*, pp. 185–239. New York: Basic Books, 1966.

Court, David, and Kenneth Prewitt. "Nation as Region in Kenya: A Note on Political Learning." *British Journal of Political Science* 4 (1974):109–114.

Currie, Kate, and Ray Barry. "State and Class in Kenya: Notes on the Cohesion of a Ruling Class." *Journal of Modern African Studies* 22 (1984):559–593.

Gertzel, Cherry J. *The Politics of Independent Kenya, 1963–68*. Evanston: Northwestern University Press, 1970.

Gertzel, Cherry J., Maurice Goldschmidt, and Donald Rothchild, eds. *Government and Politics in Kenya*. Nairobi: East African Publishing House, 1969.

Goldsworthy, David. *Tom Mboya: The Man Kenya Wanted to Forget*. Nairobi: Heinemann, 1982.

Gordon, David. *Decolonization and the State in Kenya*. Boulder: Westview Press, 1986.

Hornsby, Charles. "The Social Structure of the National Assembly in Kenya, 1963–83." *Journal of Modern African Studies* 27 (1989):275–296.

Hyden, Goran, Robert Jackson, and John Okumu, eds. *Development Administration: The Kenyan Experience*. Nairobi: Oxford University Press, 1970.

Jackson, Tudor. *The Law of Kenya: An Introduction*. New York: Rowman and Littlefield, 1971.

Karimi, Joseph, and Phillip Ochieng. *The Kenyatta Succession*. Nairobi: Transafrica Book Distributors, 1980.

Kenyatta, Jomo. *Harambee: The Prime Minister of Kenya's Speeches, 1963–1964*. Nairobi: Oxford University Press, 1964.

————. *Suffering without Bitterness: The Founding of the Kenya Nation*. Nairobi: East African Publishing House, 1968.

Lamb, G. *Peasant Politics, Conflict, and Development in Murang'a*. Lawes, Sussex: Julian Friedman, 1974.

Leonard, David K. *Rural Administration in Kenya*. Nairobi: East African Literature Bureau, 1973.

————. *Reaching the Peasant Farmer: Organization Theory and Practice in Kenya*. Chicago: University of Chicago Press, 1977.

Leys, Colin. *Politics in Kenya: The Political Economy of Neo-Colonialism, 1964–1971*. Berkeley: University of California Press, 1974, and London: Heinemann, 1975.

————. "State Capital in Kenya: A Research Note." *Canadian Journal of African Studies* 14 (1980):307–318.

————. "Accumulation, Class Formation and Dependency: Kenya," in Martin Fransman, ed. *Industry and Accumulation in Africa*, pp. 170–192. London: Heinemann, 1982.

Mboya, Tom. *Freedom and After*. London: Andre Deutsch, 1963.

————. *The Challenge of Nationhood*. New York: Heinemann, 1970.

Mueller, Susanne. "Government and Opposition in Kenya, 1966–69." *Journal of Modern African Studies* 22 (1984):399–427.

Murray-Brown, Jeremy. *Kenyatta*. London: George Allen and Unwin, 1972.

Mutiso, G.C.M. *Kenya: Politics, Policy and Society*. Nairobi: East African Literature Bureau, 1975.

Nellis, John. "Expatriates in the Government of Kenya." *Journal of Commonwealth Political Studies* 11 (1973):251–264.

Odinga, Oginga. *Not Yet Uhuru: An Autobiography*. New York: Hill and Wang, 1967.

Ojwang, J. B. *Constitutional Development in Kenya: Institutional Adaptation and Social Change*. Nairobi: African Centre for Technology Studies Press, 1990.

Rothchild, Donald S. "Ethnic Inequalities in Kenya." *Journal of Modern African Studies* 7 (1969):689–711.

————. *Racial Bargaining in Independent Kenya*. London: Oxford University Press, 1976.

Schatzberg, Michael. "Two Faces of Kenya: The Researcher and the State." *African Studies Review* 29 (1986):1–16.

Tamarkin, M. "The Roots of Political Stability in Kenya." *African Affairs* 77 (1978):297–320.

Wasserman, Gary. *The Politics of Decolonization: Kenya Europeans and the Land Issue, 1960–1965*. Cambridge: Cambridge University Press, 1976.

Werlin, Herbert H. *Governing an African City: A Study of Nairobi*. New York: Africana Publishing House, 1974.

Widner, Jennifer. *The Rise of a Party-State in Kenya: From Harambee to Nyayo*. Berkeley: University of California Press, 1992.

ECONOMICS AND DEVELOPMENT

Allen, Christopher, and Kenneth King, eds. *Development Trends in Kenya*. Edinburgh: Centre of African Studies, University of Edinburgh, 1973.

Barkan, Joel D., and Michael Chege. "Decentralising the State: District Focus and the Politics of Reallocation in Kenya." *Journal of Modern African Studies* 27 (1989):431–453.

Barkan, Joel D., ed. *Beyond Capitalism and Socialism in Kenya and Tanzania*. Boulder: Lynne Rienner, forthcoming.

Bennell, Paul. "Engineering Technicians in Africa: A Kenyan Case-Study." *Journal of Modern African Studies* 21 (1983):273–291.

Blunt, Peter, and Merrick Jones. "Managerial Motivation in Kenya and Malawi: A Cross-Cultural Comparison." *Journal of Modern African Studies* 24 (1986):155–176.

Bradshaw, York W. "Reassessing Economic Dependency and Uneven Development: The Kenyan Experience." *American Sociological Review* 53 (1988):693–708.

————. "Perpetuating Underdevelopment in Kenya: The Link between Agriculture, Class, and State." *African Studies Review* 33 (1990):1–28.

Coughlin, Peter, and Gerrishon K. Ikiara. *Industrialization in Kenya: In Search of a Strategy.* Nairobi: Heinemann Kenya, and London: James Currey, 1988.

Ergas, Zaki. "Kenya's Special Rural Development Program (SRDP): Was It Really a Failure?" *Journal of Developing Areas* 17 (1981):51–66.

Ghai, Dharam, Martin Godfrey, and Franklin List. *Planning for Basic Needs in Kenya: Performance, Policies, and Prospects.* Geneva: International Labour Office, 1979.

Godfrey, E. M., and G.C.M. Mutiso. "Political Economy of Self-Help: Kenya's 'Harambee' Institutes of Technology." *Canadian Journal of African Studies* 8 (1974):109–133.

Godfrey, M. "Kenya: African Capitalism or Simple Dependency?" in M. Bienefeld and M. Godfrey, eds. *The Struggle for Development: National Strategies in an International Context,* pp. 265–291. New York: Wiley, 1982.

Godfrey, M., and S. Langdon. "Partners in Underdevelopment: The Transnationalization Thesis in a Kenya Context." *Journal of Commonwealth and Comparative Politics* 14 (1976):42–63.

Greer, Joel, and Erik Thorbecke. *Food, Poverty, and Consumption Patterns in Kenya.* Geneva: International Labour Office, 1986.

Grosh, Barbara. *Public Enterprise in Kenya: What Works, What Doesn't, and Why.* Boulder: Lynne Rienner, 1991.

Harbeson, John W. *Nation Building in Kenya: The Role of Land Reform.* Evanston: Northwestern University Press, 1973.

————. *Structural Adjustment and Development Reform in Kenya—The Missing Dimension.* UFSI Reports 1984/7. Hanover, NH: Universities Field Staff International, 1984.

Hazlewood, Arthur. *Economic Integration: The East African Experience.* London: Heinemann, 1975.

————. *The Economy of Kenya: The Kenyatta Era.* London: Oxford University Press, 1979.

————. "Kenyan Land-Transfer Programmes and Their Relevance for Zimbabwe." *Journal of Modern African Studies* 23 (1985):445–461.

Helleiner, G. J. "Agricultural Development Plans in Kenya and Tanzania, 1969–1974." *Rural Africana* 13 (1971):36–42.

Heyer, Judith, J. K. Maitha, and W. M. Senga, eds. *Agricultural Development in Kenya: An Economic Assessment.* Nairobi: Oxford University Press, 1976.

Holtham, Gerald, and Arthur Hazlewood. *Aid and Inequality in Kenya: British Development Assistance to Kenya.* London: Croom Helm, 1975.

Hosier, Richard. "The Informal Sector in Kenya: Spatial Variation and Development Alternatives." *Journal of Developing Areas* 21 (1986):383–402.

Hunt, D. *The Impending Crisis in Kenya: The Case for Land Reform.* Aldershot, Hants., U.K.: Gower, 1984.

Hyden, Goran. *No Shortcuts to Progress: African Development Management in Perspective.* Berkeley: University of California Press, 1983.

————. *Agriculture and Development in Africa: The Case of Kenya.* UFSI Reports 1987/21. Indianapolis: Universities Field Staff International, 1987.

Kaplinsky, Raphael, ed. *Readings on the Multinational Corporations in Kenya.* Nairobi: Oxford University Press, 1978.

———. "Capitalist Accumulation in the Periphery: Kenya," in Martin Fransman, ed., *Industry and Accumulation in Africa,* pp. 193-221. London: Heinemann, 1982.

Killick, Tony, ed. *Papers on the Kenyan Economy: Performance, Problems, and Politics.* London: Heinemann, 1981.

Kongstad, Per, and Mette Monsted. *Family Labour and Trade in Western Kenya.* Uppsala: Scandinavian Institute of African Studies, 1980.

Land Resources Development Centre. *Kenya: Profile of Agricultural Potential.* Surbiton, U.K.: British Overseas Development Administration, 1986.

Langdon, Steven W. *Multinational Corporations in the Political Economy of Kenya.* New York: St. Martin's Press, 1981.

Lele, Uma. "Sources of Growth in East African Agriculture," in Uma Lele, ed., *Managing Agricultural Development in Africa: Three Articles on Lessons from Experience,* pp. 9–28. Managing Agricultural Development in Africa Discussion Paper 2. Washington, DC: World Bank, 1989.

Lele, Uma, and L. Richard Meyers. *Growth and Structural Change in East Africa: Domestic Policies, Agricultural Performance, and World Bank Assistance, 1963–1986.* Parts 1 and 2. Managing Agricultural Development in Africa Discussion Paper 3. Washington, DC: World Bank, 1989.

Leo, Christopher. *Land and Class in Kenya.* Toronto: University of Toronto Press, 1984.

Livingstone, Ian. *Economics for Eastern Africa.* London: Heinemann, 1980.

Lofchie, Michael F. *The Policy Factor: Agricultural Performance in Kenya and Tanzania.* Boulder: Lynne Rienner, and Nairobi: Heinemann Kenya, 1989.

Lubeck, P., ed. *The African Bourgeoisie: Capitalist Development in Nigeria, Kenya, and the Ivory Coast.* Boulder: Lynne Rienner, 1987.

MacWilliam, Scott, and M. P. Cowan, eds. *Essays on Capital and Class in Kenya.* London: Longman, 1976.

Marris, Peter, and Anthony Somerset. *African Businessmen: A Study of Entrepreneurship and Development in Kenya.* London: Routledge and Kegan Paul, 1971.

Marten, David. "The Transition in Smallholder Banking in Kenya: Evidence from Rural Branch Bank Loans." *Journal of Developing Areas* 16 (1981):71–86.

Matthews, Ron. "The Development of a Local Machinery Industry in Kenya." *Journal of Modern African Studies* 25 (1987):67–93.

Muller, Maria. "The National Policy of Kenyanisation of Trade: Its Impact on a Town in Kenya." *Canadian Journal of African Studies* 15 (1981):293–302.

National Christian Council of Kenya. *Who Controls Industry in Kenya? Report of a Working Party.* Nairobi: East African Publishing House, 1968.

Njonjo, A. L. "The Kenyan Peasantry: A Re-Assessment." *Review of African Political Economy* 10 (1981):27–40.

Oboler, Regina S. *Women, Power, and Economic Change: The Nandi of Kenya.* Stanford: Stanford University Press, 1985.

Ogendo, R. G. *Industrial Geography of Kenya.* Nairobi: East African Publishing House, 1970.

Richardson, Harry. "An Urban Development Strategy for Kenya." *Journal of Developing Areas* 15 (1980):97–118.

Ruthenberg, Hans. *African Agricultural Production Development Policy in Kenya, 1952–1965.* Berlin: Springer-Verlag, 1966.

Schneider, Harold. *Livestock and Equality in East Africa: The Economic Basis for Social Structure.* Bloomington: Indiana University Press, 1979.

Stichter, Sharon. *Migrant Labour in Kenya: Capitalism and African Response 1895–1975.* London: Longman, 1982.

Swainson, Nicola. *The Development of Corporate Capitalism in Kenya, 1918–1977.* London: Heinemann, 1980.

Wasow, Bernard. "The Working Age-Sex Ratio and Job Search Migration in Kenya." *Journal of Developing Areas* 15 (1980):435–444.

World Bank. *Kenya: Into the Second Decade.* Baltimore: Johns Hopkins University Press, 1975.

Acronyms

AIDS	Acquired Immunodeficiency Syndrome
CNC	Coalition for a National Convention
COTU	Central Organization of Trade Unions
CPK	Church of the Province of Kenya
DGIPE	Department of Government Investment and Public Enterprise
DP	Democratic Party
EAC	East African Community
EEC	European Economic Community
ELC	Environmental Liaison Centre
FAO	Food and Agriculture Organization
FORD	Forum for the Restoration of Democracy
FRELIMO	Frente de Liberação de Moçambique (Front for the Liberation of Mozambique)
GEMA	Gikuyu, Embu, Meru Association
GSU	General Services Unit
HIV	Human Immunodeficiency Virus
IBEAC	Imperial British East Africa Company
IBRD	International Bank for Reconstruction and Development
IDA	International Development Association
ILO	International Labour Office
IPK	Islamic Party of Kenya
IUCN	International Union for Conservation of Nature and Natural Resources
KADU	Kenya African Democratic Union
KANU	Kenya African National Union
KCA	Kikuyu Central Association
KENDA	Kenya National Democratic Alliance
KMC	Kenya Meat Commission
KNC	Kenya National Congress
KNUT	Kenya National Union of Teachers
KPU	Kenya People's Union
NCCK	National Christian Council of Kenya

NCPB	National Cereals and Produce Board
NES	National Environment and Human Settlements Secretariat
OAU	Organization of African Unity
ODA	Overseas Development Administration
OPEC	Organization of Petroleum Exporting Countries
PCEA	Presbyterian Church of East Africa
PLI	Public Law Institute
PTA	Preferential Trade Area
RDF	Rural Development Fund
RENAMO	Movimento da Resistência Nacional de Moçambique (Mozambique National Resistance Movement)
SDP	Social Democratic Party
SONU	Student Organisation of Nairobi University
SPIN	Student Peace Initiative of Nairobi University
SPLA	Sudanese People's Liberation Army
SRDP	Special Rural Development Programme
STOP	Student Opinion
UNCHS	United Nations Centre for Human Settlements
UNEP	United Nations Environment Programme
UNICEF	United Nations International Children's Emergency Fund
USAID	United States Agency for International Development
USACDA	United State Arms Control and Disarmament Agency

About the Book and Authors

Kenya, at the equator on the Indian Ocean, is one of Africa's most important and controversial nations. It has simultaneously been heralded for its political stability and economic success and criticized as a wellspring of elitism and class exploitation. Kenya remains a close ally of the West and a symbol of capitalism in Africa, and it occupies a position of strategic importance to the Middle East and the Indian Ocean. Yet all of these distinctions are now coming under question in the fourth decade of independence.

Kenya's exquisite natural beauty and renowned wildlife refuges hide a more mundane reality. The country is vast, rural, poor, and without oil or other mineral wealth. It is dependent on smallholder agriculture and export earnings from international tourism, tea, and coffee. Although the population is only 28 million, less than 20 percent of Kenya's land area is readily available for dense human settlement. Population growth has slowed from the time when it was the highest in the world, but demographic pressures still pose very serious socioeconomic, ecological, and environmental challenges.

In this second edition of a critically acclaimed profile, Miller and Yeager address these and other social issues while tracing political and economic developments from early precolonial times to the contemporary period and the recent fourth-term reelection of President Daniel arap Moi. The book captures the aggressive, self-confident spirit that characterizes Kenya and provides unique insights into how this nation of contemporary Africa is faring in its continuing quest for prosperity.

Norman Miller is professor at Dartmouth College and president of the African-Caribbean Institute. He has published extensively in the fields of African environment, health, and politics and currently serves as editor of the international research and policy bulletin *AIDS and Society*. He has taught at the University of Nairobi and has lived and worked in East Africa for long periods since 1960.

Rodger Yeager is professor of political science, adjunct professor of African history, and director of international studies at West Virginia University. He is the author of the Tanzania volume in Westview's Profiles/Nations of Contemporary Africa series. His current research is focused on public-policy problems of natural resource conservation, rural development, and demographic change in eastern and southern Africa.

Index